POSITIVELY MEDIEVAL

The Surprising, Dynamic, Heroic Church
of the Middle Ages

POSITIVELY
Medieval

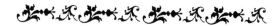

THE SURPRISING, DYNAMIC, HEROIC CHURCH of the MIDDLE AGES

JAMIE BLOSSER

Our Sunday Visitor

www.osv.com
Our Sunday Visitor Publishing Division
Our Sunday Visitor, Inc.
Huntington, Indiana 46750

Our Sunday Visitor Publishing Division
Our Sunday Visitor, Inc.
200 Noll Plaza
Huntington, IN 46750
1-800-348-2440

ISBN: 978-1-68192-028-3 (Inventory No. T1785)
eISBN: 978-1-68192-031-3
LCCN: 2016946074

Cover design: Lindsey Riesen
Cover art: Musee Dobree, Nantes, France/Bridgeman Images
Interior design: M. Urgo

PRINTED IN THE UNITED STATES OF AMERICA

CONTENTS

Preface

When I went off to college at the age of eighteen, I hadn't put much thought into what medieval Christianity was like, but in the back of my mind were images of dirty, sickly people living in mud huts and worshiping statues of Mary, opulently dressed churchmen hawking relics and indulgences, and sneering Inquisitors burning witches and Protestants. I'm not sure who, exactly, was responsible for putting these images into my head, but I'm pretty sure it was a collective effort.

I was a Protestant, though not a very good one, and that probably had something to do with it, although I don't remember my parents or pastors talking like this. It was more of an unstated historical dogma of American Protestantism: Martin Luther had restored authentic, Bible-believing, Jesus-centered, morally pure Christianity in 1517, and all that had gone before was superstitious, insincere, and morally corrupt.

My enrollment as a religious studies major in college, and the Church history courses I took subsequently, dealt a serious blow to this assumption. As it turns out, I found a good deal of authentic, Bible-believing, Jesus-centered, morally pure Christianity in the 1,400 years between the apostles and Martin Luther. I devoured the books I was given: St. Thomas Aquinas' *Summa*, St. Benedict's *Rule*, the lives of St. Francis, the *Imitation of Christ*, St. Bernard's commentaries, and all the rest. When I converted to Catholicism two years later, it wasn't so much that I renounced the religion in which I had been raised. Rather, I had found it all over again, but in a purer, richer, and more abundant form than I had ever known existed.

Even up to the dawn of the Reformation itself, medieval Christians had shown an encyclopedic knowledge of the Bible that would have put my Sunday School teachers to shame. Their writings evidenced a heartfelt, personal love for Jesus and His cross that made my own faith seem tepid in comparison; thousands of them had devoted their lives, and even given them up in martyrdom, to plant the seeds of the Gospel throughout the world. These were the values that my parents and pastors had taught me to love and cherish: How could I resist?

Even more, as my academic studies advanced, I found that many of my personal efforts at theological reflection had been spent, as it were, reinventing the wheel. After countless hours spent trying to produce (very bad) arguments for God's existence for my atheist friends, I discovered the brilliant ones written by Aquinas and Anselm. After spending as many hours puzzling out the meaning of obscure passages of Scripture, I picked up the commentaries of Augustine and Origen and the difficulties vanished. My reaction was very nearly one of betrayal. All these years, this vast storehouse of Christian wisdom had been right under my nose, and no one had told me about it?

My historical assumptions had been all wrong. In *every* generation—including the Middle Ages—faithful Christians had passed on the torch of the Christian faith, keeping the flame alive even in the most difficult moments. The Reformation had not rediscovered an authentic Christianity long since vanished from the earth: that authentic Christianity had been there all along. Now, I have no misty-eyed nostalgia for the medieval Church, which was just as sin-infected and scandal-ridden as the Church in our own day. Nor do I have any personal disdain for the Prot-estant Reformers, who in many ways were doing their best to ad-dress the legitimate problems of medieval Christianity, even if (in my own view) their radical solutions ended up ripping out the very foundations of the medieval Church they were trying to reform.

So why is it worth giving medieval Christianity a second look? The momentous events of the early modern era—the Ref-ormation, the Renaissance, the discoveries of the New World, the Enlightenment, and the Scientific Revolution—so completely reworked Western civilization as to remove almost every ves-tige of medieval Christianity. And the gifts of the modern age are innumerable: technological innovation, economic prosperity, widespread literacy, and a thousand other undeniably beneficial developments.

Yet underneath this new superstructure, modern civilization has always been fueled by an unstated set of humane moral values such as a belief in human dignity and a broad sense of what counted as good and bad human conduct; a general (if vague) recognition of a divine Creator and a respect for the integrity of His creation; a deeply felt desire for justice and fair play; and the need to make personal sacrifices for the common good.

These values, however, were not modern inventions. They were not invented by the Protestants or the Enlightenment philosophers. Inasmuch as they are part of the Gospel message itself, they were the legacy of medieval Christianity, carefully and heroically preserved and transmitted to the modern world by medieval Christians, often at great cost.

Yet many observers have noted that these very beliefs and values, in the last half century or so, seem to be drying up, and the social and institutional structures of medieval Christendom which once sustained them no longer exist, or at least no longer have the cultural influence they once had.

Medieval Christendom can't be rebuilt, and probably shouldn't be even if it could. But the timeless values and beliefs that lay at the heart of medieval Christianity must be rediscovered, sustained, and preserved, if modern society itself is to be preserved.

Introduction

What Are the Middle Ages?

The term *Middle Ages*, or its adjectival form *medieval*, refers to a chronological period covering roughly a thousand years, from AD 500 to AD 1500. The beginning of the period is marked by the end of the Late Antique World in Western Europe, and in particular by the collapse of the Western Roman Empire in the fifth century under the weight of barbarian invasions. Its end is marked by the rise of Modernity, and in particular by the Renaissance, the Protestant Reformation, and the discovery of the New World.

These demarcations should make clear that the term Middle Ages exclusively describes *Western* Europe, as these events had little direct effect upon Eastern Europe, sub-Saharan Africa, or other regions of the world.

A book about the Middle Ages is thus necessarily a book about Western Europe, although this book will attempt to incorporate some figures from outside this region—Greek Byzantium, for example—mainly for the purposes of comparison. Most historians tend to subdivide the medieval period into the Early Middle Ages (sixth through tenth centuries), the High Middle Ages (eleventh through thirteenth), and the Late Middle Ages (fourteenth and fifteenth) in order to draw attention to the full flowering of economic, political, and literary culture that occurred in the middle period.

The term *Dark Ages* is often erroneously used to describe the Middle Ages as a whole, whereas if the term should be used at all (which is doubtful), it should be used only for the earlier period.

Three dominant tasks occupied medieval Christians during this thousand-year period: the rebuilding of civilization, the missionary work of the Church, and the pursuit of the glory of God. Some background regarding those tasks will help us better appreciate the dynamic Christians discussed in this book.

The Rebuilding of Civilization

Whatever its defects, the civilization of Late Antiquity, as found in the fourth-century Roman Empire, boasted a set of cultural achievements which were the envy of the world. The Greek culture upon which Rome was built supplied a foundation of literary and philosophical wisdom: the teachings of Plato and Aristotle, the poetry of Homer, the science of Galen and Ptolemy, the mathematics of Euclid and Pythagoras, and a fine-tuned liberal-arts curriculum designed to transmit this wisdom to future generations. The Romans themselves had added a superstructure of legal precision, military skill, and political apparatus that allowed the Caesars to place the whole Mediterranean world under their sway.

All of this, however, was gone by the end of the fifth century. What used to be called the barbarian invasions, but which are now more kindly referred to as the Germanic immigration movements, strained the Roman infrastructure beyond what it could handle. The city of Rome itself was sacked by Goths in AD 410. The empire lingered on, with diminishing borders, until the last emperor was deposed in 476. What was once the empire, at least in the West (in the East, the empire survived in Greek Byzantium), was replaced by a patchwork of barbarian kingdoms that knew nothing of Greek or Roman culture.

With no one to maintain it, the intellectual and civic infrastructure of Western Europe rapidly collapsed—schools, libraries, hospitals, roads, bridges, garrisons, urban centers, and everything that depended on them.

One of the central tasks of the Early Middle Ages was to rebuild this structure. Governments had to be erected, law codes written, borders defended, fields cleared, trade routes reestablished, cities rebuilt, schools and hospitals founded, libraries stocked—in short, civilization had to be established from the ground up. While the Dark Ages has become the stuff of jokes for its low level of culture, it was in fact a miracle that culture survived at all. But survive it did. By the High Middle Ages, Western Europe could boast of an organized system of schools and universities; a highly efficient—if imperfect—social, economic, and political system (collectively known as feudalism); precise law codes; centralized nation-states (some complete with parliaments and elected officials); an impressive array of scientific and technological developments; and a strong corpus of original artistic, musical, literary, and architectural works.

Hostile ethnic groups which had invaded, looted, and ravished the countryside—barbarians, Vikings, Magyars, and Turks—were subjugated, assimilated, converted, or at least held at bay. And all of this was engineered not by some centralized, coordinating secular state power, but largely by bishops, monks, priests, nuns, and ordinary Christians.

Before proceeding, it may be worthwhile to consider the map on Page 21, which will give a sense of the geographic shape of Europe at the dawn of the Middle Ages. Note the Roman Empire lingering on in the East, stretching from Greece in the northwest through modern-day Turkey and Palestine, all the way to Egypt in the south, with its capital at Constantinople (later Byzantium) on the Black Sea.

Note also the various Germanic, barbarian kingdoms covering North Africa, Spain, France, Britain, and Germany. Within two centuries, Spain, North Africa, Egypt, and modern-day Palestine and much of Turkey would be transformed into Muslim caliphates, and Viking (Norman) incursions would reshape much of the northern coasts of Western Europe. But this, more or less, is the region in which medieval Christianity took shape.

The Missionary Work of the Church

Many Christians in the fourth-century Roman Empire could boast that the command of Christ to "make disciples of all nations" (Mt 28:19) had been fulfilled in their own day, which many of them called "our Christian times" (*tempora Christiana*). After all, the vast majority of the population—from the emperor down to the lowest servants—were professing Christians. Yet the tumultuous period of the Early Middle Ages would flip this situation upside down, as Christians often found themselves as small minorities being ruled by new, non-Christian populations such as Goths or Muslims. Additionally, deep disagreements over theology meant that even some purportedly Christian populations were somewhat less than orthodox—the Arians, Monophysites, Albigensians, and many others.

The work of proclaiming the Gospel to these populations was another central task of the Middle Ages. But the work of missionaries was only the beginning. It had to be followed up with the task of catechizing the converts, forming them in the faith and establishing permanent pastoral structures—parishes, dioceses, seminaries, monasteries, and so forth—to guarantee that the faith would be passed on effectively and in its entirety. The hard work of theological debate and apologetics was necessary to bring back into the fold heterodox and wayward believers.

As Christian populations expanded, Church structures had to grow more centralized and coordinated—witness, for example, the unprecedented work of the medieval papacy in coordinating the growth of the medieval Church. These structures themselves, of course, were not immune from corruption and abuse, necessitating constant work on the part of Church reformers. Even more, political rulers were always eager to manipulate the Church and her structures for their own ends, requiring clear safeguards to maintain the purity of the Church's spiritual mission.

The Pursuit of the Glory of God

Aside from these urgent tasks necessitated by the changed social conditions of the Middle Ages, we should not forget the most central goal of the Church, "that in everything God may be glorified" (1 Pt 4:11)—the regular work of prayer, contemplation, and worship that must go on in any and all historical conditions. While rarely registering on the radar of historians, this work was clearly at the very heart of medieval Christianity, as all of the sources bear witness. The tireless and unceasing prayer of Christians in chapels and shrines, the journeys of pilgrims, the chanting of the Divine Office in the monasteries, the solemn meditation of contemplatives and hermits, and the daily Eucharistic sacrifice formed and crowned it all.

The fervency and sincerity of medieval piety is proven by the great monastic movements that flourished in this period (the Benedictine, Franciscan, and Dominican orders, for example), the soaring architectural achievement of medieval cathedrals, and the unparalleled intellectual accomplishments of the medieval scholars such as St. Thomas Aquinas and St. Anselm.

The cultivation of knowledge and love of God was not just an extraneous hobby of the medieval world: it was its beating heart.

The Scope and Purpose of This Book

I am convinced that many of the challenges that Christians face today are not new, and not terribly different from the challenges that Christians faced in the Middle Ages. Medieval Christians also faced an often hostile and secularizing culture, the tensions of religious pluralism, an aggressive state eager to usurp the religious liberty of the Church, the scandal caused by immoral and worldly clergy, and many other issues. In that era, Christians rose to these challenges in heroic, intelligent, creative, and dynamic ways, and I am convinced that their responses can inspire and prepare us to face the similar challenges of our own times.

It may seem odd to some that I view the Middle Ages as relevant at all. After all, the popular culture has reduced the medieval Church to a crude caricature—a primitive, superstitious, ignorant, violent, and backward lot that we would all do better to shove under the carpet: irrelevant at best, and embarrassing at worst. As a matter of fact, the very term *medieval* was an invention of fifteenth-century Renaissance scholars who wished to denigrate this historical "valley" between the twin cultural peaks of ancient and modern civilizations.

But in my ten years of teaching Church history, I have witnessed time and time again—and these times are among my favorite moments as a teacher—that my students, after picking up and reading medieval literature firsthand, are captivated by its relevance. Contrary to the typical narrative peddled by the contemporary secular culture, sources reveal medieval Christianity to be intellectually inquisitive, spiritually vibrant, dynamic and world-affirming, sincerely held, and culturally diverse.

This is why, as a writer and a teacher, I have always preferred to use primary texts from the historical period in question, rather than substituting modern scholarship. In other words, I would a thousand times prefer that a young reader actually pick up Augustine's *Confessions* and hear this wonderful saint tell his own life story than resort to a textbook on Augustine purchased at a bookstore. I have found that the lives of men and women from the past come to life when we read about them *in their own words*. This is even more true of the saints, whose writings seem to exude a sanctity all to themselves, which often gets lost when it is reduced to a paragraph summary in a contemporary textbook.

Even more, I have found that history works best when its focus is on *concrete individuals*, real personalities, rather than a broad survey of dates, events, and vague generalizations. This is why I have chosen to structure this book not so much chronologically or thematically, but around the lives of real persons—the lives of the saints.

The faithful men and women of the Middle Ages—those who passed on the Faith so heroically and at such great cost—still retain their power to inspire, to capture imaginations, and to teach those willing to learn.

Who Are the Medieval Saints?

Narrowing down the list of candidates for inclusion in this book was nothing short of agonizing. Every name crossed off the list, to my mind, represented a piece of the brilliant mosaic of medieval Christianity. Numerous readers will groan to find their favorite figure excluded and can take consolation that I groaned twice as loudly. Allow me to share a few brief considerations that I took into account.

First, not all the figures in this book are canonized saints. It was not until the year 1234 that the Catholic Church developed a centralized, organized procedure for declaring people saints. Until that time sainthood functioned more informally: if enough people began to treat someone as a saint—recalling her virtues, for example, or preserving her relics, visiting her tomb, praying to her, saying Masses in her honor—and if this pattern continued for long enough and spread widely enough, the person began to be called a saint, and that was that.

But some of the figures in this book wouldn't even be considered saints by this less formal procedure. Usually there are good reasons: no one knew enough about the personal lives of Julian of Norwich or pseudo-Dionysius (though their writings were impeccable), Justinian's and Charlemagne's personal lives left something to be desired (though they did more for the Church than anyone else in their eras), Meister Eckhart's and Gregory of Palamas' writings were controversial in some places (though their sincerity was never in question), and so on. But it seemed better to include figures of great historical and religious significance, and who generally led praiseworthy lives, than to be overly rigid about survivors of the canonization process.

I have taken great effort to include Doctors of the Church whenever possible, although some have been regrettably omitted. The term *Doctor*, Latin for "teacher," is used to recognize those saints who have made particularly important contributions to the Church's theological tradition: usually they are theologians, though sometimes mystics or pastors have received the honor.

A greater effort has been made to ensure that the book presents a representative sampling of medieval Christianity. Too many treatments of this period resemble a roll call of celibate male clerics. Without casting doubts upon the immense contributions carried out by churchmen during the Middle Ages, it would be a shame to overlook the work done by laity, and by women in particular, in carrying on the faith in this period. For this reason, I have included six women as subjects of this book, and six married persons.

As a professional theologian, I have worked hard to overcome a prejudice for my own discipline, and to fight the tendency to write nothing but biographies of university professors. Instead, to capture the diversity of contributions made by the medieval saints, I have come up with several categories into which to group them. Admittedly, they are somewhat superficial; most of these personalities are so multifaceted that they are hard to pin down!

First are the missionaries, those who devoted their lives to the spread and proclamation of the Gospel.

Next is the group I call the leaders—those who founded institutions, ruled nations, or simply rose to the occasion when intelligent and creative leadership was needed in the Church or society.

Third, we have the martyrs, those who paid the cruel price of fidelity to the Gospel, shedding their blood in the name of Christ.

Fourthly, those I call monastics, who dedicated their lives to the values of poverty, chastity, and obedience to give witness to the kingdom of God.

Next, mystics who excelled at a life of prayer and communicated to others the path to a mature spiritual life.

Sixth, the thinkers, the intellectuals who helped to develop, clarify, and defend the Church's theological and philosophical traditions.

I have ended the book with a seventh group, Eastern Christians, who carried out some of these same tasks in the regions of the Middle East and Eastern Europe. Of course, some figures fit in more than one category, and a rather arbitrary judgment call had to be made. For example, Boethius is undeniably a thinker, a martyr, and a leader.

As for the specific writing selections, I have tried—as with the choice of writers—to find a balance between high quality selections and diverse, representative samples. The reader will find theological and philosophical tracts, commentaries, dialogues, homilies, letters, scientific treatises, last wills, judicial transcripts, biographies and autobiographies, prayers, hymns, poetry, legislation, and much more. I have tried to select writings from the saints themselves, but when this was not possible (Elizabeth of Hungary, for example, left no writings) I have opted for the writings of their friends or associates, or at least near contemporaries.

The vast majority of Western medieval writers wrote in Latin, of course; Eastern writers, in Greek. In some cases I have made my own translations; in a few cases permission has been graciously granted to use those of others. In the majority of cases I have simply adapted older, public-domain translations, updating them for readability. Readability has to be balanced against fidelity to the original texts, and I have consistently favored the former without (I hope) doing violence to the latter.

This book is not written with scholars in mind, and those who wish to use these texts for scholarly ends will likely complain of the absence of some elements they have come to expect (reference to critical editions, footnotes with variant translations, and similar material). My aim throughout has been to produce writing samples that are clear, concise, and enjoyable to read, yet which remain substantially true to the original texts. A bibliography at the end of the book indicates which sources I consulted for each chapter.

Mediterranean World, Early Middle Ages, c. AD 500

BLACK SEA

BYZANTINE
(ROMAN) EMPIRE

MEDITERRANEAN SEA

OSTROGOTHIC KINGDOM

VANDAL KINGDOM

ANGLO-SAXON
KINGDOMS

FRANKISH
KINGDOM

VISIGOTHIC
KINGDOM

ATLANTIC
OCEAN

MEDIEVAL MISSIONARIES

No Christian would deny that missionary work is part of the fundamental charter of the Christian Church. The call to "go therefore and make disciples of all nations" (Mt 28:19) echoes throughout the centuries as Jesus' last and greatest charge, and Christians of every generation have responded to it generously. The bold example of the original apostles, especially the globe-trotting St. Paul, served to inspire hundreds of missionaries during the patristic period, including great names like St. Patrick, the Apostle of Ireland, and St. Martin of Tours. By the close of the patristic age, churches had been planted from Ethiopia to Ireland, from Spain to India.

Yet the medieval period brought new missionary challenges. The "barbarian" immigrants, mostly of Germanic races, had flooded the European continent from the northeast, carrying with them their devotion to pagan gods and hostility to the Catholic religion of their Roman adversaries. Even as these were receiving the first seeds of the Christian religion, new fiercely pagan immigrants arrived in the form of Vikings and Magyars.

To complicate matters further, the initial missionary successes among the barbarians had been carried out by non-Catholic missionaries, the heretical Arians, who denied the divinity of Christ. Then there was the problem of Islam, which had overcome the Christian communities in Asia and North Africa by the eighth century. As for mainland Europe, while there were certainly still scattered communities of Catholic Christians, the institutional structures of the Church had been shattered by the invasions: many Christians had not seen clergy for decades and thus lapsed easily back into the pagan superstitions of their past.

In short, by the time of the great missionary awakenings of the seventh century, many among the Christian leadership probably saw themselves as starting from scratch, re-evangelizing an utterly de-Christianized continent.

In some ways medieval missionary work looks very different from the way it is typically carried on today. In the Middle Ages there was a shared cultural assumption that the general population would hold the same religion as the ruler, so a common pattern resurfaces where the conversion of a king would result in the mass baptisms of a nation's entire population.

Another cultural assumption was that a religious figure would legitimize his message by performing miracles, often "outperforming" the representatives of rival religions, as Elijah did on Mount Carmel (see 1 Kgs 18), or Moses before the Pharaoh (Ex 7). Further, because the primary religious alternative to Christianity was paganism, which the New Testament itself describes as demonic in inspiration (1 Cor 10:20), Christian missionaries were often seen as striving against Satanic powers, winning souls from devil-worship. These patterns or themes are, it seems, rarely stressed today.

But in other ways the missionary work of the Middle Ages looks very familiar to us. Then as now, the task of evangelizing was usually combined with the task of civilizing, so that missionaries would spend as much time teaching agricultural methods and basic literacy and providing medical care as they did preaching the Gospel. Also, we see medieval missionaries wrestling with the question of inculturation, or how Christianity would fit into distinctive cultures, balancing a respect for the inherent goodness of every culture with the need to preserve the essential message of the Gospel without watering it down.

Readers will also note how the preaching of the Gospel is most effective when it is combined with a pattern of generosity, charity, and sincere holiness on the part of the missionaries who bring it. And finally, in the Middle Ages as today, missionary work is sustainable only when it is part and parcel of a larger effort to establish lasting Church structures—schools, seminaries, and charitable institutions, for example—rather than being seen as the conversion of individual souls.

Although tens of thousands of individuals probably devoted their lives to missionary work in the Middle Ages, the constraints of space permit the treatment of only a handful. We will first meet St. Columba, a standout among the Irish seafaring saints; then the three dominant figures who worked under the patronage of the bishop of Rome and the protection of the Frankish kingdom: St. Augustine of Canterbury (the Apostle to the English), St. Willibrord (the Apostle to the Frisians), and St. Boniface (the Apostle to the Germans); and, finally, Sts. Cyril and

Methodius, the Greek brothers who missionized the Slavic peoples in the East.

Together, a study of these figures shows us not only how Christians won thousands of souls for the kingdom of heaven, but how the Christian Church built and shaped Western civilization in the process.

ST. COLUMBA (521–597)

It is not without reason that the Scots carried the relics of St. Columba ahead of their armies in the Scottish Wars for Independence. This was a saint, after all, whose missionary career was launched when he was exiled from his Irish homeland for instigating too many brawls. He had first gotten into trouble when he picked a fight with his teacher, St. Finnian, over whether he deserved to keep a copy of the psalter he had been assigned to copy: several men died in the ensuing scuffle. Shortly afterward, he ended up in the middle of a blood feud which broke out at a sporting event, and which resulted in the death of an Irish prince. It should surprise no one that Columba used a stone as a pillow.

Columba's early life actually fits neatly into the Irish tradition of the *peregrini*, or exiles. Irish Christianity was known for its harsh standards for penance: it was not unusual for those who engaged in mortal sin in the Middle Ages to be publicly flogged as penance. And those who had carried out particularly egregious sins often volunteered to undergo what, for the Irishman, is the greatest punishment of all—self-banishment from Ireland. Thus at the age of forty-four Columba, presumably in penance for his violent past, set sail with twelve companions in a wicker boat covered with animal skins.

Landing in nearby Scotland, Columba returned to the boat and cast off again, complaining that he could still see his homeland from the first landing spot. When finally out of sight of his beloved Ireland, Columba began preaching the Gospel to the native barbarians (the Picts), whose king responded by donating the island of Iona to the monks. The monastery they built there became the center of Scottish Christianity, spawning numerous other monasteries across the country and eventually transforming itself into a school for missionaries.

We know precious little about Columba's life except for the vast number of miracles that are attributed to him by his biographers, so many that one would think he did little else with his time. Many of these miracle stories are rather incredible, though without at least *some* historical basis such traditions would certainly never have sprung up. Many of the stories reflect the agrarian culture of Scotland (blessing crops to increase their fertility) and the scholarly work of the monks (detecting grammatical errors in books without opening them).

Columba and his Irish monks, the heirs of a brilliant Latin education—it is said that, at any time, three thousand scholars could be found studying under St. Finnian, Columba's teacher—brought this literary culture to Scotland. Columba's biographer claims that he wrote more than three hundred books by hand and died while transcribing a book.

Some remark ought to be made about the "style" of Christianity brought to Great Britain. While St. Augustine of Canterbury had brought Christianity to England directly from Rome, Irish—or Celtic—Christianity had developed in almost complete isolation from Rome, cut off from any communication with the rest of worldwide Christianity. Thus the Christianity Columba brought to Scotland had several distinctive features: most importantly, abbots, rather than bishops, oversaw religious matters in geographic regions of the country, and Easter was celebrated on a different date from its calculations in Rome.

Although often described as non-papal, the Irish had a great esteem for the bishop of Rome—they simply hadn't heard from him in centuries! But as a consequence, much of the literature on English Christianity during this period describes the rather unedifying feuding between so-called Roman and Celtic missionaries.

COLUMBA COMES TO SCOTLAND

The English monastic scholar St. Bede makes only brief mention of St. Columba, in connection with the founding of the monastery at Iona. But Bede draws attention to certain distinctive, Celtic features of Columba's communities which were different from the Eng-

lish customs he learned from St. Augustine of Canterbury's Roman tradition—namely, the different way of calculating Easter and the tendency of priest-abbots, rather than bishops, to govern churches. (From Bede, Ecclesiastical History of the English People)

In the year of our Lord 565 … there came into Britain from Ireland a famous priest and abbot, marked as a monk by habit and manner of life, whose name was Columba, to preach the word of God to the provinces of the northern Picts…. Columba came into Britain in the ninth year of the reign of Bridius, who was the son of Meilochon, and the powerful king of the Pictish nation, and he converted that nation to the faith of Christ by his preaching and example.

In this way he also received from them the gift of an island [Iona] on which to found a monastery. It is not a large island, but contains about five families, according to the English computation; his successors hold it to this day. He was also buried there when he died at the age of seventy-seven, about thirty-two years after he came into Britain to preach. Before he crossed over into Britain, he had built a famous monastery in Ireland, which, from the great number of oaks, is in the Scottish tongue called Derry— The Field of Oaks.

From both these monasteries, many others had their beginning through his disciples, both in Britain and Ireland; but the island monastery where his body lies has the pre-eminence among them all.

That island has for its ruler an abbot, who is a priest, to whose jurisdiction all the province is subjected, and even the bishops, contrary to the usual method. This is according to the example of their first teacher Columba, who was not a bishop, but a priest and monk, of whose life and discourses some records are said to be preserved by his disciples.

But whatever he was himself, this we know for certain concerning him, that he left successors renowned for their chastity, their love of God, and observance of monastic rules. It is true they employed doubtful cycles in fixing the time of Easter, since no one brought them the relevant decrees of councils, because of their being so far away from the rest of the world; but they earnestly practiced such works of piety and chastity as they could learn from the prophets, the Gospels, and the apostolic writings.

THE MIGHTY MIRACLES OF ST. COLUMBA
IN SCOTLAND

Columba's primary rivals were the pagan Druids, who fought hard to keep Christianity out of Scotland. Of the hundreds of miracle stories that circulated about Columba, many emphasize his demonstration of the superior power of the Christian God, over and against that of the pagan gods of the Druids. One seventh-century story has Columba driving a monster out of Loch Ness, and is often credited as the first sighting of "Nessie"! (From Adamnan's Life of Columba, Founder of Hy)

While the blessed man was stopping for some days in the province of the Picts, he heard that there was a fountain famous amongst this pagan people, which foolish men, having their senses blinded by the devil, worshiped as a god. For those who drank of this fountain, or purposely washed their hands or feet in it, were struck by demonic power, and went home either leprous or blinded, or at least suffering from some kind of weakness. By all these things the pagans were seduced, and paid divine honors to the fountain.

Having heard about this, the saint one day went up to the fountain fearlessly; on seeing this, the Druids, whom he had often sent away from him vanquished and confounded, were greatly rejoiced, thinking that he would suffer like others from the touch of that deadly water. But having first raised his holy hand and invoked the name of Christ, he washed his hands and feet; and then with his companions, drank of the water he had blessed. And from that day the demons departed from the fountain; and not only was it not allowed to injure any one, but even many diseases amongst the people were cured by this same fountain, after it had been blessed and washed in by the saint….

On another occasion also, when the blessed man was living for some days in the province of the Picts, he had to cross the Ness River. When he reached its banks, he saw some of the inhabitants burying an unfortunate man, who had been seized while swimming and bitten cruelly by a monster that lived in the water, as he learned from those who were burying the man … The blessed man, on hearing this, was not at all afraid…. The monster, far from being satisfied, was only hungry for more prey. Lying at the bottom of the stream, when it felt the water disturbed by those above, the monster suddenly rushed out, giving an awful roar with its mouth wide open….

Observing this, while all the rest, brothers as well as strangers, were stupefied with terror, the blessed man raised his holy hand, and invoking the name of God, formed the saving sign of the cross in the air. He commanded the ferocious monster…. "Thou shalt go no further, nor touch the man; go back with all speed."… Then the brothers, seeing that the monster had gone back … were struck with admiration, and gave glory to God in the blessed man. And even the pagan barbarians who were present were forced by the greatness of this miracle, which they themselves had seen, to praise the God of the Christians….

On a certain day after the events recorded in the above chapters, a Druid named Broichan, while talking with the saint, said to him: "Tell me, Columba, when are you planning to set sail?" The saint replied, "I intend to begin my voyage after three days, if God permits me, and preserves my life." Broichan said, "On the contrary, you will not be able to, for I can make the winds unfavorable to your voyage, and cause a great darkness to surround you." The saint replied, "The almighty power of God rules all things, and in His name and under His guiding providence all our actions are directed."

What more should I say? That same day the saint, accompanied by a large number of followers, went to Loch Ness as he had determined. Then the Druids began to rejoice, seeing that it had become very dark, and that the wind was very violent and contrary. (We should not be surprised at this: we know that God sometimes allows them, with the aid of evil spirits, to raise storms and agitate the sea.)

Our Columba, therefore, seeing that the sea was violently stirred up, and that the wind was most unfavorable for his voyage, called on Christ the Lord and set out in his small boat; and while the sailors hesitated, he all the more confidently ordered them to raise the sails against the wind. No sooner was this order carried out, while the whole crowd was looking on, than the ship ran against the wind with extraordinary speed. And after a short time, the wind, which until then had been against them, shifted to help them on their voyage, to the intense astonishment of all. And thus throughout the remainder of that day the light breeze continued most favorable, and the ship of the blessed man was carried safely to the port he was seeking.

A HYMN TO GOD THE CREATOR

The astonishing miracles for which Columba was remembered should not cause us to forget his work in spreading art, literacy, and education. Scotland was also devoid of any developed intellectual culture, and the Irish missionaries brought with them the Latin intellectual culture they had learned from Catholic missionaries from the days of St. Patrick. The following is a hymn written by Columba, called "Altus Prosator": it is "abecedarian," meaning that, at least in the original Latin, each stanza begins with a different letter of the alphabet.

> High Creator, Unbegotten,
> Ancient of Eternal days,
> Unbegun ere all beginning,
> Him, the world's one source, we praise:
> God who is, and God who shall be:
> All that was and is before:

Him with Christ the Sole-Begotten,
And the Spirit we adore,
Co-eternal, one in glory.
Evermore and evermore:—
Not Three Gods are They we worship.
But the Three which are the One,
God, in Three most glorious Persons:—
Other saving Faith is none.

* * *

All good angels and archangels,
Powers and Principalities,
Virtues, Thrones, His will created—
Grades and orders of the skies,
That the majesty and goodness
Of the Blessed Trinity
In its ever bounteous largesse
Never might inactive be;
Having thus wherewith to glory.
All the wide world might adore
The high Godhead's sole-possession
Everywhere and evermore.

* * *

God, the Lord Most High, foreseeing
Nature's concord full and sweet.
Molded Heaven and Earth and Ocean
To one harmony complete:
Sprang the grasses, fair unfolding.
Copses burgeoned in the sun:
Beamed the sunlight, starlight, moonlight,
Firelight: all of need was done—
Birds for brake, and fish for waters.
Wild or tame kine for the sward—
Last, the highest, first created,

Man, Creation's crown and lord.

* * *

When together, ethereal wonder,
Shine the Stars, the Angels sing;
To th' Immensity's Designer,
Host on host, their anthems ring:
Songs right meet for adoration,
Glorious harmonies they raise;
Since they move not from their courses
Never-ending is their praise.
Noble concert in the highest
Is their offering full and free:—
'Tis of love's sincerest rapture
Not of natural decree.

* * *

From the Lord the rain's soft showerings
Ever fall at need below:
Closely stored behind their barriers
Lest their bounty overflow:
Slowly, surely fertilizing,
Never failing at His will.
They as if from breast maternal
O'er the earth their balm distill:
So the rivers in their season.
From the winter to the spring.
To the autumn from the summer
Their inflowings ever bring.

ST. COLUMBA'S LEGACY:
CELTIC VS. ROMAN CHRISTIANITY

The Irish (Celtic) missions penetrating England from the north-west and the Roman missions penetrating from the southeast were destined to clash. In most matters they were identical, but on several minor points—such as the date of celebrating Easter—they differed sharply, mainly because the Irish Church had developed in isolation for centuries, with virtually no contact from the rest of Europe. St. Bede describes how England settled the matter, by a debate about which saint was greater—Columba or Peter! (From Bede, Ecclesiastical History of the English People*)*

At this time a significant and fiercely debated question arose about the celebration of Easter: those Christians from Kent or France claimed that the Irish celebrated Easter on a day differently than the custom of the universal church…. This had the unfortunate consequence that Easter was celebrated twice every year in England, and sometimes when the king, having ended his fast, was celebrating Easter, the queen and her followers were still fasting on Palm Sunday…. This reached the ears of the rulers, King Oswy and his son Alchfrid … who decided that this and other ecclesiastical questions should be settled once and for all at a council. The kings, both father and son, came there, and the bishops, the priests, and an interpreter….

King Oswy first made an opening speech in which he said that it was proper for those who served one God to observe one rule of life, and as they all expected the same kingdom in heaven, so they should not differ in the celebration of the heavenly mysteries. Rather, they should inquire which was the truer tradition, so that it might be followed by everyone together….

Wilfrid, having been ordered by the king to speak, began in this way: "The Easter which we keep, we saw celebrated by all at Rome, where the blessed Apostles, Peter and Paul, lived, taught, suffered, and were buried; we saw the same done by all in Italy and in France, when we traveled through those countries for the purpose of study and prayer. We found it observed in Africa, Asia, Egypt, Greece, and all the world, wherever the Church of Christ is spread abroad, among different nations and tongues, at one and the same time; save only among those here and those who join them in their stubbornness—the Picts and the Britons, in these remote islands of the ocean, and only in part of these islands, who foolishly insist on contradicting all the rest of the world."...

To this Colman rejoined.... "Are you suggesting that our most reverend Father Columba and his successors, men beloved by God, who kept Easter after the same manner, judged or acted contrary to the sacred writings? On the contrary, there were many among them, whose holiness was affirmed by heavenly signs and miracles which they worked, whom I, for my part, do not doubt to be saints, and whose life, customs, and discipline I never cease to follow."...

Wilfrid responded, "If that Columba of yours (and, I may say, ours also, if he was Christ's servant) was a holy man and powerful in miracles, yet could he be preferred before the most blessed chief of the Apostles, to whom our Lord said, 'You are Peter, and upon this rock I will build my Church, and the gates of hell shall not prevail against it, and I will give to you the keys of the kingdom of Heaven'?"

When Wilfrid had ended thus, the king said, "Is it true, Colman, that these words were spoken to Peter by our Lord?" He answered, "It is true, O king!" Then said he, "Can you show any such power given to your Columba?" Colman answered, "None."... Then the king concluded, "And I also say unto you, that he is the doorkeeper, and I will not decide against him, but I desire, as far as I know and am able, in all things to obey his laws, for if I do otherwise, I may come to the gates of the kingdom of Heaven, and there should be none to open them, since I have made an enemy of the one who has the keys."

The king having said this, all who were seated there or standing by, both great and small, gave their assent, and renouncing the less perfect custom, quickly accepted the better one.

ST. AUGUSTINE OF CANTERBURY (d. 604)

Although we know little or no personal detail about the life of St. Augustine of Canterbury, we do know that there would probably never have been an English Church without him. From the sources we get the impression of an unassuming man content to work quietly in the fields, patiently building an edifice that would dominate the English landscape for over a millennium.

Although Christian missionaries had reached the native Britons in England by the early fourth century, the Church there was in tatters by the sixth. The withdrawal of Roman legions in 410 to protect the Imperial capital had led to an immediate invasion by the Saxons, as ruthless in their pagan religion as in their barbaric behavior. The few Christians who lingered among the now-conquered Britons were disheartened and gave up all hope of convincing their conquerors to accept the Gospel. While the Irish had some luck missionizing the northern coasts, they could not penetrate the interior. It seemed that all hope for a Christian England was lost.

Yet that great missionary pope, St. Gregory the Great, would not be daunted. A legend traces his brainchild of an English mission to an encounter with English slaves in a Roman slave market: Gregory nourished a lifelong scheme to buy slaves, free them, convert them, and send them back to their homelands as missionaries. Struck with the beauty of the fair-haired English, Gregory was horrified to hear that they had no missionaries among them. He thus hatched the most carefully conceived and well-organized missionary strategy since the days of St. Paul, forming a missionary team of forty handpicked monks from his own Roman abbey under the leadership of Augustine, their prior at the time.

Augustine was the right man for the job. His sharp wit, his delicate pastoral touch, and the natural knack for administration he had shown as prior would all be necessary in the mission field. Augustine's first task was to establish a support network in the nearest Christian community, bringing his team to France to gather resources, including interpreters and local information. His next task was to rally the spirits of his team: the horror stories they heard in France of the savageries of the Saxons made the team unwilling to go on!

Next, after convincing the team to continue, he carefully plotted out the mission strategy. It may have been Augustine's choice to begin the mission in Kent, where rumor had it that the local king, Ethelbert, was sympathetic to Christianity, having wed a Christian wife. Plus, situated next to the channel, Kent would put the team in close geographical proximity to its French support network. Augustine's tactic of working closely with the royal couple meant it was only a matter of time before the king—with the gentle pressure of his wife—converted, and once the king converted, so would the nation. Within a year Augustine was able to baptize ten thousand Saxons in a Christmas ceremony.

From this point onward, Augustine left a profound legacy in the English Church. He fostered a strong devotion to the pope among the English—in fact, he considered his team an extension of the papacy itself, constantly asking the pope for advice on missionary strategies. A Benedictine monk himself, he quickly built a monastery on English soil, and with it a school for training missionaries, laying the foundations for an English monastic and missionary tradition that would reshape Europe.

His correspondence shows a profound sensitivity to local customs and a willingness to allow English Christianity to take its own distinctive cultural shape, rather than be supplanted by Roman Christianity. Perhaps he learned from his own mistakes: his failure to stand up to greet Irish missionaries during a meeting, probably due to his Roman aristocratic background, was a huge cultural faux pas and caused a decades-long schism between the Roman and Irish churches. Nonetheless, the Apostle to the English has always been seen as the founder of Christianity in England and a model missionary.

THE LAUNCHING OF THE ENGLISH MISSION

Bede, an English monastic scholar, tells of how Pope Gregory the Great first conceived of the plan for a mission to England, its rocky start, and its gradual successes. (From Bede, Ecclesiastical History of the English People*)*

Around AD 596, Gregory, a man famous for his holy life and solid education, became bishop of Rome, an office he held for over thirteen years. Through divine inspiration, he sent that servant of God, Augustine, along with several other God-fearing monks, to preach the word of God to the English nation.

But as soon as they had begun that work in obedience to the pope's commands, they suddenly were seized with fear and planned to return home, terrified of proceeding to a fierce, barbaric, and pagan nation, whose language they did not even know. In unanimous agreement that this would be the safest course, they sent back Augustine—who was supposed to be ordained a bishop in England if the mission were a success—to beg St. Gregory that they might be allowed to abandon such a dangerous, burdensome and risky journey. The pope replied by sending the entire group a letter, insisting that they proceed with their labor on behalf of God's word, trusting in the assistance of Almighty God….

Augustine, encouraged by Gregory's letter, returned to the work of God's word, and arrived at Britain with nearly forty companions and Frankish interpreters. The mighty Ethelbert was at that time king of Kent…. They sent a message to him, indicating that they came from Rome and brought a joyful message of eternal life in heaven with God for anyone who was willing to listen to it. The king heard this and ordered them to stay put for a while until he could decide what to do about them. For he knew about the Christian religion, having a Christian wife from France named

Bertha: she had been raised a Christian and married Ethelbert only on the condition that she could continue to practice [the Faith].

A few days later he came to them, inviting them to sit in his presence in the open air. (He was afraid to meet them indoors because of an ancient superstition that, if he did so, their magical powers might be able to overpower him. But they brought divine power, not magic.) They carried a silver cross for a banner, an image of our Lord and Savior painted on a board, singing a litany and praying to the Lord for the salvation of themselves and the English people.

After Augustine had preached the word of life to the king and his attendants, the king answered: "You speak pleasantly and make attractive promises, but they are new to us and confusing, and I cannot accept them, since this would mean breaking with ancient English custom. But because you have traveled so far to my kingdom, and seem very eager and sincere in your desire to share this message, I won't harass you, but will act as your host, providing you with supplies and allowing you to preach and gain any converts who will listen to you." So the king allowed them to stay in the city of Canterbury, and gave them liberty to preach.

As soon as they moved into the residence he gave them, they began to imitate the practices of the early Church: frequent prayer, fasting, preaching to as many as possible, practicing self-denial, eating only the food they needed for subsistence, which they received from their converts, living exactly in the way which matched the message they were preaching, always willing to suffer and even die for the truth they preached. Because of this, several believed and were baptized, admiring the simplicity and innocence of their life, and the beauty of their teaching ... until eventually the king himself was converted to their faith.... After he was baptized, greater numbers began to gather to hear the word, abandoning their pagan rituals, believing and joining the unity of Christ's Church. The king encouraged such conversions but did not force anyone to convert: he contented himself with showing more personal affection to those who did, because he had learned from Augustine and his companions that serving Christ ought to be done voluntarily, not by force.

ONE CHURCH, MANY CUSTOMS

Augustine maintained a steady line of communication with his patron, Pope Gregory, in Rome, asking him questions about Church policy and allowing the pope to influence the basic shape of the newly born English Church. One question that confused Augustine was the sharp divergence in customs between Christians in Rome, where he had been raised, and those in France. (Some French Christians had immigrated to England, so at this time England had been influenced by French customs.) As a Roman missionary, how aggressive should he be in forcing the English to accept Roman customs? (From Bede, Ecclesiastical History of the English People*)*

Augustine's second question: Even though the Christian faith is one and the same everywhere, why are there different customs in different churches? Why is the Mass said one way in the Roman churches, and another way in the French churches?

Pope Gregory's answer: You know, my brother, only the customs of the Roman Church in which you were raised. But if you found anything more acceptable to God in *any* church—Roman, French, or any other—it would make me happy if you made use of it. You should carefully teach the English people, who are very new to Christianity, anything useful you can gather from the various churches. For things are not to be loved for the sake of the places they are found, but places for the sake of good things found in them.

Therefore, you should choose things that are devout, holy, and orthodox from every church, and make them into one body, so to speak, and only after that should you introduce them to the English.

THE SLOW AND PATIENT TASK OF THE MISSIONARY

Every missionary faces the question of pace: How quickly should one try to move a convert from his false opinions and practices to true ones? Should the convert be pushed to abandon his old life "cold turkey," all at once, or can he be allowed to take more gradual steps, growing accustomed to his new life more slowly? Pope Gregory gave clear instructions to Augustine that he should opt for a more gradual pace in England, hoping that this would draw in more converts than an all-or-nothing approach. (From Gregory's Letter no. 76)

I have put a lot of thought into the case of the English. I have decided that their pagan temples should not be destroyed, but only the idols that are inside them. Instead, just sprinkle these temples with holy water, and put new altars in them with Christian relics inside. After all, if the temples are well-built, they can simply be transferred from the worship of idols to that of the true God.

This way, when the people see their beloved temples not destroyed but preserved, they might be more willing to abandon their error. They can continue to visit the places they are comfortable with, and can gradually learn to adore the true God there. Since they have a long habit of offering animal sacrifices to demonic idols, they might be allowed to continue some similar practice, in a different form. For example, on the anniversary of the saints whose relics are in the temple, they might carry out some ceremony using branches from the trees around the temple, once that temple has become a church, and thus celebrate the saint's feast day.

They might even continue to kill animals, but not to sacrifice them to the devil, but rather to eat them, while giving thanks to God for giving all things to them. In this way, they can outwardly carry out some of the same activities they have always enjoyed doing, while inwardly we can gradually steer their minds toward other enjoyments. The reason is that it is no doubt impossible to remove all bad habits immediately from hardhearted people. Someone who wants to get to a high place must get there by small steps, not by huge leaps.

After all, God treated the people of Israel this way. They had grown accustomed to offering animal sacrifices to demonic idols while in Egypt, and He did not prevent them from offering such sacrifices, but simply instructed them to offer them to himself, in order to change their hearts. In this way, some elements in their sacrificial worship changed, but others remained the same, and since they were offered to God and not to idols, while they may have looked the same as before, they were actually quite different.

ST. WILLIBRORD (658–739)

Though little is known of Willibrord's life, this has not stopped the citizens of Luxembourg from their rather quirky celebration of his life, the annual Procession of Holy Dancers, wherein every year thousands hop in a coordinated dance for a mile to the abbey church at Echternach which Willibrord founded. Perhaps it is an appropriate celebration for the life of a man whose miracles, nearly half of the time, involved the multiplication of wine flasks for festivities.

An Englishman of Saxon stock, Willibrord joined the Benedictines at the young age of fifteen, studying for over a decade under the best and brightest of his day, both in England and in Ireland: he had both St. Egbert and St. Wilfrid for educators. His burning desire to preach to the barbarians in Frisia (modern-day Holland) couldn't be quenched, however, and in his thirties he journeyed to Utrecht with eleven companions to establish a missionary headquarters there.

Willibrord set the example for later European missionaries by seeking out the military protection of the strongest Catholic kingdom of the day—that of the French rulers Charles Martel and Pepin—and by voluntarily submitting their missionary endeavors to the patronage of the bishop of Rome.

Willibrord struggled to establish a functional church in Frisia, even collaborating with the young St. Boniface for several years. When the pagan king Radbod seized power, however, he destroyed almost all of the churches Willibrord had built, replacing them with pagan shrines and killing any missionary he could lay hands on. Patiently, Willibrord returned and rebuilt the devastated churches once the Frankish king could guarantee his safety.

Though well trained as a scholar, the only confirmed writing we have from Willibrord is a note in the margin of a calendar, where he scribbled the date of his arrival in Frisia. Thankfully, St. Alcuin of York, Willibrord's blood relative and the greatest scholar of his day, wrote a biography to record Willibrord's legacy for later generations.

THE BEGINNINGS OF THE DUTCH MISSION

St. Alcuin's biography of his relative St. Willibrord shows how the monastic schools of England could become breeding grounds for future missionaries. We also see, in these selections, how French military power served as a necessary support for European missions.

By the age of thirty-three [Willibrord's] religious fervor had reached such a pitch of intensity that he decided it was not worthwhile to continue to increase his own holiness, unless he could also preach the Gospel to others and increase their holiness as well. He had heard that in the northern regions of the world "the harvest is plentiful, but the laborers are few" (Lk 10:2). Therefore, in fulfillment of his mother's dream, Willibrord, knowing only of his own decision, and not of God's preordination, decided to sail for these parts, so that if God willed it he would bring the light of the Gospel message to those whose unbelief had not been stirred by its warmth.

So he departed on a ship, taking eleven others who shared his enthusiasm for the faith. Some of these companions gained a martyr's crown through their constant preaching of the Gospel; others later became bishops and have since died in peace, after their labors in the holy work in preaching.

Thus the man of God and his brothers, as we have said, set sail, and after a successful crossing they moored their ships at the mouth of the Rhine River. Then, after resting, they set out for the castle of Utrecht, which lies on the bank of that river, and where some years later, after God had increased the faith of the people, Willibrord built his cathedral church.

But the Frisian people, and Radbod their king, still preferred their pagan practices. So Willibrord set out for France instead and met with its king, Pepin, a man of immense energy, military success and high moral character. Pepin received him respectfully, and not wanting to lose the services of so great a scholar, he invited him to preach within his own kingdom, to uproot idolatry and to teach the newly converted.

THE POPE ORDAINS AND COMMISSIONS WILLIBRORD

The English Church, founded by the Roman missionary St. Augustine of Canterbury, possessed a strong loyalty to the papacy. It is no surprise, then, that missionaries from England often stopped by Rome for authorization and a blessing from the pope.

After a time, the man of God had carefully visited several places and carried out the task of evangelization, and the seed of life, watered by the dews of heavenly grace, had born great fruit in the hearts of many souls. Then the king of the Franks, pleased with Willibrord's burning zeal and the extraordinary growth of the Christian faith, which he sought to expand even further, decided to send him to Rome to be ordained a bishop by Pope Sergius, one of the holiest men of that time. In this way, having the apostolic blessing and papal mandate, he would return to preach the Gospel with even greater confidence and vigor....

The pope, warned in advance by a heavenly dream, welcomed Willibrord with great joy and showed him every courtesy. For he saw in Willibrord a sincere faith, a religious devotion, and a profound wisdom. Therefore, he appointed a day for the ordination when all the people could assemble together.

He invited holy priests to take part in the ceremony, and in accordance with apostolic tradition and with great reverence, he publicly ordained him archbishop in the church of St. Peter, prince of the apostles. At the same time he renamed him "Clement" … and whatever he asked for (relics of saints, liturgical vessels, etc.) the pope gave him without hesitation, so that he was sent back to preach the Gospel loaded with gifts and strengthened with the apostolic blessing.

WILLIBRORD DESECRATES A PAGAN SHRINE

Like his protégé, St. Boniface, St. Willibrord had little patience for the pagan superstitions of the German natives. His dismissive treatment of pagan shrines did much, however, to impress the inhabitants, who expected their gods to punish such violators of shrines.

Now while this energetic preacher of God's Word was continuing his journey he came to a certain island on the Frisian-Danish boundary, which the natives had named Fositeland after a god named Fosite, whom they worshiped and whose temples stood there. The pagans held that place in great awe, so that none of the natives would venture to touch the cattle that fed there, and would only draw water from the spring that bubbled up there in complete silence.

Willibrord was driven ashore on that island by a storm, and had to wait for some days until the wind died down and fair weather made it possible to set sail again. He cared nothing for the superstitious "sacredness" of that spot, or for the savage cruelty of the king, who was said to condemn to the most cruel death those who violated those sacred objects. Instead, Willibrord used the water from the sacred springs to baptize three people in the name of the Blessed Trinity and slaughtered several of the cattle as food for his companions.

When the pagans saw this they expected the strangers to become mad or be struck with sudden death. But they were astounded and terror-stricken when they saw that Willibrord and his companions suffered no harm at all.

ST. BONIFACE (d. 754)

That St. Boniface was hacked to death by a mob of frenzied pagans while preparing for a confirmation service probably surprised no one. As a man of determination, with an iron will, tact and diplomacy had not exactly been his strong suit. Once, when pagan villagers would not stop worshiping an oak tree believed to be sacred to Thor, Boniface snatched up an axe and chopped it down. When he was not (as the villagers had expected) struck by Thor's lightning, they agreed to convert, but such tactics were not likely to make him many friends.

Boniface, named Winfrid by his parents, was born among the Saxon tribes in England who had been so patiently won for the Church by the efforts of St. Augustine of Canterbury. Sometime after joining a Benedictine monastery over the objections of his parents, he turned down election as its abbot, departing for mainland Germany to preach the Gospel to his kinfolk there, never to return to his native land again. He worked under the tutelage of the elderly missionary St. Willibrord for some years in the forests of the German interior and took up that saint's mantle upon the latter's death.

Like most great missionaries, however, Winfrid knew he needed support. St. Augustine of Canterbury had impressed on the English a strong devotion to the papacy, and of his own initiative Winfrid traveled to Rome and sought the pope's blessing and commission for his missionary endeavors. (It was the pope who, apparently impressed with this missionary's eagerness, renamed him Boniface, from *bonum facere*, "to do good.")

The pope encouraged him to secure the military protection of the French, whose armies could guarantee his safety among the savage German tribes, and it was probably Boniface's close collaboration with both Rome and the French kings that set the stage for the later alliance which would emerge in the age of Charlemagne.

Boniface worked patiently in the German hinterlands, building church structures from the ground up, establishing monasteries, seminaries, and bishoprics while presiding over Church synods to enforce strict moral standards on local clergy. Boniface's pattern of convincing entire tribes to convert, often through extraordinary acts like the felling of the sacred oak, and then leaving until later the work of catechesis and Christian instruction, meant that the Christian religion in mainland Europe was often only superficial, with paganism and barbarism lurking just below the surface.

Yet Boniface, known today as the Apostle to the Germans, was a pioneer, furrowing new ground and planting the seeds so that later generations could cultivate and nurture the growth.

THE POPE COMMISSIONS BONIFACE
AS A MISSIONARY

*The fateful meeting between Boniface and Pope Gregory II would forge lasting links between the German people and the papacy, links of faith and charity that would bear significant fruit throughout the Middle Ages. (*From Willibald's *Life of Boniface)*

When [Winfrid] read a letter carried to him by a messenger, he learned that he was summoned to Rome, and in a spirit of complete obedience, he got ready as quickly as he could…. Eventually he came into sight of the walls of Rome, and giving praise and thanks to God on high, he went quickly to the Church of St. Peter, where he strengthened himself in long and earnest prayer. After he had rested his weary limbs for a brief time, he had a message sent to blessed Gregory [II], bishop of the Apostolic See, saying that he had arrived….

A convenient day was fixed for a meeting, and at the appointed time the pope came down to the Basilica of St. Peter the Apostle, and the servant of God was summoned to his presence. After they had exchanged a few words of greeting, the bishop of the Apostolic See asked him some questions on his doctrine—on the creeds, traditions and beliefs of his church….

They discussed and debated many other matters relating to holy religion and the true faith, and in this exchange of views they spent almost the whole day.

At last the pope asked how successful he was in preaching the true faith to a people so rooted in error and sin. On learning that a vast number had been converted from the sacrilegious worship of idols and admitted to the communion of the Church, the pope told him that he intended to ordain him a bishop and set him over people who up to that time had been without a leader to guide them….

When the holy day for the sacred solemnity arrived, which was both the feast day of St. Andrew and the day set aside for his ordination, the holy pope of the Apostolic See ordained him a bishop and gave him the name of Boniface…. He also offered to him and to all his subjects the friendship of the holy Apostolic See from that time on and forever. Also, by means of his most sacred letters, the pope placed the holy man, now strengthened by ordination as a bishop, under the protection and devotion of the glorious leader Charlemagne.

BONIFACE FELLS THE SACRED OAK

Whereas St. Augustine of Canterbury had taken a milder approach, preserving and remodeling pagan temples into Christian churches, St. Boniface preferred tough love. His preference for outright destruction of pagan shrines, as a way of testifying to the superior power of the Christian God, was the far more common method. (From Willibald's Life of Boniface)

Now many of the Hessians who at that time had accepted the Christian faith were confirmed by the grace of the Holy Spirit through the laying on of hands. But others, weaker in spirit, still refused to accept the pure teachings of the Church in their entirety. Moreover, some continued—some secretly, others openly—to offer sacrifices to trees and springs, to inspect the entrails of victims, to practice divination, magic and sorcery, to attend to auguries, auspices and other sacrificial rites, even though others who were more reasonable abandoned all of these pagan customs and committed none of these crimes.

It was on the advice of these latter persons that Boniface endeavored to cut down, at a place called Gaesmere, a certain oak of extraordinary size called the Oak of Jupiter in the old pagan languages. Summoning up all his courage—for a great crowd of pagans stood by, watching and cursing this "enemy of the gods" in their hearts—he cut the first notch. But after the first, superficial cut, the vast trunk of the oak crashed to the ground, shaken by a mighty blast of wind from above, its topmost branches shattering into fragments. As if by God's will, for the brothers who were there had done nothing to cause it, the oak burst apart into four parts, each of equal length.

At the sight of this extraordinary spectacle, the heathens who had been cursing ceased to do so, and rather believed and praised the Lord. After this, that holy bishop discussed with his brothers, and then built a church from the wood of the oak, dedicating it to St. Peter the Apostle.

THE MARTYRDOM OF BONIFACE

Boniface's first missionary journey had been to Frisia (modern-day Holland), where the native barbarians were more fierce and savage than any others on the continent. Having had little success, he always dreamed of returning, and as an elderly bishop he finally determined to go back to Frisia, having no doubt he would be killed there. (From Willibald's Life of Boniface)

When the Lord willed to deliver his servant from the trials of this world and set him free from the vicissitudes of this mortal life, it was decided, under God's providence, that he should travel in the company of his disciples to Frisia, from which he had departed in body but not in spirit. And this was done so that in dying there he might receive the divine reward in the same place where he had begun his preaching….

This, then, is how he traveled throughout the whole of Frisia, destroying pagan worship and turning people away from their pagan errors by his preaching of the Gospel. The pagan temples and gods were overthrown and churches were built in their place. Many thousands of men, women, and children were baptized by him….

When the faith had finally been firmly planted in Frisia and the glorious end of that saint's life drew near, he took with him a handpicked group of his personal followers and … set a date when he would confirm through the laying on of hands all those who had recently been baptized….

But events turned out otherwise than expected. When the appointed date arrived and the morning light was breaking through the clouds after sunrise, enemies arrived instead of friends, new executioners instead of new worshipers of the faith. A vast number of foes armed with spears and shields rushed into the camp brandishing their weapons. In the blink of an eye the attendants sprang from the camp to meet them, snatching up weapons here and there to defend the holy band of martyrs (for that is what they would soon be) against the insane fury of the mob.

But the man of God, hearing the shouts and the onrush of the mob, called all his clergy to his side and emerged from his tent, gathering up the relics of the saints that he always carried with him. At once he scolded his attendants and forbade them to continue fighting, saying: "Sons, cease fighting. Lay down your arms, for we are told in the Scriptures not to render evil for good but to overcome evil by good."….

While he was encouraging his disciples with these words to accept the crown of martyrdom, the frenzied mob of pagans rushed suddenly upon them with swords and every kind of deadly weapon, staining their bodies with their precious blood.

HOW TO ARGUE WITH A PAGAN

St. Boniface's close collaborator throughout his life, Bishop Daniel of Winchester, wrote, about 723, to advise him on the best way of arguing with a pagan. Daniel's advice—don't argue, just keep asking them questions about their beliefs until they realize just how absurd they are—is timeless. (From Letters of St. Boniface, *no. 11)*

To Boniface, honored and beloved leader, from Daniel, servant of the people of God.

My joy is great, brother and fellow-bishop, that your good work is finally achieving results. Supported by your deep faith and great courage, you have undertaken to convert pagans whose hearts have until now been stony and barren, and with the Gospel as your plow you have labored tirelessly day after day to transform them into fields fertile for harvest…. Moved by affection and good will, I am taking the liberty of making a few suggestions, in order to show you how, in my opinion, you may overcome with the least possible trouble the resistance of these barbaric people.

Do not start arguing with them about the genealogies of their false gods. Accept their premise that each god and goddess was begotten by other gods through sexual intercourse: then you can point out that, if these gods have a beginning, being born like humans are, they must be human and not gods. Once they admit that their gods have a beginning, you should ask them whether the world had a beginning or whether it has always existed. For before there was a universe, there was no place for the gods to live….

But if they answer that the universe has no beginning, then try to prove otherwise, or simply ask them more questions: Who ruled the universe, then? How did the gods come to rule the universe, if it existed before them? Where did the *first* gods and goddesses come from? Do the gods and goddesses continue to reproduce? If not, when did they stop, and why? If so, the number of gods must be infinite. If they are, which god is the most powerful? How can we possibly know this? But we had better know, or else we might offend this god, who is more powerful than the rest, by not honoring him.

 Ask whether they think that the gods should be worshiped only for the sake of some earthly benefit, or for a future, eternal reward? If for an earthly benefit, point out that pagans are no better off than Christians in earthly benefits, so what good is it to be a pagan? Ask them why their gods even want to be worshiped, if they already rule the universe? Then ask how we know what kind of sacrifices they want, and why they do not choose more suitable sacrifices.

These and similar questions, and many others that it would be tedious to mention, should be put to them, not in an offensive and irritating way, but calmly and with great moderation. From time to time their superstitions should be compared with our Christian doctrines and touched upon indirectly, so that the pagans, more out of confusion than exasperation, may be ashamed of their absurd opinions and may recognize that their offensive rituals and ridiculous legends have not escaped our notice.

They must face this conclusion: If their gods are omnipotent, beneficent, and just, they must reward their worshipers and punish those who despise them. Why then, if they act thus in earthly affairs, do they spare the Christians who cast down their idols and turn away from their worship the inhabitants of practically the entire globe?

CHRISTIAN HYPOCRISY: THE GREATEST OBSTACLE
TO MISSIONARY WORK

Boniface's continuous letters to his supporters reveal that his greatest headaches came not from savage pagans but from misbehaving Christians. These letters are filled with questions as to how to discipline clergy who keep mistresses, bishops who use their offices for monetary gain, and so on. His replacement as bishop had to step down because of his involvement in a violent blood feud with another family. In this letter to a newly elected pope, Boniface complains that rumors of misbehavior of Christians in Rome have caused grumbling among his own congregations, who don't see why they have to abandon practices that Roman Christians still practice. (From Letters of St. Boniface, no. 27)

To our beloved lord Zacharias, who bears the insignia of the supreme pontificate, from Boniface, a servant of the servants of God.

We confess, Father and Lord, that after we had learned through messengers that your predecessor Gregory, of holy memory, had departed this life, nothing gave us greater comfort and happiness than the knowledge that God had appointed Your Holiness to enforce the canonical decrees and govern the Apostolic See. Kneeling at your feet, we earnestly beg that, as we have been devoted servants and humble disciples to your predecessors in the See of Peter, we may likewise be counted obedient servants, under canon law, of Your Holiness.

It is our firm resolution to preserve the Catholic faith and the unity of the Church of Rome, and I shall continue to urge as many hearers and disciples as God shall grant me on this mission to render obedience to the Apostolic See.

Be it known to you also, Holy Father, that Carloman, Emperor of the Franks, summoned me to his presence and desired me to convoke a synod in that part of the Frankish kingdom which is under his jurisdiction. He promised me that he would reform and reestablish ecclesiastical discipline, which for the past sixty or seventy years has been completely disregarded and despised….

The episcopal sees, which are in the cities, have been given, for the most part, into the possession of avaricious laymen or exploited by adulterous and unworthy clerics for worldly uses…. Among them are bishops who deny the charges of fornication and adultery but who, nevertheless, are shiftless drunkards, addicted to the chase, who march armed into battle and shed with their own hands the blood of Christians and heathens alike.

Since I am recognized as the servant and legate of the Apostolic See, my decisions here and your decisions in Rome ought to be in complete agreement when I send messengers to receive your judgment.

Because the sensual and ignorant Allemanians, Bavarians, and Franks see that some of these abuses which we condemn are rampant in Rome, they think that the priests there allow them, and on that account they reproach us and take bad example. They say that in Rome, near the church of St. Peter, they have seen throngs of people parading the streets at the beginning of January of each year, shouting and singing songs in pagan fashion, loading tables with food and drink from morning until night, and that during that time no man is willing to lend his neighbor fire or tools or anything useful from his own house.

They recount also that they have seen women wearing pagan amulets and bracelets on their arms and legs and offering them for sale. All such abuses witnessed by sensual and ignorant people bring reproach upon us here and frustrate our work of preaching and teaching….

If Your Holiness would put an end to these pagan customs in Rome it would redound to your credit besides promoting the success of our teaching of the faith.

May God protect Your Holiness and may you enjoy health and long life in Christ.

STS. CYRIL (826–869) and METHODIUS (815–885)

The story of Saints Cyril and Methodius is something of an East-meets-West fairy tale, in which Greek brothers are sent by a Byzantine emperor into Moravia, where conflicts with German clergy lead to their alliance with the Latin pope.

Born in Greece to a high-ranking Byzantine military officer, Cyril and Methodius (originally named Michael and Constantine—as was the custom, they adopted new names upon becoming monks) received the top-notch education suited to such aristocrats. While they were quickly funneled into the Byzantine civil service, they both renounced promising political careers to enter a monastery together. Their illustrious reputations, however, haunted them, and the Byzantine emperor recalled them into public service, pressing them to go on diplomatic missions into Iraq, the Caucuses and ultimately Moravia (modern-day Czech Republic).

It was in Moravia that the brothers earned the legacy that led to their being proclaimed co-patrons of Europe in the Roman Catholic tradition and equal to the apostles in the Eastern Orthodox. Frankish missionaries had labored in Moravia for years without success. Their refusal to allow the Slavic natives to worship in their own languages—they insisted on praying and preaching in Latin—came off as culturally insensitive, and the Moravians suspected an agenda of annexing their nation to the burgeoning Carolingian Empire in the West. The gravest obstacle to a Slavic liturgy, however, was that no written language existed: the phonetic sounds of the Slavic tongue had never been transcribed into a written alphabet.

Knowing Cyril's gift for languages (he knew Greek, Arabic, and Hebrew), the emperor asked him not only to master the Slavic tongue, but also to write an alphabet for the language and teach it to the Slavs. Cyril set to work, devising the alphabet and undertaking a massive translation project, producing in the end—with the help of his brother—Slavic liturgical books, large portions of the Bible, and even a civil law code. The Cyrillic alphabet, a descendent of Cyril's, is the basis of numerous modern languages today. The brothers' mission in Moravia was, therefore, part evangelization and part literacy program.

The brothers' mission was driven by the notion that the Gospel must be inculturated anew in every culture it enters, taking up and sanctifying, rather than repudiating, the positive elements of that culture, not only language but also customs, symbols, and traditions. The Moravian mission was continually harassed, however, by Frankish clergy who insisted that God could be rightly worshiped only in Latin (or Greek or Hebrew, which they also acknowledged).

The bishop of Rome, however, took the brothers' side, summoning them to Rome, endorsing the Slavic liturgy, and ordaining Methodius a priest. While Cyril died in Rome, Methodius was encouraged by the pope to expand his mission into vast regions of Austria, Hungary, Serbia, and Croatia, over which the pope eventually gave him jurisdiction as bishop.

The Franks, however, never forgave Methodius for his refusal to Latinize the Slavs, and Methodius spent many of his later years experiencing harassment, exile, and even imprisonment, being freed only upon the stern order of the pope himself. Sadly, his disciples in Eastern Europe were exiled after his death, but they simply carried on the mission work eastward, eventually resulting in the conversion of Russia to Christianity.

Given the legacy of these brothers, then, it is no surprise that they are judged by some as equal to the apostles! (Most contemporaneous texts focus on Cyril rather than Methodius, so he will be the focus of these selections.)

CYRIL IS SENT TO THE SLAVS

Cyril's biography reveals the way in which missionary work was closely dependent upon the work of education and translation, so that all peoples could worship God in their own languages. This selection also shows the work of the Byzantine emperor in directing and coordinating mission work in the East. (From Life of Constantine*)*

While Cyril, that true philosopher, was rejoicing, something happened to him that was entirely unexpected, a more challenging task than he had ever carried out before. For Rastislav, a Moravian prince, under God's inspiration, had spoken to his princes and the rest of the Slavs and sent word to the Byzantine Emperor

Michael, saying: "Our people have rejected our former paganism and now observe Christian laws, but we have no teacher who can teach us the true Christian faith in our own language. So, since God's law emanates from you into all places of the earth, please also send us a teacher."

So the emperor called together a council and summoned Cyril, saying to him: "I know you are tired, but I need you to do this. No one else can carry out this task as well as you can." Cyril replied, "Though I am tired and sick, yet I will go, for they need to be able to write in their own language."

But the emperor warned him: "My grandfather, my father and many others have tried this, but they all failed. How can we now succeed?… May God give you strength, since He gives all things to those who ask with confidence and opens the door to those who knock" (cf. Lk 11:9).

Cyril then departed and, as was his custom, devoted himself to prayers with others who would join him in his work. And suddenly God—who listens to the prayers of his servants—appeared to him, and at that very moment he began writing [in Slavic]. He wrote out the words of the Gospel, "In the beginning was the Word, and the Word was with God, and the Word was God" and so on (Jn 1:1).

The emperor, hearing this, rejoiced and praised God with his counselors. He sent Cyril out with many gifts, writing a letter to Ratislav to this effect:

> "God … who desires all men … to come to the knowledge of the truth" (1 Tm 2:4), and attain greater dignity, has seen your faith and efforts. Our goal is to teach you to read and write in your own language, which has never been done before: in this way you may take your place among the great nations who praise God in their own language.
>
> To this end, we are sending a holy and orthodox man to you, a true and wise philosopher, to whom

God has given your language. Receive this gift, greater and more precious than all gold, silver, and precious stones, and work with him diligently to bring this business to a good conclusion, to seek God with all your heart.

Do not neglect our common salvation, and let nothing hinder you, but spur all men so that they may turn toward the path of truth. In this way by your own efforts, you will not only help bring them to the knowledge of God, but also make yourself worthy and acceptable, both in this life and in the future life, to all the souls who believe in Christ, our God, from this time until the end. Even further, you will leave behind a legacy for all generations, like that great emperor Constantine.

CHALLENGES TO CYRIL'S MISSION

In Moravia, Cyril's Greek mission encountered Latin missionaries who disputed whether it was appropriate to translate sacred writings into the Slavic languages, preferring to reserve liturgical prayer only for the more ancient languages. While the Latin clergy claimed that such translations were novel, Cyril argued that it was consistent with the biblical message of evangelizing all nations. (From Life of Constantine)

Arriving at Moravia, Cyril was received with great honor, and Ratislav turned over all his students to him to be instructed. Soon Cyril had established a whole liturgical regimen, having taught them how to recite morning and evening prayer and the rituals of the sacraments. And, once the holy Scriptures began to be recited, those words of the prophet were fulfilled: "the ears of the deaf [shall be] unstopped" (Is 35:5), and "the tongue of the stammerers will speak readily and distinctly" (Is 32:4), to the praise of God and the shame of the devil.

But as divine doctrine was spreading, the devil—the wicked one, the envious one, a liar from the beginning—unable to stop this positive development, instead entered into his servants, inciting them to say, "This is offensive to God: if He had wanted people to read and write prayers in their own languages, He would have made them able to do so from the beginning. But God chose only three languages—Hebrew, Greek, and Latin—in which He may rightly be praised."

There were many who said these things: the Latin clergy, archdeacons, priests and their disciples. And Cyril began to argue with them, just as David did with the heathen, overcoming them through the words of Scripture. He mockingly named them "three-tongued worshipers" and "Pilatians" (for Pontius Pilate wrote in these three languages above the Lord's cross).… For forty months he made headway in Moravia, and then set about the task of having some of his students ordained.

When he was in Venice, the Latin bishops and priests and monks came against him as a raven comes against a falcon, raising again the "three-tongued heresy." They said, "Tell us why you have developed and taught the Slavic language, which no other man came up with before, neither the apostles, nor the pope of Rome, nor Gregory the Theologian, nor Jerome, nor Augustine. We permit only three languages for praising God: Hebrew, Greek, and Latin."

Cyril, however, said to them: "Does God not make the rain fall upon all men equally? Does not the sun shine down upon all men equally (see Mt 5:45)? Can we not all equally breathe the air? How, then, are you not ashamed to allow only three languages, declaring that all other peoples and races should remain blind and deaf to God's Word? Tell me, do you consider God to be so frail, that He is not able to give it to them, or so envious that He does not want to?

"We know, on the contrary, that many nations have come to develop their own written languages, and so to praise God in their own tongue. For example, the Armenians, Persians, Abkhazis, Iberians, Sogdians, Goths, Avars, Tirsians, Khazars, Arabs, Copts, Syrians, and many others. If, however, you do not wish to understand things from these, perhaps you will at least listen to Scripture. For David cries out, 'O sing to the Lord a new song; sing to the Lord, all the earth' (Ps 96:1) … and 'Let everything that breathes praise the Lord!' (Ps 150:6)….

"And in speaking to the doctors of law, Jesus says, 'But woe to you, scribes and Pharisees, hypocrites! because you shut the kingdom of heaven against men; for you neither enter yourselves, nor allow those who would enter to go in' (Mt 23:13). And again, 'Woe to you lawyers! for you have taken away the key of knowledge; you did not enter yourselves, and you hindered those who were entering' (Lk 11:52). Truly Paul says to the Corinthians:

> [I]f you in a tongue utter speech that is not intelligible, how will any one know what is said? For you will be speaking into the air. There are doubtless many different languages in the world, and none is without meaning; but if I do not know the meaning of the language, I shall be a foreigner to the speaker and the speaker a foreigner to me. So with yourselves; since you are eager for manifestations of the Spirit, strive to excel in building up the Church. Therefore, he who speaks in a tongue should pray for the power to interpret. (1 Cor 14:9–13).

"And again, let 'every tongue confess that Jesus Christ is Lord, to the glory of God the Father' (Phil 2:11)."

And with these words and others he confounded them, and he departed, leaving them behind.

THE POPE ENDORSES CYRIL'S MISSION

Fortunately, the bishop of Rome, undisputed head of the Latin missionaries, saw no problems with Cyril's work, and invited him to Rome to give him his blessing. The result is a shocking display of international cooperation: a Latin bishop, in a Slavic liturgy, in-

stalling Greek missionaries as bishops of Latin dioceses in the East!
(From Life of Constantine*)*

And the Pope, to strengthen Cyril's case, summoned him to
Rome. And when he came to Rome, Pope Hadrian himself went
out to meet him with all the citizens, carrying candles, because
Cyril had brought with him the relics of St. Clement, martyr and
Roman pope....

Then the pope placed Cyril's Slavic books in the Church
of St. Mary, which is called Phatne, and celebrated a holy liturgy
over them. Afterwards the pope had two bishops, Formosum and
Gondricuni, ordain the students from among the Slavs, and after
being ordained, they celebrated a liturgy in the church of St. Peter the Apostle in the Slavic language ... and through the whole
night they sang, glorifying God in Slavic....

Cyril with his disciples did not cease to give thanks to God
on account of these things. The Romans, however, did not cease
to go to him and interrogate him about all sorts of things, and
seek from him a second and third explanation.

THE OFFICIAL DECREE AUTHORIZING CYRIL'S TRANSLATIONS

Eleven years after Cyril's death, the bishop of Rome solemnly en-
dorsed the great missionary's efforts to bring the Gospel to the Slavs
by authorizing his liturgical texts. (From Pope John VIII's Indus-
triae tuae, *AD 880)*

We rightly praise the Slavonic letters invented by Cyril in which
praises to God are set forth, and we order that the glories and
deeds of Christ our Lord be told in that same language. Nor is it
in any wise opposed to wholesome doctrine and faith to say Mass
in that same Slavonic language, or to chant the holy Gospels or
divine lessons from the Old and New Testaments duly translated
and interpreted therein, or the other parts of the Divine Office:
for He who created the three principal languages, Hebrew, Greek,
and Latin, also made the others for His praise and glory.

MEDIEVAL LEADERS

꙳ꙮ꙳ꙮ꙳ꙮ꙳ꙮ꙳

The Catholic vision of life has always resisted the poison of secularism, or the tendency to reduce religion to a private, individual, interior experience in complete isolation from the "real life" of work, politics, and social life. As the great medieval theologian St. Thomas Aquinas would put it, "Grace does not replace nature, but perfects it": every area of life that is truly human—political, economic, civic, literary, family, and such—is lifted up, elevated, and perfected by the grace of Christ.

By implication, the Catholic Church needs more than full congregations on Sunday mornings: she needs men and women to take the "salt" of the Gospel and season the professional and civic spheres of human life.

This was never truer than in the Middle Ages, a period that began with all of these areas in utter disarray. The robust civic infrastructure of the Roman Empire in Western Europe had collapsed during the barbarian invasions of the fourth century, and thereafter found itself ruled by men who had little interest in the promotion of literacy, peace and justice, and law and order. As Catholic missionaries took up the task of proclaiming the Gospel to the barbarian tribes of Western Europe, these missionaries had to do more than announce the Good News of Christ's resurrection. They had to establish schools, teach literacy, and draft law codes—in short, they had to evangelize *and civilize.*

New nations had to be built on the rubble of the Roman Empire: nations with leaders who were strong and just, able to rule as Christ had ruled. In the absence of strong governments and just laws, the strong were able to oppress the weak, the wealthy to exploit the poor. Tyrannical warlords had to be subjugated; law codes had to be updated and enforced; and hospitals, orphanages, and other charitable institutions had to be built to care for the poor, the sick, and the desperate.

Even more, culture depends upon literacy, and the barbarians had had little use for books except as fuel for fires. Books had to be copied and collected into libraries, schools had to be rebuilt, and children taught to read and write, all in the hope that the vast storehouses of knowledge built up in the age of the Fathers would not vanish from history, but could be transmitted to future generations.

Without such patient work on the part of thousands of teachers, lawyers, kings, and parents—from the grandest emperor to the anonymous peasant farmer—the Dark Ages would never have ended. Yet by the thirteenth century Western Europe could boast of burgeoning universities, busy parliaments, and a solid civic infrastructure excelling anything the Roman Empire had ever known.

Those who built, revised, and reformed these institutions—those we will call leaders—came in many stripes. We will look at only a few: two Christian kings of France (Charlemagne and Louis IX); the quintessential schoolmaster Alcuin of York; Gregory, the pope who so revolutionized the papal office that he is known as the "first medieval pope"; and Elizabeth of Hungary, whose private work on behalf of the poor and sick inspired countless generations after her.

ST. GREGORY THE GREAT
(540–604)

Gregory lived his whole life in the shadow of intense suffering. Rome, his birthplace, was sacked by barbarians when he was only six years old, and barbarian raids around the Italian countryside brought throngs of dirt-poor refugees flooding into Rome, carrying with them a plague that wiped out a third of the region's population. Gregory was himself constantly sick from fever, indigestion, and gout, and in his later years claimed that his only consolation was the hope that death might come soon.

Yet Gregory knew that difficult times call for heroic activity. His family's noble background (his father was a senator) marked him out for a brilliant political career, but after a brief stint as Rome's governor he renounced public office and entered a monastery, where he spent what he later called "the happiest years" of his life. When the reigning pope was struck down by the plague, however, the city's populace elected Gregory pope against his will, disrupting his plans to flee the city and intercepting his letter of refusal. (Forcible ordinations were not unusual in this period, as odd as they sound to modern ears.)

As the first pope from a monastic background, Gregory brought an intense spirituality to that office. It was Gregory who first conceived of a global plan of spreading the Gospel to the empire's barbarian conquerors, sending St. Augustine of Canterbury, the prior of his former monastery, to England as the head of a mission team. He organized the first universal system of relief for the poor in Rome, harvesting produce from the Church's lands and sending teams patrolling the streets to distribute prepared food to the indigent refugees.

Gregory's revisions to the Mass (later incorporated into the Gregorian Sacramentary) and fondness for liturgical chant (later known as Gregorian chant) so influenced the universal Church that he became known as the "father of Christian worship." Meanwhile, his immense corpus of writings (854 letters survive!) inevitably led to his being named a Doctor of the Church. Perhaps his most influential writing was the only contemporaneous biography of St. Benedict, a monk whose life he desired to imitate.

Gregory is of significant historical importance because of his westward reorientation of European Christianity. With the collapse of the Western Roman Empire, most Christians in the West continued to look to the East for their inspiration, where a thriving and materially successful Roman Empire still flourished in Byzantium. Having spent eight years as the papal ambassador to Constantinople, where his mission of securing military aid for Rome from the emperor proved fruitless, Gregory returned to the West somewhat disillusioned with the great Eastern hope.

If Western Christianity were to survive, it had to find its own independent basis, and Rome was as good a basis as any other. (His successors would also look to the great Frankish kings, such as Charlemagne, for military aid.) Gregory worked hard, therefore, to elevate the significance of Rome in the West, encouraging churches throughout Western Europe—including those in mission lands—to take their cues from Rome rather than Constantinople.

He did not hesitate to venture even into political affairs to protect the city of Rome: When the political offices of Rome fell vacant as a result of the endless wars and violence in the region, Gregory himself—he had, after all, once been governor!—took charge of the city's defenses, carried out diplomacy, maintained relief for the poor, and established treaties with the barbarian tribes in the countryside.

It was thanks to Gregory's tireless efforts that Rome, the Eternal City, would emerge from the ashes to become the center of a new, Christian civilization in Western Europe.

THE LEGACY OF POPE GREGORY

The English monastic historian Bede felt a special debt of gratitude to the pope who had first sent Christian missionaries to his country. (From Ecclesiastical History of the English People*)*

In AD 605, having magnificently served as bishop of Rome for over thirteen years, blessed Pope Gregory died and was taken up to his eternal home in heaven. And it is appropriate that I mention him in this history of the English people, since it was through his zeal that our English nation was brought from bondage to Satan into the faith of Christ, and we consider him our own "apostle." Because during his papacy, even while he was exercising supreme authority over all the Christian churches that had already long been converted, he still managed to transform our idolatrous nation into a Church of Christ....

Gregory was born a Roman, son of Gordion, a member of a noble and devout family.... By God's grace he used his high worldly position only for the glory of heavenly honor, for he soon retired from his secular life and entered a monastery. There he began a life of such perfection in grace that, as he would later recall with tears, his mind was focused on higher things, soaring above all that is temporary, and he was able to devote himself entirely to the spiritual life....

He would talk about this later, not to brag about his virtue, but to regret how much virtue he had lost in his spiritual life when he took up his responsibilities as pastor. One day, in conversation with his deacon Peter, Gregory was recalling his former spiritual state, and sadly went on: "My pastoral responsibilities now force me to deal constantly with men of the world, and when I remember how peaceful life was before, it seems that my mind is sunk in the swamp of daily affairs. For when I am tired from constant attention to the worldly affairs of countless people and wish to meditate on spiritual things, I seem to turn to them with undeniably diminished strength. So when I compare what I now endure with what I have lost, and when I weigh that loss, my burden seems greater than ever."

The holy Gregory spoke in this way from deep humility, but I personally doubt that he lost any of his monastic perfection through his pastoral cares; instead, I think he gained even greater merit by his labors for the conversion of souls than by his former peaceful life, especially because, when he became pope, he transformed his house into a monastery....

His body was laid to rest on March 4 in the church of St. Peter the Apostle before the sacristy, from which he will one day rise in glory with the other shepherds of Holy Church. On his tomb was written this epitaph:

> Receive, O earth, the body that you gave,
> Till God's life-giving power destroy the grave.
> His heaven-bound soul no deadly power, no strife
> Can harm, whose death is but the gate of life.
> The tomb of this high Pontiff, now at rest,
> Recalls his life and deeds for ever blest.
> He fed the hungry, and he clothed the chill,
> And by his message saved their souls from ill.
> Whate'er he taught, he first fulfilled in deed,
> And proved a pattern in his people's need.
> To Christ he led the Angles, and by grace
> To Faith and Church he added a new race.
> O holy pastor, all your work and prayer
> To God you offered with a shepherd's care.
> High place in heaven is your just reward,
> In triumph and in joy before the Lord.

I have to tell a story that shows Gregory's deep desire for the salvation of our nation. One day some merchants, recently arrived in Rome, displayed their wares in a crowded marketplace. Among their merchandise Gregory saw some boys being sold as slaves. They had fair complexions, fine-cut features, and fair hair. Looking at them with interest, Gregory asked what country and race they came from. He was told, "They are from Britain, where everyone looks like this."

He then asked whether the people there were Christians or were still pagans, and was informed that they were pagans. "Alas!" said Gregory, with a heartfelt sigh: "How sad that such handsome people are still in the grasp of the Author of darkness, and that behind such beautiful faces are minds ignorant of God's grace! What is the name of this race?" "They are called Angles," he was told. "No," he said, "for they have the faces of angels, and should become fellow heirs of heaven with the angels.

"And what is the name of their province?" "Deira," he was told. "Good," said Gregory, "They shall indeed be saved *de ira* ["from wrath" in Latin] and called to the mercy of Christ. And what is the name of their king?" "Aella," he was told. "Then 'Alleluia' must be sung in their land to the praise of God the Creator," said Gregory.

Not yet pope himself, Gregory approached the pope of Rome to beg him to send preachers of God's word to the English people in Britain to convert them to Christ and eagerly volunteered himself for the task, if the pope would agree to send him. But permission was not given, although the pope was willing, for the citizens of Rome so loved Gregory that they would not let him depart so far from the city.

But as soon as Gregory became pope himself, he took up this long cherished project and sent other missionaries in his place, assisting their work by his own prayers and encouragement.

THE QUALITIES OF A CHRISTIAN MINISTER

Gregory's most widely read work was his Book of Pastoral Rule, *a set of moral, spiritual, and practical guidelines for Christian ministers. The fruit of a lifetime of experience in pastoral ministry, it would serve as a handbook for thousands of clergy in later centuries.*

The conduct of a minister should be as superior to the conduct of his people as the life of a shepherd is superior to his flock. For someone who is in a position over a flock should take serious thought to the urgency of his maintaining an upright life. It is necessary, then, that he should be pure, decisive in his action, discreet in his silence, profitable in speech, sympathetic to all around him, excelling in contemplation, a close friend to others in humility, relentless in opposition to vice through his zeal for holiness, not neglecting to take care of external things in his focus on what is interior.

He should always be pure in thought, so that no impurity pollutes the one whose job is to wipe away the stains of pollution from the hearts of others, for a hand that is not clean itself cannot clean others but will only make them filthier. A minister must always be an active leader, so that he can point out the way of life to others by the way he lives, more by example than by words, so that the flock may learn how to walk by imitating the voice and manners of the shepherd.

For the man who, due to his position, is required to speak of exalted matters should also carry out exalted things. This is because a voice will more easily penetrate into the heart of a hearer when the speaker's life is commendable, since what he commands in his speech he also shows how to do by his actions.

The minister should be discreet in keeping silence and profitable in speech, lest he express what should be suppressed or suppress what he ought to express. For just as incautious speaking leads to error, so indiscreet silence leaves in error those who should receive instruction.

The minister ought to understand how often vices appear in the form of virtues. For often stinginess excuses itself under the name of thriftiness and wastefulness hides itself under the name of generosity. Often excessive carelessness is believed to be affection and unbridled wrath is seen as spiritual zeal. Often hastiness is mistaken for punctuality and laziness for thoughtfulness.

Thus it is necessary for the minister of souls to distinguish virtues from vices with great care, lest stinginess be given free reign, or lest he congratulate someone for wastefulness. He must not overlook what he should have corrected, or else he might draw those under his care to eternal punishment; but he also must not be ruthless in correcting in others what he does himself.

ON RESERVATIONS ABOUT WHAT ONE HAS WRITTEN

Gregory was highly self-conscious of his writing, as is evident from this closing section of his famous commentary on the Book of Job. Note how his profound monastic spirituality and concern for the interior life penetrate every aspect of his work.

Now that I have finished this work, I see that I must recollect my thoughts. For even when we try to speak rightly, our mind is often scattered and fragmented when we are trying to think of the right words to say, diminishing our mind's power, as it were, by plundering it from the inside.

So I must return from the forum of speech to the council chamber of the heart, to summon together the thoughts of my mind for a kind of council to deliberate how I may best watch over myself, to see to it that in my heart I do not speak any heedless evil, or speak any good in a poor fashion. For good is well spoken when the speaker seeks with his words to please the person who has been good to him. And if I discover that I have not spoken any evil, still I will not claim that I have never spoken evil at all. And if I have received some good from God and spoken it, I freely admit that I have spoken it less well than I should have (from my own fault, to be sure).

For when I turn inward to myself, pushing aside the leafy verbiage and the branches of arguments, and examine my intentions at the very root, I know that even though my intention was to please God, some little desire for the praise of men crept in (I do not know how) and intruded upon my desire to please God. And when later (too much later) I realize this, I find out that I have done what I set out not to do.

In this way, we often begin with good intentions in the eyes of God, but a secret desire to be liked by others creeps along and waylays our intentions. For example, we eat food out of necessity, but while we are eating, a gluttonous spirit creeps in and we begin to take excessive delight in eating for its own sake, so that what began as nourishment to protect our health ends by becoming an excuse to merely gratify our pleasures. We have to admit that our intention, which seeks to please God alone, is sometimes treacherously accompanied by a less righteous intention that seeks to exploit God's gifts to please other men.

If God should strictly examine us in these affairs, what excuse can we offer? For we see that our evil is always evil, pure and simple, but the good that we think we have cannot really be good, pure and simple.

But I think it is worthwhile for me to reveal unhesitatingly to the ears of my brothers everything I secretly hate in myself. As a commentator, I have not hidden what I felt, and as a confessor, I have not hidden what I suffer. In this commentary I reveal the gifts of God, and in my confession I uncover my own wounds. In this vast human race there are always little ones who need to be instructed by my words, and there are always great ones who can take pity on my weakness once they hear about it.

Thus in this commentary I can offer help to some of my brothers (as much as I can) and seek the help of others. To the first I speak to explain what they should do, to the second I open my heart to ask them to forgive. I have not withheld medicine from the former, nor have I hidden my wounds from the others.

So I ask that whoever reads this should pour out their prayers to the strict judge on my behalf, so that his tears may wash away every stain that is found on me. When I balance the power of my commentary with the power of prayer, I suspect that the reader will have more than paid me back for what he hears from me, if he offers his tears for me.

ON THE DANGER OF PRIDE IN HIGH POSITIONS

Having desired to avoid the papal office himself, Gregory detested nothing more in his fellow clergy than ambition and pride: his pre-

ferred title as pope was servus servorum dei, *"servant of the servants of God." When word reached him that his colleague in the East, Bishop John of Constantinople, had begun using the title "universal bishop," Gregory wrote a series of letters to chastise him, including the following letters to John himself and to the Byzantine emperor.*

From Gregory to John, Bishop of Constantinople

You will remember what peace and harmony you found among the churches at the time when you were ordained a bishop. But how many of your brothers may now take offense now that you have, with what pride and audacity I do not know, attempted to seize for yourself a new title. I am astounded at this, since I remember how once you wished to flee from the office of bishop rather than attain it. But now that you have the office, you seem to want to exercise it as though you had rushed into it out of pure ambition!

Once you confessed that you were unworthy to be called a bishop, but now you have arrived at the point where, despising your brother bishops, you desire to be named the *only* [universal] bishop…. I beg you, I beseech you, and with all the sweetness in my power I demand of you, that you ignore all those who flatter you by offering you this erroneous title, that you do not foolishly agree to be called by this proud title.

For truly I say it weeping, and out of inmost sorrow of heart attribute it to my own sins, that this brother of mine, who has been raised to the office of bishop to bring others to humility, has become unable to be brought to humility by others, that he who teaches truth to others has not agreed to teach himself, even when I beg him.

For what are all of your brother bishops of the universal Church but stars of heaven, whose life and speech shine forth amid the sins and errors of men, as though shining amid the shadows of night? And when you desire to raise yourself above them by this proud title, and to tread down their name in comparison with yours, what else are you saying but, "I will ascend to heaven; above the stars of God I will set my throne on high" (Is 14:13)....

As you know, the council of Chalcedon offered the bishops of the Apostolic See I serve by God's providence [that is, Rome] the honor of being called "universal." But not one of them has ever wished to be called by such a title, or seized this ill-advised name, lest, by seizing for himself the title, he would seem to deny it to all of his brothers.

From Gregory to Mauricius Augustus

Everyone who knows the Gospel is aware that by the Lord's voice the care of the whole Church was committed to the holy Apostle and Prince of all the Apostles, Peter. For to him it is said, "Peter, do you love me? Feed my sheep" (see Jn 21:17). To him it is said, "Behold, Satan has desired to sift you as wheat, and I have prayed for you, Peter, that your faith not fail. And when you are converted, strengthen your brothers" (see Lk 22:31). To him it is said, "You are Peter, and on this rock I will build my Church, and the gates of Hades shall not prevail against it. I will give to you the keys of the kingdom of heaven, and whatever you bind on earth shall be bound in heaven, and whatever you loose on earth shall be loosed in heaven" (Mt 16:18–19).

Look! He has received the keys of the heavenly kingdom, and power to bind and loose is given to him, the care and dominion of the whole Church is committed to him, and yet he is not called the "universal bishop," while the most holy man, my fellow priest John, attempts to be called "universal bishop." I am compelled to cry out and say, *O tempora, O mores!* ["What times! What customs!"]

For all of Europe is given up to the power of barbarians, cities are destroyed, camps overthrown, provinces depopulated, no farmers live on the land, worshipers of idols rage daily and slaughter the faithful, and yet priests, who ought to lie weeping on the ground in ashes, are seeking for themselves pompous names, and glory in new and sacrilegious titles.

Am I, most holy Lord, seeking to push my own agenda in this matter? Am I taking some personal offense? No: I am defending the cause of Almighty God, the cause of the Universal Church.

ST. ALCUIN OF YORK (735–804)

Known by his contemporaries as the smartest man in the world, St. Alcuin was personally responsible for the greatest revolution in learning in the early Middle Ages, leading to the saying, "Wherever literary activity is to be found, there is a student of Alcuin."

Virtually nothing is known of Alcuin's early life, save that he claimed to be a blood relative of St. Willibrord, the great missionary to the Frisians. He was trained in the famous cathedral school of York under Archbishop Egbert, who was himself a disciple of the Venerable Bede, the greatest medieval historian in England. Showing no particular desire for an ecclesiastical career—he never seems to have received priestly ordination but was content to remain a lifelong deacon—Alcuin's only desire was to learn and teach.

Alcuin might have been just one of many English scholars scribbling away in monastic libraries, save for a chance meeting with the Frankish emperor Charlemagne in Italy in 781. Impressed by Alcuin's education, the emperor invited him to be master of the palace school at his court in Aachen, Germany. Under Alcuin's direction, what had been established as a place for teaching courtly manners to royal children became a center of international education.

Alcuin expanded the curriculum at Aachen to include the full scope of liberal arts—grammar, logic, rhetoric, mathematics, geometry, astronomy, and music—culminating in the study of sacred Scripture. Charlemagne himself, along with his wife and children, enrolled as pupils, and it was not long before nobility and clergy from all over the empire began submitting candidates for enrollment.

Alcuin drafted the best and brightest scholars from Europe to teach at Aachen. Similar schools were set up throughout Charlemagne's empire, following Alcuin's model, and a scheme was even developed to offer universal primary education in every village in Europe. According to legislation issued by Charlemagne, but almost certainly drafted by Alcuin, all clergy throughout the empire were compelled to receive an education, with literacy tests for ordination and the threat of suspension for clergy who refused. Priests were then expected to set up primary schools in every diocese to teach reading and writing at no cost.

Alcuin's pupils at Aachen, including the legendary Rabanus Maurus, were sent out to oversee these schools, using textbooks written by Alcuin himself. Alongside schools, Alcuin worked to establish libraries throughout Europe, requesting, copying, and collecting manuscripts from across the world to preserve and advance scholarship.

The resulting "Carolingian Renaissance" of learning was the largest burst in creative scholarly activity until the foundation of the medieval universities almost four centuries later. Among the achievements of Alcuin's schools include the invention of the lower case (absent in ancient Latin), the first Western system of musical notation, and several developments in Romanesque architecture. Alcuin himself is credited with inventing the question mark!

One of Alcuin's most cherished projects was the improvement of the liturgy, which in his day was often mumbled in bad Latin with excessive regional variations by barely literate priests. Alcuin promoted the Roman liturgy, as found in the Gregorian Sacramentary, as the basis for a uniform and universal text of liturgical prayers, which did much to standardize the Mass in Western Europe.

ALCUIN'S TRAINING AT YORK

Alcuin built up an extensive corpus of poetry and included the art of writing poetry as part of his educational curriculum, helpful for teaching grammar and literary style. In this personal piece, he reflects

*back on his education at the School of York in England, where Arch-
bishop Aelbert taught Alcuin and other pupils both the liberal arts
and theology. (From Alcuin,* On the Saints of the Church at York)

There the Eboric scholars felt the rule
Of Master Aelbert, teaching in the school.
Their thirsty hearts to gladden well he knew
With doctrine's stream and learning's heavenly dew.

To some he made the grammar understood,
And poured on others rhetoric's copious flood.
The rules of jurisprudence these rehearse,
While those recite in high Eonian verse,
Or play Castalia's flutes in cadence sweet
And mount Parnassus on swift lyric feet.

Anon the master turns their gaze on high
To view the travailing sun and moon, the sky
In order turning with its planets seven,
And starry hosts that keep the law of heaven.

The storms at sea, the earthquake's shock, the race
Of men and beasts and flying fowl they trace;
Or to the laws of numbers bend their mind,
And search till Easter's annual day they find.

Then, last and best, he opened up to view
The depths of Holy Scripture, Old and New.
Was any youth in studies well approved,
Then him the master cherished, taught, and loved;
And thus the double knowledge he conferred
Of liberal studies and the Holy Word.

ALCUIN'S MINISTRY OF EDUCATION

*After a lifetime spent building schools all over Charlemagne's Frank-
ish empire, Alcuin retired to a monastery. Yet even there he could
not surrender his great task of advancing scholarship and learning.*

In this letter, written a few years before his death, he writes the emperor to request more books and to reflect upon the place of learning and philosophy in the grand scheme of things.

Your Flaccus [that is, Alcuin], in response to your requests and kindness, is busy at St. Martin's Abbey, feeding my students the sweet honey of the Holy Scriptures. I am excited that others should drink deeply of the old wine of ancient learning. I will soon begin to feed others with the fruits of grammatical skill, and some I am eager to enlighten with a knowledge of the constellations of the stars, which seem, as it were, painted on the dome of some mighty palace. "I have become all things to all men" (1 Cor 9:22), so that I may train up many to work for God's holy Church and the glory of your Empire, so that the grace of Almighty God in me should not be in vain (cf. 1 Cor 15:10), and your great generosity wasted for nothing.

But I am missing some rare books of scholarship, which I used to have when I lived in my own country (thanks to the generous support of my teacher, and in some part due to my own humble efforts). I mention this to Your Majesty so that, perhaps, if it pleases you who are so eagerly concerned about the advance of scholarship, you will let me send some of our young men to get us some necessary books. If so, they can bring to France the flowers of England, so that a graceful garden will exist not only in York, but also in Tours, like a Paradise blossoming with abundant fruit....

In your gracious zeal, you will not overlook the fact that every page of the Holy Scriptures urges us to acquire wisdom. For nothing is more honorable, nothing so ensures a happy life, nothing is more praiseworthy in any state in life, than that men live according to the teachings of the philosophers. Further, nothing is more essential to the people's government, nothing better for the guidance of life toward upright character, than the grace which wisdom gives, and the glory of education and the power of learning. Therefore, Solomon, the wisest of all men, exclaims, "Better is wisdom than all precious things, and more to be desired" (cf. Prv 8:11).

You must encourage the young men who are in Your Majesty's palace, my lord king, to seek and gain this by every possible effort, every single day, especially when in the flower of their youth, so that they may become worthy to gain an honorable old age, and, eventually, everlasting happiness. For my part, I will not be idle in sowing the seeds of wisdom among your servants in this land…. In the morning of my life and in the most fruitful period of my studies I sowed seed in Britain, and now that my blood has grown cool in the evening of life I have not ceased, but sow seed in France, desiring that both gardens may spring up by God's grace.

Whoever wishes to can read so many things about the scientific pursuits of the ancients, and come to understand how eager they were to gain the grace of wisdom. I have noticed that you are zealous to advance toward this wisdom and take pleasure in it, and that you are decorating the splendor of your worldly rule with an even greater intellectual splendor. In this may our Lord Jesus Christ, who is himself the supreme realization of divine wisdom, guard and exalt you, and cause you to attain to the glory of His own blessed and everlasting vision.

ON HAVING ONE'S GRAMMAR CORRECTED BY ONE'S STUDENT

Alcuin had once been Charlemagne's grammar teacher, and the emperor delighted in returning Alcuin's letters to him with all of the grammatical mistakes circled, accompanied with a recommendation of a proofreader. One can almost feel the friendly sarcasm in Alcuin's reply.

Flaccus [Alcuin], "wounded with the pen of love" (cf. Sgs 5:7–8), sends greetings to the most pious and excellent lord King David [that is, Charlemagne].

I am so thankful that, in your profound piety, you have had the booklet I sent you read aloud into your most wise ears. I am also thankful that you had the errors in it carefully noted and sent it back so that I could correct them. It would have been even better had you corrected them yourself, because mistakes are always more readily noted by another reader, rather than the author himself.

The deficiencies in the booklet, both in its grammar and punctuation, are simply the normal results of thinking too quickly, because my mind is moving faster than my hands can write. My bad headaches prevent me from proofreading the words once they are written, and if you do not want to be blamed for my negligence, you should not blame me for it….

I have taken the liberty of sending Your Excellency some written phrases, with examples and verses from the Church Fathers, and also some mathematical puzzles for your amusement, which I have written on the blank part of the paper you sent to me. It seemed best to me to send back clothed what you sent me naked, so to speak….

Careful observance of the detailed rules for punctuation does a great deal to enhance the beauty of sentences, but this is often completely lost due to the lack of sophistication of our scribes. It is my hope that the right usage of punctuation will be restored to scribes now that you have begun to renew learning and education throughout your kingdom. For my part, despite my failings, I continue the daily fight against unsophisticated writing here at Tours.

For your part, use your authority to teach the youth in your palace school to use the most elegant style possible to transcribe what you dictate, so that documents that circulate in the name of the king may emanate the nobility of royal wisdom.

EXERCISES IN MATH AND LOGIC

Alcuin was known for developing clever mathematical and logic problems to stimulate the minds of young students. A collection of these, attributed to Alcuin, has come down to us under the title Problems to Sharpen the Young. *Note how much of the back-*

ground deals with everyday issues in medieval life: inheritance disputes, raising cattle, crossing rivers, and supporting clergy.

If two men, one after the other, marry each other's sisters, then tell me, how will their sons be related to each other?

When the father of a family died, he left as an inheritance to his sons thirty glass flasks, of which ten were full of oil, ten only half full, and another ten empty. Divide, if you can, the oil and the flasks, so that each of the three sons receives an equal share, both of the wine and of the flasks.

Two men were leading oxen up the road, when one said to the other, "Give me two of your oxen. Then I will have as many as you have." And the other replied, "Instead, you give me two of your oxen. Then I will have twice as many as you." Tell me, if you will, how many oxen each man had.

There were three men who each had a sister, and they wished to cross a river, but there was only a small boat there, in which only two at a time could cross. But each of the men had his eye on the sisters of the others, and none of the men trusted his sister to be left alone with any of the others. Tell me, if you can, how they can all cross the river without jeopardizing the honor of any of the sisters.

A man wished to cross a river, having in his possession a wolf, a she-goat, and a sack of cabbages. But the boat would only carry two of these at a time, and he could not figure out how to get across without endangering any of his possessions. Tell me, if you can, how he could get across with his possessions intact.

There was a man and a woman, each of whom weighed about the same as a loaded cart, and two children who, taken together, weighed the same. But they had to cross a river in a boat that would only carry the weight of a single loaded cart. Tell me, if you are able, how they will able to cross on the boat.

Upon his death, the master of a house left his children and his pregnant wife 960 coins. He had ordered that, if a boy were born to his wife, he should receive three-fourths of the inheritance (that is, nine-twelfths), and the mother should receive a fourth (three-twelfths). However, if a daughter were born to his wife, she should receive seven-twelfths of the inheritance, and the mother five-twelfths. But it came to pass that she gave birth to twins, a boy and a girl. Solve, if you can, so that the mother, the son and the daughter each receive their fair share.

A bishop ordered that twelve loaves of bread be divided among his clergy. He stipulated that each priest should receive two loaves, each deacon half a loaf, and each lector a fourth of a loaf. And it turned out that the total number of clergy equaled the number of loaves, that is, twelve. How many priests, deacons and lectors must there have been?

CHARLEMAGNE (742–814)

Though not considered a saint, Charlemagne was the kind of Christian statesman without whom Europe never would have emerged from the Dark Ages and become a center of medieval Christianity. The basic shape of Christian Europe—its odd inter-mingling of politics and religion, the central role of the papacy, its uneasy relationship with the Greek East, its eccentric combination of Gothic barbarism and Roman nobility, and its zeal for scholar-ship and learning—emerges under the guiding hand of Charles the Great.

Charles (*Karolus*) emerged as the unlikely heir of the first Catholic nation in Europe, the Kingdom of the Franks, an oasis of Catholic Christianity in an ocean of paganism, Islam, and he-retical Arianism. His rise had occurred through a series of unex-pected historical events: Clovis, an early Frankish chieftain, had converted to Christianity under the influence of his Catholic wife. Charles "the Hammer" Martel, Charles' grandfather, had driven the Muslims out of France, and Charles' father, Pepin the Short, had seized the royal throne from the "do-nothing" Merovingian dynasty. Pepin had asked the pope to crown and anoint himself and his sons in order to establish their rather dubious legitimacy to rule, and in return Pepin promised that he and his sons would forever be protectors of the Roman Church.

Emerging as King of the Franks in 768, Charles knew that he needed the pope as much as the pope needed him. He wanted a *Christian* kingdom, with all the benefits that came with it— Christian schools, Christian culture, and, above all, the protection of the Christian God—and he understood the bishop of Rome to be the spokesman for Christianity.

Meanwhile, in Rome, the pope had his own problems: constant threats to his rule from the unruly Roman population and the menacing Lombard tribes threatening invasion from the outside. Charles needed the spiritual aid of the papacy, and the papacy needed the military aid of the Franks. Thus an unlikely alliance was formed that would last for nearly a thousand years.

More than once Charles would come to the rescue of Rome, crushing the Lombard armies and delivering their territories up as a personal gift to the pope (the origin of the Papal States, and the modern Vatican City State), and traveling to Rome personally to ensure that the pope received a fair trial when false accusations were leveled against him.

Not only that, but Charles gave the papacy a central role in Church and monastic affairs throughout his kingdom: in some measure the spread of Gregorian chant, the Roman Rite of the Mass, and Benedictine monasticism across Europe are due to Charles' attempts to be sure Christianity throughout his kingdom was patterned after Roman Christianity. The popes began to see Charles as a divinely given protector of the Roman Church, in the same way early Christians had seen the Roman Emperor Constantine.

Accordingly, it was no surprise to anyone but Charles himself (who at least *acted* surprised) when Pope Leo III stood up in the middle of Mass on Christmas Day and bestowed an imperial crown on Charles, dubbing him "Roman Emperor." Charles' own reservations were due to how this would play out in the East, where the Greek emperors in Byzantium still considered themselves the legitimate successors of the Roman emperors and saw Charles as a mere barbarian upstart.

But Charles—or Charles the Great (Charlemagne), as he came to be called—was undeniably sincere in his Christianity. His biographer records his daily Mass attendance, his temperance and piety, and his concern for good behavior on the part of himself, his household, and his court. He personally presided over a steady stream of Church synods and councils to regulate liturgy, monastic life, and doctrine throughout the kingdom: in fact, his constant interference even in doctrinal matters was worrisome to many churchmen, and established a troublesome standard for the future.

Charlemagne promoted not only Christianity, but also education and culture, importing the best scholars from all over Europe (including his own personal tutor, St. Alcuin of York) to build schools in every region, presiding over a Carolingian Renaissance that was largely responsible for the scholarly impetus that climaxed in the medieval universities four centuries later. By the end of his reign, Charlemagne's empire covered most of mainland Europe: rightly has he been called the "father of Europe."

As noted earlier, Charlemagne is probably not a saint. Several aspects of his reign are problematic from a modern standpoint—his multiple illegitimate marriages (eight to ten wives or concubines!) and his pattern of forcibly baptizing those he defeated in battle, among other things. But his role in Christianizing Western Europe meant he would inevitably be treated as a saint. He was briefly canonized, but that declaration was later retracted (the pope who canonized him was rightly recognized as an antipope, or false pope), and though devotion to "St. Charlemagne" continued unopposed in some quarters up until modern times, the Church has never formally recognized him as such.

THE LIFE OF A CHRISTIAN EMPEROR

We know more about Charlemagne's life than about the lives of any of his contemporaries, thanks to the excellent biography written by his advisor and diplomat, Einhard. With a genuinely human touch,

Einhard shows the personality of Charles, his struggles to educate himself in the liberal arts, and his devotion to the Christian religion. Note especially his personal attachment to the papacy.

Charles was large and strong, fairly tall … with a laughing, joyful face. Thus he always had a stately and dignified appearance … a firm gait, a manly stature, and a clear voice…. Following the national custom, he frequently rode on horseback for exercise and went hunting, which the Franks do better than anyone in the world. He enjoyed breathing the air of natural hot springs and often went swimming, which he did better than anyone else. For this reason he built his palace at Aix-la-Chapelle, near such springs, where he lived constantly during his later years until his death.

Charles was very moderate in eating, and especially in drinking, for he hated drunkenness in anyone, especially in himself and among the members of his household. But he had a hard time holding back from good food, and often complained that fasts injured his health…. His favorite dish was the roasts that his huntsmen would bring in on a spit. Whenever he ate, he always listened to reading or music. He preferred the readings of stories and deeds from older times, but he was also fond of the books of St. Augustine, especially *City of God*.

Very articulate, Charles was fluent and quick in speech. He knew not only his native language, but studied foreign ones. He mastered Latin to the extent that he knew it as well as his native tongue, but he never quite mastered Greek…. He eagerly cultivated the liberal arts, deeply respected those who taught them, and gave great honors to such teachers.

He learned grammar lessons from the deacon Peter of Pisa and other subjects from another deacon, a Saxon named Alcuin, the greatest scholar of his day. He spent much time with Alcuin learning rhetoric, logic, and especially astronomy, such that he grew very proficient at investigating the movement of the planets. He tried hard to learn how to write, and kept tablets under his pillow to practice during his free time, but since he started so late in life, he never really had any success at it.

Having been raised as a child in the Christian religion, he cherished its principles with the greatest fervor and devotion. For example, he built a beautiful basilica at Aix-la-Chapelle and adorned it with gold and silver, lamps, and rails and doors of solid brass. Not finding any suitable materials nearby, he imported columns and marble for the basilica from Rome and Ravenna. He worshiped constantly at this church whenever his health permitted, not only attending Mass but also visiting in the morning and evening and even after nightfall to pray. He showed great concern that all services there be conducted with the greatest possible reverence….

He took great care to aid the poor, including generous almsgiving, not only in his own country and kingdom, but elsewhere. For when he found out that there were impoverished Christians living in Syria, Egypt, and Africa, in Jerusalem, Alexandria, and Carthage, he was moved with compassion and sent aid overseas to them….

But above all other holy and sacred places he cherished the Church of St. Peter the Apostle at Rome, and he filled its treasury with vast amounts of gold, silver, and precious stones. He sent many generous gifts to the popes, and throughout his whole reign his greatest wish was to use his own care, influence, and wealth to reestablish the ancient authority of the city of Rome, to defend and protect the Church of St. Peter, and to beautify and enrich it above all other churches.

CHARLEMAGNE'S IMPERIAL CORONATION
BY THE POPE

A second biography of Charlemagne was written by a monk known as Notker the Stammerer, the kind of eclectic genius who flourished in monastic libraries during the Carolingian Renaissance. Notker records how Charles came to the assistance of the pope in a time of crisis, and how the pope repaid him by naming him Emperor of Rome.

Now since the envious are never anything but envious, so those who live in Rome often rise up and protest whenever a strong pope is raised to the apostolic see. In this fashion, a group of envious Romans rose up against Pope Leo III, falsely accusing him of a horrible crime and attempting to blind him as punishment. The pope had a message secretly sent by his servants to Michael, the Emperor of Constantinople, but he refused all assistance…. Therefore the holy Leo invited the invincible Charles to come to Rome….

Now Charles, always prepared for war, though he had no idea why he was being summoned, came at once with his soldiers and attendants, coming as head of the world to the city that had once been head of the world. And when the envious Romans heard of his sudden coming, they immediately fled and hid in various hiding places, cellars, and dens, just as sparrows hide themselves when they hear the voice of their master….

Afterwards Charles stayed and visited Rome for a few days. During this time, the pope called together everyone who could come from the surrounding area and then, in the presence of these and of the knights of the invincible Charles, the pope declared him to be the Emperor of Rome and the Defender of the Roman Church.

Now Charles had no idea this was coming: he couldn't exactly turn it down, since he recognized it had been divinely preordained for him, but he made it clear that he was not exactly grateful for his new title. For his main concern was for the Greeks in the East, who would probably be envious of his title and plan some harm against his kingdom of the Franks.

CHARLEMAGNE'S IMPERIAL LEGISLATION

As emperor, Charles went to great lengths to restore law and order to a region that had been lawless for nearly four centuries. He also worked hard to promote Christian ideals and advance the missionary efforts of the Church in an area that had hitherto been flooded with pagan shrines. The following brief selections from various legal documents show some of the typical patterns found in Carolingian legislation: a concern for justice and the promotion of Christian values, and the use of clergy and monks as civil servants.

First, the Lord Emperor has sent embassies throughout his whole kingdom, composed of the wisest and most prudent nobles, including bishops and archbishops, abbots and pious laymen, to facilitate just laws for all men, enforced through local chapters. Moreover, anywhere that laws are found not to be right and just, he has ordered these embassies to inquire into these cases most diligently and report back to him, so that, God willing, he can reform them.

And let no one, through ingenuity or cleverness, dare to oppose or disobey the written law or the verdicts decided upon, as so many are inclined to do. And let no one do injury to God's churches, to the poor, to widows, wards of the state, or to any Christian.

But all shall live entirely in accordance with the laws of God, justly and under a just rule, and everyone shall be told to live in peace with his neighbors in his business or profession. The monastic clergy ought to observe their monastic rules in every way without greedily and unjustly seeking profit, nuns ought to keep diligent watch over their lives, laypersons and clergy ought to observe the laws carefully and without malicious fraud, and all ought to live in mutual charity and perfect peace.

And let the embassies make a diligent investigation whenever any man claims that he has been treated unjustly by anyone, just as they hope to deserve the grace of Almighty God and keep faith with Him, fearing and obeying His will. In this way, in all cases without exception, the law will be administered justly and in its entirety, not only in regard to the churches of God, the poor, widows, and wards of the state, but in regard to all people.

And if there is ever any case which neither these embassies nor the provincial courts are able to correct justly, they shall immediately refer this case, together with their reports concerning it, to the judgment of the emperor himself. And never shall the straight path of justice be blocked by anyone through flattery, bribery, on account of any special relationship, or through fear of the powerful.

First, since the Lord Emperor is unable to give the necessary care and discipline to each person individually, each person shall strive voluntarily, in accordance with his own knowledge and ability, to live entirely in the holy service of God, in agreement with His laws and His own promise.

Also, no one shall presume to rob or do any injury to the churches of God, to widows, to orphans, or to pilgrims, for the Lord Emperor himself, after God and his saints, considers himself their protector and defender.

Also, on Sunday, the Lord's Day, no meetings or public judicial assemblies shall be held, except in cases of great necessity or when war compels it. Instead, all shall go to the church to hear the word of God and shall be available for prayers or good works. Likewise, also, on feast days they shall devote themselves to God and church services, and shall refrain from secular assemblies.

THE CAROLINGIAN RENAISSANCE

Not content with enforcing law and order and promoting the Christian religion, Charlemagne sought to bring his kingdom out of the Dark Ages, the collapse of intellectual culture in the wake of the Roman Empire's collapse in Western Europe. He worked to establish a network of schools throughout the empire and to promote learning and scholarship generally. (From Charlemagne's Letter to Baugulf *of Fulda)*

Charles, by the grace of God King of the Franks and Lombards and Patrician of the Romans, to the Abbot Baugulf and to all his congregation, and also the faithful committed to you, greetings through our ambassadors in the name of Almighty God.

Please know that we, together with our faithful, consider it useful that the dioceses and monasteries which Christ's favor has entrusted to our care should eagerly teach reading and writing to those who are able to learn them, according to the God-given capacity of each individual.

In this way, just as obedience to your monastic rule gives order and grace to your good morals, so eager teaching and learning may do the same for literature, so that those who seek to live rightly in a way that pleases God can also please Him by speaking correctly. For it is written, "For by your words you will be justified, and by your words you will be condemned" (Mt 12:37). For although good behavior may be better than a good education, nevertheless, good behavior often follows from a good education....

For all men should shun errors, especially those who carry out the task of education, since they are meant to be especially servants of the truth. For recently we received letters from several monasteries telling us that their monks were offering up their holy and pious prayers, and in most of these letters we found grammatically incorrect and poorly expressed sentences! This is clearly because pious thoughts which were conceived in the mind could not be translated into written speech without error, due to a tongue uneducated because of the lack of adequate study.

After this, we began to fear that, if the skill of good writing was diminishing, so the ability to understand the Holy Scriptures might also be diminishing, and we all know that errors in understanding are far more dangerous than errors in speech.

Therefore we encourage you not only to avoid the neglect of reading and writing, but also to study humbly and earnestly so that you will be able to penetrate more easily and correctly the mysteries of the divine Scriptures. For everyone knows that the various images, metaphors, and figures of speech in the sacred pages will be interpreted more accurately, in a spiritual sense, if the interpreter has mastered good reading and writing. Men who have both the will and the ability to learn and a desire to teach others should be chosen for this task. This should be done with a zeal that matches the sincerity with which we command it.

For we desire you, as soldiers of the Church, to be devout in mind, educated in expression, chaste in conduct, and eloquent in speech, so that whoever shall seek you out, on account of reverence for God or because of your holy reputations, will be instructed by your wisdom just as he is edified by your appearance. Having learned this wisdom from your reading or singing, he may go away joyfully, giving thanks to Almighty God.

Be sure that, if you wish to retain our favor, you send copies of this letter to all your other monasteries and bishops. Farewell.

ST. ELIZABETH OF HUNGARY (1207–1231)

Elizabeth seems to have been born in the wrong place at the wrong time. From her childhood she wanted nothing more than to be a nun, living in quiet poverty and celibacy. She ended up as a princess, marrying into one of the wealthier dynasties in Europe, and living a life of luxury and pomp. That she played the hand dealt to her, so to speak, seeking sanctity in the life she had rather than in the life she wished to have, made her the "greatest woman of the German Middle Ages," as she was called at her canonization.

The beginnings of St. Elizabeth's life have the makings of a fairy-tale story: When she was barely able to walk she was brought to be raised in the royal Hungarian court, pledged to marry the king's oldest son in a marriage arranged to cement political alliances between Catholic families allied against the excommunicated Emperor Otto IV.

But Elizabeth's youth was flooded with pain and sorrow. Her mother was murdered by jealous Hungarian nobles when Elizabeth was only six; the king slipped into insanity, turned against the Church, and died excommunicated when she was ten; and at the same time her fiancé was found dead before the marriage could be finalized. She was hastily married to his younger brother, Ludwig, at age fourteen.

The couple had a happy marriage, raising three children together. While Ludwig did not seem to share the intensity of her piety, he happily put up with it, even holding her hand at night while she prayed at their bedside. When, at twenty years of age, she heard the news that he had died en route to the Sixth Crusade, she is said to have cried, "The whole world is dead to me," and refused to remarry despite violent pressure from her uncle, who feared that her celibacy would ruin the family's political ambitions—she apparently threatened to cut off her nose to ruin her beauty and thwart any suitors he sent her.

Elizabeth was a contemporary of St. Francis, and when she first met his friars in Germany, she knew him to be a kindred spirit. Though initially prevented from joining the order due to her marriage and financial endowments, she became a fervent collaborator, taking a Franciscan as her spiritual director and helping the order found a monastery in Germany in 1225. Francis sent her a letter of blessing shortly before his death to thank her for her support. While married Elizabeth founded hospitals and poorhouses, selling her jewelry and state clothes to feed the poor on her estates. After her husband's death she seems to have entered the Franciscan Third Order, which was founded to facilitate the living of Francis' ideals for those "in the world."

Her husband's death and her departure from the royal Hungarian court allowed her to give full scope to the charitable ideals that had been frustrated in her early life. She used her dowry to found a Franciscan hospital in Marburg, where she worked personally among the sick and poor until her death at age twenty-four. Her reputation for humility and charity was so great that pilgrims streamed to her tomb from all over Christendom, making it one of the busiest pilgrimage sites in Europe.

Only a few decades after Elizabeth's death, her biography was included in a large collection of saints' lives known as The Golden Legend, *a bestseller throughout the Middle Ages and well into the modern period. The few selections here give a general outline of her life.*

Elizabeth was of noble birth, the daughter of the king of Hungary, but she was nobler through her faith and religion than through her lineage. She was noble by her example, by her miracles, and by her beautiful holiness, for the Author of Nature had raised her, in a sense, above nature itself.

Though she had remained perfectly chaste in her youth, her father pressured her into marrying because he wanted her to have children. She had no desire for marriage, but she would not disobey her father. Instead, she went to Father Conrad, her confessor and spiritual director, and vowed to him that, if her husband died before she did, she would remain celibate afterwards. Then she was married to the landgrave of Thuringia, as God had preordained that she would bring many people to the love of God and teach the untaught people.

She got up often during the night to pray, even though her husband would ask her to lie back down and rest a little. She had asked one of her female attendants, who was very close to her, that if she happened to fall asleep during her prayers, she should shake her foot to wake her back up. But once, when this attendant thought she had taken her lady's foot, she had mistakenly taken her husband's foot, which startled him awake, wondering why she had done so! When the situation had been explained to him, he let it pass and put up with it without complaining.

And she often spun wool with her attendants and made cloth, donating it to the Church, and thereby giving an example to others. Once when her husband was away visiting the emperor's court, she assembled all the wheat harvested that year and began distributing it to all the people, for there had been a great famine that year in that region. And sometimes, when she ran out of money to give away, she would sell her jewelry to raise money.

She built a hospital below the castle where she invited a great number of the poor. There she visited them every day, no matter what sickness they had, and washed them with her own hands, despite the protestations of her attendants. And she was so sweet with the children of the poor families that they called her "mother." She had coffins made for the poor and attended their funerals personally, and would help to bury them with her own hands, often in the clothes that she had made for them.

Though her husband was occupied with other things, he was still devout in serving God also, and even if he didn't have time to do all of the things personally that she was doing, he fully supported her doing so, and thus his devotion should be praised as well. St. Elizabeth wanted her husband to use his power and influence to defend the true faith, and encouraged him to go on a Crusade to the Holy Land. He agreed to go, but he ended up dying while he was away, receiving his reward in heaven, and making his wife a widow.

When the death of her husband was announced in the region, some of her husband's vassals called her a fool for wasting so many resources and pressured her to leave. And because she was so patient, and had long desired a life of poverty anyway, she moved into a humble house, eventually associating herself with the Franciscans, maintaining a spirit of thanksgiving in the midst of all of her suffering and poverty.… She took a religious habit and remained perpetually celibate after the death of her husband, wearing coarse and rough clothing, often patched with different colors and fabrics.

Finally she received back her dowry, of which she gave a portion to the poor, and with the other she founded a hospital, for which others called her a squanderer and a fool, which she put up with joyfully. Once this hospital was built she became a nurse there, serving the poor humbly, even holding the sick in her arms during the night, cleaning their filthy clothes and sheets, bringing their meals to their bedsides, and washing their sores. And when there were no sick to care for, she would spin wool, [and give] clothing to the poor.

When the time approached for her to die, as God had ordained it, she lay sick with fever.… She said, then, that it was near midnight when Jesus was born, and time for God to call His servant to a heavenly wedding. Thus, in the year 1231, she gave up her spirit and slept in the Lord.… And the poor people cried loudly, and snatched up scraps of her clothing and clips of her hair to keep as relics. Her body was put in a tomb, where many miracles were performed after her death.

ST. LOUIS IX (1214–1270)

Louis IX recalled how, as a young child, his mother had told him, "I love you, my dear son, as much as a mother can love her child; but I would rather see you dead at my feet than that you should ever commit a mortal sin." The words seem to have had their effect. The child who heard them would become the only king of France to be canonized.

Louis became king while still a teenager, his mother gradually surrendering her role as regent, yet he would maintain a life of piety and holiness that would shame most Catholics. He attended Mass and heard the Divine Office daily, and his biographer claims that he routinely invited beggars to share his table, spending so much money on the poor in his kingdom that his relatives accused him of wasting their inheritance. His marriage to Margaret of Provence was by all accounts a happy one, so much so that his mother allegedly became profoundly jealous of his wife; the couple had eleven children together.

But Louis was conscious that God had raised him to the throne for a reason, and he devoted his reign to a reform of the laws and customs of his country, determined to leave the laws of the kingdom more fair and just than he had found them. He attempted to put a stop to immoral and unhealthy practices that undermined the public good, such as gambling, prostitution, bribery, blasphemy, private vendettas, and the custom of trial by combat.

He instituted the practice of "royal justice," where the person of the king became the supreme judge, and anyone could appeal to him at any time: his biographer says that he held court at an oak tree in the forest, where the poor and ill-treated lined up to speak to him. When one of his nobles hanged three squires for poaching, Louis had him arrested, using his fine of 12,000 livres to pay for perpetual Masses to be said for the souls of the men he had hanged. Louis did more than any other European legislator to introduce the notion of "innocent until proven guilty" into criminal law.

He also did more than any prior king to bring peace to France, so heavily battered by wars and feuds. He ended the wars against the heretical Albigensians in the south and abandoned the ancient feud with England in the north, angering his own countrymen by the land settlement he gave to the English king to gain a cessation of hostilities. But his reputation for putting peace and justice over personal gain made him a sort of international adjudicator throughout Europe: King Henry III of England asked him to negotiate a truce between himself and his barons some years later.

King Louis is perhaps best known for his personal involvement in the Crusades, which by his day had continued for almost two centuries, ever since the Greek emperor of Byzantium had requested military aid from the Franks in liberating his Christian kingdom from hostile Muslim invaders. Louis finally decided that the defense of Christendom and the well-being of the Christian communities in the Holy Land (which, he heard, would collapse without assistance) were more important than his domestic affairs. He brought 35,000 men personally to Egypt on the so-called Seventh Crusade in hopes of using gains there to negotiate for the safety of Christians in the Holy Land.

The expedition was a failure, and Louis himself was captured and ransomed back at an expense that nearly bankrupted his kingdom. Yet he never gave up hope for the cause of the Holy Land, spending four more years there donating funds and negotiating for the safety of Christians there.

By the end of his reign, King Louis IX had done as much as his predecessor Charlemagne to cement the role of the French nation as the greatest ally of the Church. So much so that within thirty years of Louis' death the papacy would actually relocate from Rome to France for nearly sixty years, the somewhat infamous Avignon Papacy.

Louis' manner of death reflected his way of life. He embarked on yet another Crusade in 1267, taking his three sons with him to North Africa. But his armies were struck with dysentery, and he succumbed to the disease himself in 1270, summoning his sons to his deathbed to beg them not to forget the cause of his beloved poor in France. So loved was Louis across Europe that his body was accompanied by huge crowds as it passed back to France, and prayers were offered to him at his tomb long before he was canonized.

THE LIFE AND RULE OF A SAINTLY KING

A close friend of the king, Jean de Joinville, was asked to write a biography of his personal reminiscences for submission to the papacy as evidence in support of Louis' eventual canonization.

This is the way King Louis ruled his dominions. Every day he heard the Liturgy of the Hours, a Mass for the dead, and either the Mass for the day or for a saint's feast. Every day, after dinner and a rest, he would hear the prayers for the dead read by a chaplain in his room, and afterwards Vespers and Compline.

He scheduled things in such a way that he and his councilors, after hearing Mass, would go and listen to the "Pleas of the Gate," or legal petitions. And when he came back, he would call us all to his bedroom, have us sit around him, and would ask us whether there were any cases that required his personal attention. And once we had named these, he would send for those who were involved … and convince them to arrive at a reasonable agreement.

Often during the summer months he would go and sit in the forest of Vincennes after Mass, leaning against an oak tree, and everyone who had business would go talk to him without anyone interfering. He would ask, "Is there anyone here who has a case?" and those with cases stood up. Then he would say, "Everyone keep quiet, and I will deal with you each in order."

Once he returned to France from overseas, he was attentive to Our Lord and upright with his subjects, and thought it would be a good idea to reform the laws of the realm. Here are a few of the laws he made:

- We, Louis, by the grace of God king of France, do order that all the king's officials … must take an oath that, no matter what is at stake, they will give justice to every person without exception, rich and poor, stranger and friend, and will maintain all customs and laws that are tried and true. And if any officials are proven to act contrary to their oaths, we order that they be punished suitably.…

- They must swear not to take any bribes, directly or indirectly, neither gold, nor silver, nor anything else, save perhaps a little fruit, bread, or wine worth less than ten shillings a week.… If they ever find that such gifts have come into their possession, they must return them as soon as possible.…

- They must swear that if they know any official under their care to be dishonest, addicted to plunder, usury, or any other vices which makes him unworthy to serve the king, they will not support him in any way, but will punish and judge him justly.

- They must not curse, swear, or say anything offensive toward God, Our Lady, or the Saints. They must abstain from gambling and taverns. Promiscuous women should be put out of their houses, and whoever rents a house to a promiscuous woman should be fined a month's rent.

Before he went to bed, he would call all his children and tell them stories of the good deeds done by kings and emperors, and he would tell them to follow these examples. And he would also tell them about the wicked deeds of rich men who by plunder and greed had lost their kingdoms. "And these things," he used to say, "I tell you as a warning to avoid them, lest you incur God's anger." He had his children taught prayers to the Virgin Mary and had them recite the Liturgy of the Hours, so they would get into the habit of hearing them.

The king was so liberal in giving alms to the poor that wherever he went in his kingdom he made gifts to poor churches, to poorhouses, to asylums and impoverished families…. It was his custom that, wherever he went, over a hundred poor people would be fed in his house with bread and wine, and either meat or fish. In Lent and Advent he fed even more, and often the king would wait on them personally, serving their dishes, carving their meat, and even personally giving them money as they left….

Also, every day he invited the elderly to eat with him, serving them the same food he was eating…. Some of his relatives complained at how much money he was giving away and how much time he was wasting doing this sort of thing. But he replied, "I would rather be excessive in giving alms out of love for God than in the pomp and swagger of this world."

A LETTER FROM A KNIGHT ON CRUSADE

This letter from an otherwise unknown knight who joined the king on the Seventh Crusade in 1249 gives an intriguing picture of Louis' behavior among his troops in wartime.

From Guy, a knight of the household of the viscount of Melun, to master B. of Chartres, his dear half-brother and beloved friend, greetings.

Because I know how worried you are about the state of the Holy Land and of our lord king of France, and that you are interested in the general welfare of the Church and of the fate of many relatives and friends who are fighting for Christ under the king's orders, I thought I would write to give you a detailed update of events that you've probably already heard about from others.

After a council, we left Cyprus and headed east.... One night a violent storm blew us over the waves, and when the sky cleared toward morning our ships came together, and it turned out we were exactly at our destination.... Our lord the king, hearing of our position, tried to keep the men calm by keeping up a confident spirit. "My faithful soldiers and friends," he said to them all:

> As long as we are inseparable in our love of one another, we will be undefeatable. It is only by God's blessing that we have come to our destination so quickly. I am not myself the king of France, nor am I the holy Church. You are both as well. I am only a man who will die like all other men whenever it pleases God.
>
> Whatever may happen to us, everything will go well. If we are conquered, we will be martyrs. If we triumph, all glory will go to France, to Christianity, and to God. It would be foolish to think that God, who foresees all things, has brought us here in vain. This is his cause, and we shall conquer for Christ. He will triumph in us; He will give the glory, the honor and blessing not to us, but to His name.

The men, seeing the firmness and immovable determination of the king, prepared for a naval combat and to land as he had ordered.... During the battle, some of our enemy's slaves and prisoners escaped, for their jailers had gone out to fight us, and they rushed to us joyfully, applauding our king and our army, saying, "Blessed is he who comes in the name of the Lord!"

These things happened on Good Friday, which we thought was a good omen. The king and the rest of the Christian army were able to disembark safely and joyfully. We rested until the next day, when we were able to gain possession of the rest of the land with the help of the slaves who knew the country and roads.

The king entered the city [of Damietta] amidst cries of joy and went immediately to the mosque of the Saracens to pray and thank God, whom he believed had brought about all that had happened. Before eating, all the Christians solemnly sang that angelic hymn, the *Te Deum*, weeping sweet tears of joy.

Then the Mass of the Blessed Virgin Mary was celebrated in that place where Christians had celebrated Mass and rung bells in ancient times, once it had been purified with holy water. In this very place, four days earlier, the captives told us that the prophet Mohammed had been venerated.

A KING'S ADVICE TO HIS SON

These excerpts from the elderly king's letter to his oldest son and probable heir give some sense of what he considered important in life.

To my dear first-born son, Philip, I give greetings and a father's love.

Uphold the good customs of your kingdom and tear down the bad ones. Do not oppress your people; do not burden them with tolls or taxes unless you absolutely have to.

Never let anyone be so bold as to say, in your presence, any words that tempt anyone to sin, and never let anyone cut others down behind their backs.

Dear son, if you should become king, try hard to be worthy of the title. In other words, be loyal and committed to your subjects, in both justice and integrity. No matter what happens, do not turn to the right or to the left, but always go straight ahead.

If a poor man has a quarrel with a rich man, your first instinct should be to take the side of the poor man, then to uncover the full truth of the matter, after which point you can make sure justice is done to both.

If anyone brings a case against you for some perceived injury or wrong, publicly take his side rather than your own, giving him the benefit of the doubt, and understate the strength of your own case. The reason for this is that, unless you take the lead in this way, some of your councilors might otherwise hesitate to take the side of your opponent for fear of angering you, and you should not wish that. You should let your councilors know that you do not want any special treatment: this way they will always act and judge in the right way more boldly.

If you find yourself in possession of something that rightly belongs to another, even if you inherited it from someone else, give it back instantly, no matter how valuable it is—whether land, money, or anything else. If you are unsure to whom it belongs, have wise men investigate it quickly and carefully. And if proper ownership cannot be determined, then make some settlement, with the help of wise men, so that you can walk away with a clean conscience. And if you hear that one of your predecessors already made a settlement, inquire carefully to find out if that settlement was fair, and if you find that it was not, make it right quickly, for the good of your own soul and that of your predecessors.

And if for some reason you are forced to declare war … whatever the reason may be, you must command that the poor people who have done no wrong or crime be protected from its destructive effects to their land. Even if it is necessary to seize your enemy's land, this is better than damaging the property of the poor. And be careful not to start any war until you have good counsel that it has a just cause, and not before you have asked your opponent to make amends and waited as long as you should. And if your opponent asks for mercy, you should pardon him, so that God may be pleased with you.

Finally, my son, I ask and require you that, if it pleases the Lord that I should die before you do, have Masses and prayers offered for the benefit of my soul, and send to all the churches and monasteries of the French kingdom and ask them to pray for my soul, and grant me a special part in all the good deeds which you shall do as king.

MEDIEVAL MARTYRS

A religion whose founder underwent a cruel and violent death will naturally hold in special regard those of His followers who prove willing to tread the same path. In every generation the Church has prized those who gave witness (the literal translation of the Greek *martyros*) to their supreme love by making the ultimate sacrifice. Temporary periods of great suffering have always been followed by unprecedented growth, leading the writer Tertullian to call martyrs the "seed of the Church," sown and watered by their own blood.

While the early Church is normally thought of as the "age of the martyrs," the era when thousands of Christians fell prey to the persecutions of the Roman Empire, the medieval era was not lacking in such witnesses. After all, the fall of Rome brought a resurgence of pagan religion to Europe as the barbarian immigrants built shrines and temples for the gods they brought with them from the East.

Missionaries like St. Boniface could still expect harsh opposition from pagan druids and priests, and Boniface was far from their only victim. If missionaries aroused such fury among those who held religious

power, how much would the rulers whom they converted—kings and dukes like St. Wenceslaus—protect the new faith and implement its values in law?
And even when paganism had begun to dissipate in
Europe, lingering heresies such as Arianism still held
power in some places, and St. Boethius found that he
was not safe even from baptized Christians.

Indeed, as Western Europe was Christianized,
the bigger threat to sanctity came from within the
Church, not from outside of it. Not every baptized
Christian was eager to see the principles of the Gospel carried out in the political, economic, or cultural
spheres, especially those in positions of power who
had something to lose from such a change.

This is, no doubt, equally true today, although
there has been a considerable change in the issues at
stake. St. Thomas Becket, for example, would feel the
wrath of the king of England for defending the liberty
of the Church against the all-consuming tyranny of
the state, and while the specific concern of St. Thomas
(the exemption of clergy from secular law courts) is
not the concern of many contemporary Catholics, no
Catholic today would have a hard time identifying
analogous concerns in the twenty-first century.

Often it is difficult to disentangle the specifi-
cally *religious* principle from the political complica-
tions with which it is intricately related. For example,
was it Boethius' religious views or his political stances
that got him killed? Was Joan of Arc killed because
she was a French partisan, or because she carried a divine message? But this is no doubt equally true today,
and it reminds us of the fact that religious principles
have inherent political ramifications from which it is
hard to separate them in practice.

Therefore, even if some of the most famous martyrs of the Middle Ages often seem more complex than those of the ancient period, they display the same qualities: a willingness to maintain their moral principles even at great personal risk, a profound confidence in the face of death, and a benevolent love even for those who would take from them their very lives.

ST. BOETHIUS (480–524)

It says something of Boethius' time that the descendant of two emperors and father of two consuls should be strangled and clubbed to death within sight of Rome. A noble, a scholar, and a saint, Boethius was simply born at the wrong time.

Boethius (or Anicius Manlius Severinus Boethius, his proper name) belonged to the ancient Anicii family of Rome. His father was consul, as were both of his sons, and he himself became a senator by age twenty-five. But Boethius was born after the last Roman emperor had been deposed from the throne, and Rome was ruled by a barbarian king, the so-called Theodoric the Great.

Yet Boethius' noble lineage and reputation for brilliance caught Theodoric's eye, and Boethius soon found himself a high-ranking official in the new Ostrogothic kingdom of Rome.

Boethius' fluency in Greek (a rare gift among Latin speakers at the time) made him a natural choice to serve as Theodoric's liaison to Constantinople, the capital of the Roman Empire which lingered in the East after Rome fell in the West.

Tensions remained high between East and West, and Boethius would attempt to patch up the disputes concerning both political and religious matters. Perhaps he did his job too well: he was accused of treason, of conspiring with the Eastern emperor to overthrow Theodoric and restore the imperial power in the West. Imprisoned, exiled, and eventually executed, Boethius was simply a casualty of the complicated political and religious alliances of his day.

His works, however, survived him. Given his talent with the Greek language, he had made it his lifelong goal to translate all of the works of Aristotle and Plato from Greek into Latin, so that such classical wisdom would not be lost to Western civilization. Alongside this project he wrote works on mathematics, music, and numerous other subjects, including several theological tracts.

Boethius' works served as a treasure trove for later medieval writers, who pillaged them for ancient wisdom. Indeed, when St. Thomas Aquinas struggled to come up with definitions for technical terms such as "eternity" and "person," he was content simply to quote Boethius and leave it at that.

Boethius' most famous work is his last, the *Consolation of Philosophy*, written in prison while contemplating his fall from glory and his inevitable death. Appropriately cast as a Socratic dialogue with a personified Philosophy, he muses on the fickleness of fortune and how to remain virtuous when suffering grievous loss.

Although Boethius' death was obviously brought in part by political concerns, religious motives were not absent. Theodoric was an Arian, meaning that he did not believe Christ to be equal to (consubstantial with) the Father, whereas Boethius had written extensively against the Arian position, insisting on the equality of all persons of the Trinity. The Gothic, barbarian kingdoms sought a systematic enforcement of Arian theology, and Boethius' orthodoxy (which he shared with the Eastern, Byzantine Empire on this point) was undoubtedly another factor in his death. It was sufficient, anyway, for him to be included in the Roman martyrology (an official catalogue of martyrs whose feasts were celebrated by the Roman church), and his *Consolation of Philosophy* was read throughout the Middle Ages as the last testament of a Christian martyr.

HOW TO RESPOND TO BAD FORTUNE

An early topic of the Consolation of Philosophy *is how the virtuous person should react when fate deals him a bad hand. This selection is from one of the poetic songs in Book I.*

Whoso calm, serene, sedate,
Sets his foot on haughty fate;

Firm and steadfast, come what will,
Keeps his mien unconquered still;
Him the rage of furious seas,
Tossing high wild menaces,
Nor the flames from smoky forges
That Vesuvius disgorges,
Nor the bolt that from the sky
Smites the tower, can terrify.
Why, then, shouldst thou feel affright
At the tyrant's weakling might?
Dread him not, nor fear no harm,
And thou shall his rage disarm;
But who to hope or fear gives way—
Lost his bosom's rightful sway—
He hath cast away his shield,
Like a coward fled the field;
He hath forged all unaware
Fetters his own neck must bear!

RIDING ON THE WHEEL OF FORTUNE

Another theme of the Consolation *is the fickleness of fortune. Boethius' image in Book II of the ever-turning wheel became a favorite image for fortune in the Middle Ages.*

Mad Fortune sweeps along in wanton pride,
Uncertain as Euripus' surging tide;
Now tramples mighty kings beneath her feet;
Now sets the conquered in the victor's seat.
She heedeth not the wail of hapless woe,
But mocks the griefs that from her mischief flow.

Such is her sport; so proveth she her power;
And great the marvel, when in one brief hour
She shows her darling lifted high in bliss,
Then headlong plunged in misery's abyss.

Now I would like to strike up a discussion with you, using Fortune's own words: then you can decide if her claims are just. "Man," she might say, "why do you keep complaining about me?"

What wrong have I done you? What have I taken from you? Let's agree on a judge, and we will each make our case before him as to who is the true owner of wealth and positions. If you can succeed in convincing him these are the true property of humans, then I will freely grant them to you.

When nature brought you from your mother's womb, I took you, naked and empty-handed, and nursed you with my abundance. Maybe because I was partial to you, I spoiled you, and this is what makes you rebel against me. I surrounded you with a fortune of the goods in my power: now it is my right to take it back again. You should thank me for letting you use what was not rightfully yours; now you have no right to complain, as if what you lost were your property in the first place.

Why are you complaining, then? I have not wronged you. Wealth, honor and all such things are my servants: they know their mistress, and they come and go at my command. I might dare to say that, if these things you complain of losing had been yours in the first place, you could never have lost them. Am I not allowed to do what I want with what is mine?

No one complains when the skies shine brightly one minute, and then darken the next, when the seasons cover the earth with flowers and fruit, and then disfigure it with storms and cold. We don't mind it when the sea is smooth and peaceful today, rough with waves and storms tomorrow. Are you trying, in your greed, to force me to be consistent, when this trait is foreign to me?

This is my way, the game that I will never stop playing. I turn the wheel that spins, delighting to see the high fall down and the low rise up. Rise up, if you want to, but only if you are ready to fall down again when the rules of my game require it. Were you truly ignorant of my character?

TRUSTING IN DIVINE PROVIDENCE (*BOOK IV*)

"It remains," I said, "for you to explain this apparent injustice I'm suffering now."

"The question you're asking," Lady Philosophy replied with a smile, "is the grandest of all mysteries, one which can never be explained completely to the human intellect, for, when one problem is removed, many more arise to take its place, and arise and arise unless the mind is keen and awake. For the problem you raise touches on a number of difficult questions: the simplicity of Providence, the nature of Fate, the unpredictability of Chance, divine and human knowledge, predestination, and free will. You know the difficulty involved in these questions; nevertheless, I will try to answer them in the short space allotted us."

Then, as though she were beginning for the first time, Philosophy said:

> The coming-into-being of all things, and the entire course that changeable things take, derive their causes, their order, and their forms from the unchanging mind of God. The mind of God set down all the various rules by which all things are governed while still remaining unchanged in its own simplicity. When the government of all things is seen as belonging to the simplicity and purity of the divine mind, we call it 'Providence'....

Now, your original question concerns the apparent confusion and disorder which seems to be manifestly shown forth when good men both prosper and suffer, and evil men both prosper and suffer and get both what they want and what they do not want.

First, is human judgment so perfect that it can discern who is truly good and who is truly evil? If that were true, why do humans disagree so often, so that the same person is thought by one group to deserve the highest rewards and is thought by another group to deserve the most miserable punishments?

Even if I were to grant that some people can somehow distinguish between good and evil people, would that person also be able to look inside the soul and, like a doctor examining a body, discern the inner condition of the person?... Now the health of the soul is virtue, and the sickness of the soul is vice. Now who else is the physician of the soul but God, who preserves and rewards the good and punishes the wicked, and who sees in the great panorama of Providence what is best for everyone?

Here is the great conclusion about Fate we have been tending to: divine wisdom understands and does what humanity, in its ignorance, never can understand.

Because of this ignorance, I will confine myself to explaining what your limited intellect can understand about the divine mind. You may see a man and judge him to be just and good; Providence, which sees all things, including the inner condition of the man, may view the man completely otherwise.... Therefore, when something happens which appears contrary to your opinion of right and wrong, it is your opinion that is wrong and confused, while the order of things is right.

Let me give you an example. Suppose we have a man who is so fortunate that he seems to be the beloved of God and men. This man may be so weak that were he to suffer any adversity at all, even the slightest, he would buckle and collapse and forsake all virtue and goodness if he did not feel it brought him any profit. Therefore, God in his wise governance spares this poor man any adversity that might ruin his virtue, so that he who cannot bear suffering need not suffer. Suppose we have another man, perfectly virtuous, saintly, and truly beloved of God; this man may also be kept free from illness because it is not right for him to suffer any adversity at all….

To other people, Providence mixes both prosperity and adversity according to the condition of their souls; Providence gives suffering to those who would be ruined by too much prosperity, and tests others with sufferings and difficulties who would strengthen their virtue and patience with such sufferings. Most humans are of two types: some are terrified of burdens they can easily bear, while others dismiss burdens they are, in fact, unable to bear. Providence leads both these types through various trials to self-knowledge. Some people earn fame through glorious death or by not breaking down under the most horrific torture; these people prove that evil cannot overcome goodness: it is beyond doubt that these adversities were good, just, and beneficial to the ones who suffered them.

Let us look at evil men. Sometimes their lives are easy and sometimes painful; the source of both of these effects is the divine mind and both of these effects are wrought for the same reasons. Of course, no one marvels when wicked people suffer, since everyone believes they deserve what they get, for such suffering and punishment prevents others from committing crimes and urges those who are suffering to reform their ways.

Yet, evil men who prosper are an extremely powerful argument for good people, for they see, in the prosperity of the wicked, how they should judge the good fortune the wicked often enjoy. The prosperity of the wicked leads to another good, for if it is in the nature of a particular wicked man to be driven to violence and crime if he suffers poverty, Providence prevents this by granting him great wealth. Such a man might compare his evil nature to the good fortune he is enjoying and grow terrified at the possibility of losing his good fortune; he may then reform and behave uprightly as long as he fears losing his wealth.

Some evil men who undeservedly enjoy worldly prosperity are driven to ruin by their reprobate character; some evil men have been given the right to heap adversity on the good so that the latter may be tested and strengthened. You see, there is just as much disagreement between evil men and other evil men as there is between evil and good men, because such evil men are frequently in conflict with themselves and their consciences, and are frequently wracked with guilt and self-hatred at their foolishness.

From this Providence works the great mystery in which the evil make other evil men good. For when an evil man finds himself unjustly suffering because of other evil men, that man flares with anger and loathing for those evil men and returns to virtue because he cannot stand to be like the men he hates. To the divine mind alone are all evil things good, because the divine mind brings about good effects from these seemingly evil causes.

All things are part of a predetermined order, so that when something moves from the place it has been assigned, it moves into a new order of things. As far as Providence is concerned, there is nothing, nothing whatsoever, that is left to Chance."

ST. WENCESLAUS (d. 929)

Wenceslaus was the ultimate fruit of the missions of Sts. Cyril and Methodius among the Slavic peoples: his grandfather was a personal convert of the brothers. Yet paganism was still a live force among the Slavs, and Wenceslaus' Christian father, Vratislaus, the duke of Bohemia (modern-day Czech Republic), had entered into a political marriage with the daughter of a pagan tribal chief. Although she submitted to baptism as a condition for entering the marriage, Dragomir remained committed to her ancestral paganism and harbored deep resentment toward her husband's "foreign" religion. When Vratislaus died, his heir Wenceslaus was sent to be raised by his saintly grandmother, St. Ludmila.

When the teenage Wenceslaus returned to begin his own rule, his mother, Dragomir, retained her grip on power as his maternal regent, contesting his every action and insinuating that her overly pious son was better suited for the priesthood than for the throne. Seeking to destroy any lingering Christian influence on her son, she had his grandmother Ludmila strangled to death.

When a civil war broke out in Bohemia, the devout Wenceslaus saw his greatest ally in the Christian empire in the West, the Holy Roman Empire that was then situated in Germany. He personally sought an audience with the emperor, Henry I, the successor of Charlemagne: Wenceslaus' only request was for a relic of St. Vitus, which he reposed in a church in his domains.

Wenceslaus thereafter began to implement Christian laws in his kingdom, staffing his government with Christian clergy, including Germans from the West. He then married and fathered a son, the presumptive heir who would guarantee that his pro-Christian policies would survive his own death.

Although the details still remain unclear, it seems that his own family connived his downfall, the result of a conspiracy between his scheming mother and his now-disinherited younger brother who would have become ruler after Wenceslaus, in the absence of another male heir. Knowing his predilection for honoring the feasts of saints, his brother Boleslaw invited him to a celebration of the feasts of Sts. Cosmas and Damian, striking him down outside the doors of the church itself.

Wenceslaus' reputation for innocence and piety, along with the report that his last words were of forgiveness for his brother, led to widespread veneration, and his tomb became a shrine, bringing pilgrims from afar. His own brother soon thought better of his crime and underwent public repentance, moving Wenceslaus' remains to the church of St. Vitus that Wenceslaus had built.

The German emperor showed his appreciation by posthumously declaring Wenceslaus "king of Bohemia," whereas in life he had been merely a duke. The equestrian statue of Wenceslaus in the square of Prague has long been a symbol of national pride, and the nineteenth-century carol "Good King Wenceslaus" remains a fitting remembrance of the saint, who had served throughout the Middle Ages as a model of a Christian king.

THE LIFE OF ST. WENCESLAUS

The Life and Passion of Saints Wenceslaus and Ludmila *was writ-ten in the form of a homily only a few decades after the martyr's death. It pays special attention to the tensions caused by Wenc-eslaus' desire to adhere to Christian standards in the face of his family's opposition. The selections that follow are translations from this text.*

Blessed Wenceslaus was named duke—his actions very pleasing to Christ—while still in the blossom of youth. Yet he had risen far above boyhood, having reached the summit of education at the hands of his schoolmaster, retaining in his deep memory and his passionate soul the desire to do every good work that had come into his ears. For this very reason, his own mother began to pon-der treachery with other sons of Satan.

Full of envy at his works, she said to others in her council: "Alas, what are we going to do? How will we turn things back the way they were? Our little prince, who has been raised up to the very highest seat in the house, perverted by clergy and behaving like a monk, continues to oppose the traditional customs of our fathers. And if this is how he acts in his youth, what do you think you will have to bear once he grows up?" So from that day on they began to harass him: threats, scolding, mockery, and count-less other evils.

But as this was happening, that man beloved of God armed himself with the shield of faith, patiently protecting himself so that his soul remained unaffected. In fact, their wicked plots even reached to the point of attempting to murder the clergy and reli-gious whose teachings he listened to, attempting to terrify them and thus prevent them from gaining access to him.

But conscious of all of these things, he would meet secret-ly with faithful men to make plans about the future, on occasion sending secretly for a cleric when the sun went down, and dis-cussing all those things which were beneficial to him all night, from dusk until dawn, and then allowing his cherished teachers to leave secretly. And covering up his notebook under the clothing he was wearing, he would take it out again in a quiet place, and read it with diligence and with interior sighs of duress, as he ached for the hearts of his people due to their unbelief and blindness.

Finally, strengthened by the power of God that encircled him, he summoned his mother and those under her influence, and rebuked them…. "The sayings of the wise are like goads, and like nails firmly fixed" (Eccl 12:11). Thus said the blessed Wenceslaus: "Why, sons of criminals, offspring of liars and men of iniquity, have you hindered me from learning the law of the Lord Jesus Christ and obeying His commandments? Just because you tire of serving Christ, why should you hinder the rest of us? Although I have been under your power up until now, yet now I reject it, and I choose instead the omnipotent God whom I desire to serve with all my heart."…

From his boyhood he did not depart in the smallest degree from the Lord's teaching: true in his speech, just in his judgment, faithful in every enterprise, his piety exceeding all human measure. When anyone was undergoing a trial in the council of judges and was awaiting his judgment as chief judge, he took every opportunity to quietly withdraw himself, remembering the threats of Christ put forward in the Gospel: "Judge not, and you will not be judged; condemn not, and you will not be condemned" (Lk 6:37).

He destroyed gallows and prisons that had been built in ancient times but still remained standing. He tirelessly comforted orphans, widows, the poor, the groaning and the wounded, fed the hungry, revived the thirsty, covered the naked, visited the sick, buried the dead, welcomed neighbors, friends, and strangers, honored priests and clergy as the Lord, honored monks, and opened the way of truth to those who had gone astray. He observed truth, humility, patience, meekness, and above all things charity, seizing nothing by force or deceit….

THE MARTYRDOM OF ST. WENCESLAUS

His brother Boleslaw, who had his own house in the city called by his name, was inflamed by the devil and stung from all sides by darts of greed. He seized the occasion of the feast of the blessed martyrs Cosmas and Damian, two days before that of St. Michael the Archangel, since there was a church in those parts consecrated in honor of those saints. He invited his brother to the feast, sending for him on the pretense of being hospitable, but as reality would soon show, his real purpose was to slaughter him….

Blessed Wenceslaus, soon to be a victim of Christ, then went up to the church as was his custom, hoping to sneak in some time for private prayer before the people were assembled, like a good shepherd among his flock. As he sought to recite or hear the morning prayer, the noose was suddenly drawn tight. For the priest of the church, one of those whose wickedness sprung from Babylon, shut tight the door of the church as soon as he saw the man of God approaching, as he had been instructed by the treacherous men. Then they rose up from ambush, the brother plainly appearing in all his armor.

And seeing his brother, the chosen soldier of God went up to greet him, embracing his neck with his arms and kissing him, saying, "May you always be well, brother, and may you be enriched in both this life and the future one, and may Christ receive you to his eternal banquet, as you have received me and those who come with me."

In response, with proud spirit and fierce eyes his brother lifted up his sword in his hand, which he had carried under his cloak, and answered, "Yesterday I treated you as the circumstances required, but today this is the way one brother will serve another!" And he swung his sword and struck his brother in the head, but thanks to the Lord's help he was barely able to draw blood. For the miserable man was so struck with horror at the very thing he was doing that he was unable to strike as a strong man could.

Blessed Wenceslaus, however, grasped the sword in his naked hand: "You do wrongly," he said, "to attack me in this way!" But when he saw that his protests would do nothing to stop what was happening, he finally spoke his mind, saying: "Ah, how your judgment has perished! For far be it from this servant of God to crush even the smallest of animals with his hand, and yet you dare to stain your hands with the blood of your own brother!"

And he restored to his brother the sword he had seized, taking his hand back covered with blood, and quickly ran to the church. But the brother cried out in a loud voice to his friends: "Where are you, I say?! You do a poor job of aiding your lord when he has need of your help!"

Then the whole mob of the wicked, who had until then lurked in hiding, broke forth, many armed with swords and spears, and struck Wenceslaus down with harsh blows, slaying him in front of the church door. Thus that holy soul fell on the field of battle, freed from the burdens of this life, crowned with blood as with a laurel wreath.

He departed to his Lord, entering into triumph, while heaven rejoiced and the earth wept, on the last day of the new moon in October, in the year 929 of our Lord's Incarnation.

ST. THOMAS BECKET (1118–1170)

Even if the principles for which Thomas Becket died seem somewhat obscure and perplexing from a modern perspective, the iconic nature of his death—his head hacked open by a band of knights while he was presiding at the altar—make him a perfect model of the medieval martyr, and the universal popularity of his shrine as a pilgrimage site (as immortalized in Chaucer's *Canterbury Tales*) did much to cement his reputation.

A Norman of humble birth, Thomas received enough legal education to become a competent secretary, climbing the clerical ranks until King Henry II of England chose him as the royal chancellor. He and Henry seem to have been the closest of companions, often hunting and hawking, fighting and feasting together, so much so that the king sent his own son to be raised in Thomas' household. Thomas excelled at nothing, however, so much as increasing the king's revenues, especially by squeezing the ample wealth of the Church to the extent that he became despised by most of the churchmen in England.

With the death of the archbishop of Canterbury, the highest ranking churchman in England, Henry saw a chance that wasn't to be missed and used his power to put his crony Thomas in the position. A fox minding the henhouse, Thomas would be in an unprecedented position to facilitate the royal wishes regarding the Church, bending it further and further under the king's sway.

His unexpected and unwilling ordination as a bishop seems to have sparked something of a conversion in the heart of Thomas, who immediately began acting strangely, at least from the king's point of view. Now instead of hunting and hawking, he spent his hours praying and fasting, wearing a hairshirt (a popular medieval penitential practice) and journeying barefoot. And to Henry's great dismay, when conflicts arose between the court and the Church, Thomas began taking the side of the Church!

The issue at the time, once again, is difficult for us to understand. The Church had always had her own legal system—known as canon law—which included provision for punishing those who broke her laws. While today these punishments are exclusively spiritual in nature—for example, excommunication—at the time they included physical punishments such as imprisonment and floggings but, by ancient custom, not execution, which remained the sole prerogative of the state.

The primary purpose of these punishments was to discipline clergy who broke their vows; almost never were they used on laity. This created, however, the problem of double jurisdiction: a priest who committed a serious theft might face punishments from both his Church and his king. To avoid this injustice, the Church had insisted that, as the higher court, her jurisdiction prevailed over the secular courts, such that clerical malefactors should be exempt from secular justice.

The kings of England had perpetually complained about this, ostensibly because it was unjust—the king would routinely execute even common criminals, but the Church would not, supposedly being "soft on crime." More likely, though, the kings complained because it created a limit to their absolute power, a class of people exempt from their will. What looks on the surface like a mere political dispute turns out to be a serious issue about church-state relations: are the Church and her laws to be submitted entirely to the whim of the state like every other political organization, or does she have a claim to rights and liberties that transcend the power of the state?

Thomas, in any case, thought so, and he had come to believe that the traditional liberty of the Church was in danger of being trampled by the greedy tyranny of the absolutist king. He rallied the clergy against the king on this issue, and for his troubles was found in contempt of court and fined exorbitant sums by the king.

When Thomas' friends at court advised him that the furious king sought his life, he fled the country and sought refuge with the pope in Rome. After four years in exile, all Thomas' property confiscated and his blood relatives dispossessed and banished, the pope arranged a temporary compromise and Thomas returned to his see. Yet trouble soon stirred: Thomas had excommunicated several bishops for usurping his privileges in his absence, and when the king demanded that he reverse the edict, he refused, insisting once again that the king did not rule the Church—Christ did.

Grumbling on his throne, the king's courtiers heard him complain that his life would be easier if Thomas were dead ("who will rid me of this troublesome priest," according to some), and a group of knights volunteered for the task. It is not clear whether the king ordered them to or not: clearly they thought they were carrying out his will. They interrupted Thomas during prayers and cut him down at the altar.

The universal outcry over his murder raised international outrage, and the pope acted quickly to declare Thomas a martyr and a saint within two years, requiring the humiliated King Henry to do penance for his crime, submitting to be publicly flogged at the tomb of Thomas. Since that time Thomas has become something of a symbol for the vigilant defense of the freedoms and rights of the Church over and against the state—although the issues have certainly changed over time, the central concern has not.

THE OUTBREAK OF THE CONTROVERSY

This account was penned by Roger of Hoveden, a clerk in the royal court who had access to all the relevant documents. A contemporary of Becket, Roger wrote the following selections about twenty years after the martyr's death.

In the same year [1163], a great controversy arose between the king of England and Thomas, archbishop of Canterbury, regarding the rights of the Church, which the English king was trying to disrupt and diminish, whereas the archbishop was trying by any means necessary to keep them intact. It was the king's desire that if priests, deacons, subdeacons, or other Church ministers were arrested for theft, murder, felony, arson, or similar crimes, they would be taken before secular judges and punished like the laity.

On the contrary, the archbishop of Canterbury maintained that if any cleric in holy orders, or any other minister of the Church, should be charged with a crime, he should be tried by churchmen in the Church's courts, and if he be convicted, he should be removed from office; and if he committed yet another crime after being removed from office, *only then* would he be handed over to the king and his deputies.

In the year 1164 … the king called a great council and assembled all the archbishops and bishops of England in his presence, requesting them, out of love and obedience to him, and for the good ordering of the kingdom, to confirm and faithfully observe the laws of King Henry, his grandfather. But Thomas, archbishop of Canterbury, answered for himself and the others that they would accept the laws which the king said were made by his grandfather, and would obey them faithfully, with the exception of those laws regarding Church ministers, the honor of God and of his holy Church. But this exception angered the king, and he used every means possible to force the bishops to promise to accept the laws without any exception. Yet the archbishop of Canterbury would not by any means agree to this….

The king, paying no attention to Thomas, swore that he would demand justice and judgment from him. The barons of the king's court therefore sentenced Thomas to be fined by the king … five hundred pounds…. To annoy him still more, the king immediately summoned Thomas to appear before him on the following day, prepared to give an account of the stewardship he had held in the kingdom before his consecration. The archbishop, however, aware that the heavy sentence of banishment awaited him if he hastily arrived at court, tried to give excuses to delay…. Then it was told him, and word was brought to him by those in the king's household, that if he appeared at the king's court, he would either be thrown into prison or executed….

However, the archbishop of Canterbury refused to put down his cross, but said, "If the king's sword physically slays the body, my sword pierces spiritually, and sends the soul to hell." Now while he was sitting there waiting, some people secretly told him that the king's followers had sworn to kill him. From that moment on, therefore, he tried to find an excuse for departing from the court, and he tried to facilitate this by appealing to the Supreme Pontiff, putting the cause of the Church and himself under the protection of God and of our lord the Pope.

BECKET'S SPEECH TO KING HENRY
AT THE COUNCIL OF CHINON

With great longing have I desired to see your face and speak with you, both for my own benefit, and especially for yours. For my own benefit, so that you might remember the obedient services which I devoutly carried out for you to the best of my ability (so help me God, at the last judgment, when all will stand before his judgment seat to be judged according to what they have done in the body, whether for good or for evil [cf. 2 Cor 5:10]).

Also, so that I might move you to have pity on me, forced as I am to live on the charity of others, among those of a foreign land (although, by God's grace, I still have more than sufficient provisions). It is also comforting that the apostle says, "all who desire to live a godly life in Christ Jesus will be persecuted" (2 Tm 3:12), and the prophet says, "I have not seen the righteous forsaken or his children begging bread" (Ps 37:25).

Yet also for your own benefit, for three reasons: because you are my lord, because you are my king, and because you are my son in the Spirit. Because you are my lord, I owe and offer you my best advice, as every bishop owes his lord, due to the honor of God and of the holy Church. Because you are my king, I am bound to respect you and to instruct you. Because you are my son, I am bound by the duties of my office to scold you and to correct you. For a father corrects his son, sometimes in kind words and sometimes in harsh words, so that in one way or another he may convince him to do what is right.

You should understand that God's grace has made you king for the following reasons: first, because you have a duty to govern yourself, to correct your life with the practice of good manners, so that by your example others may be convinced to reform their lives—as the wise man says, "the world is formed after the example of a king." Second, for encouraging some and punishing others by virtue of the power you have received from the Church with the sacrament of anointing, and with the sword which you wield through your office for the destruction of the enemies of the Church.

For kings are anointed in three places: on the head, breast, and the arms, signifying glory, knowledge, and strength. The kings in ancient times who did not obey God's judgments but sinned against His commandments were deprived of ... glory, knowledge, and strength, as were their children after them—for example, Saul, Nebuchadnezzar, Solomon, and many others. But those who humbled themselves before the Lord in contrition of heart received the grace of God all the more abundantly and effectively, together with all the blessings we have mentioned—for example, David, Hezekiah, and many others.

Christ founded the Church and gained its liberty with His own blood, by enduring the scourging, spitting, nails, and death itself, and thereby left us with an example to follow in His footsteps. As the apostle says, "If we have died with him, we shall also live with him; if we endure, we shall also reign with him" (2 Tm 2:11–12).

The Church of God is composed of two orders—the clergy and the laity. The clergy includes the apostles and their successors, the bishops and other ministers of the Church, to whom have been given the care and government of that Church, and who oversee the concerns of the Church, in order to facilitate in all things the salvation of souls. For this reason it was said to Peter, and in him all the other ministers of the Church: "You are Peter, and on this rock I will build my Church, and the gates of Hades shall not prevail against it" (Mt 16:18).

The laity include kings, dukes, earls, and other rulers who oversee secular business in order to facilitate in all things the peace and unity of the Church. And because kings most certainly receive their power from the Church, and the Church does not receive it from them but rather (I say it with your permission) from Christ himself, you ought not to order bishops around....

Do not then attempt, my lord, if you wish for the salvation of your soul, to rob the Church in any way of what belongs to it, or to act unjustly towards it; instead, allow it to enjoy the same freedom in your kingdom that it enjoys in others. Remember also the promise you made and placed in writing on the altar at Westminster, to preserve the liberties of the Church of God, at that time when you were consecrated and anointed king by my predecessor….

Finally, let me freely and peacefully return to my diocese, and I am ready to serve you loyally and dutifully as my most dear lord and king, in whatever way I can, leaving aside the honor of God, of the Roman Church, and of the Church's ministers. But if you will not do this, then know for certain that you will feel the severity of God's vengeance.

THE MARTYRDOM OF THOMAS BECKET

Thomas had not even been back in his diocese for a month when, on the fifth day of the feast of Christmas, four knights came to Canterbury—or rather, four sworn servants of Satan—whose names were William de Tracy, Hugh de Morville, Richard Brito, and Reginald FitzUrse, men of respectable families, but destined to stain the reputations of their ancestors with perpetual shame by daring to commit such a horrific crime.

These men forced their way into the presence of the archbishop, and, having no good message to bring, they maliciously omitted any polite greeting but addressed him in an insolent and arrogant manner. Threats were exchanged on both sides, threat answered with threat. At last they departed, hurling behind them abuse and insults; but immediately they returned and broke into the monastic cloister, not only armed themselves but at the head of a large group of armed men.

The archbishop, meanwhile, had meekly yet deliberately gone off to the church choir, since the monks had begged him (rather, coerced him) to lead a vespers service due to the solemnity of the season. When he saw these armed men behind him, amidst the cloisters, he must have expected that their violent feelings would cause them to leave the church, but neither the solemn occasion nor the bishop's innocence dissuaded them from their crime of shedding his blood.

Indeed, they were so blinded and possessed by their shameless determination to commit this crime that they thought nothing of the disgrace to their chivalry, nor of any danger to themselves. Therefore, they followed the archbishop with bold and firm steps and drawn swords, entering the church and crying aloud, "Where is the traitor?" When no one answered, they repeated, "Where is the archbishop?" Hearing this, he—already a confessor and soon to be a martyr for the cause of Christ—knowing himself to be falsely accused of treason and rightfully holding the office of archbishop, descended the steps to meet them. Showing no agitation or fear in either mind or body, he responded, "Here I am," with full composure.

One of these evil knights retorted in a frenzy, "Now you will die, for we cannot let you live any longer!" The bishop answered with the same composure: "I am ready to die for my God, and for defending the justice and liberties of the Church. But if you seek my life, in the name of Almighty God and under pain of excommunication, I forbid you to hurt anyone else who is here—either monk, priest, or layman, but let them be as safe from the penalty as they have been innocent of the crime."….

On this, the knights instantly grabbed and held him, attempting to drag him out of the church to carry out their crime, but failed to do so. The archbishop, seeing his murderers with drawn swords, bowed his head as if in prayer, uttering these last words: "I commend myself and the cause of the Church to God and to St. Mary and to the saints, to the patrons of this church and to St. Denis." Then, even amidst all the violence, the martyr did not utter a word or a cry, even a sigh, nor did he lift his arms in defense, but bowed his head, which he exposed and kept unmoved until the deed was completed.

Seeing this, these knights acted quickly, afraid of all the crowd who were running to the spot, and fearing that they would be stopped and their crime left incomplete. While one was raising his sword over the archbishop, he struck off the arm of a cleric named Edward Grim, while badly wounding the archbishop in the head. (For the cleric had raised his arm over the bishop's head, to ward off the blow or at least receive it himself.)

The holy man still stood upright, suffering like an innocent lamb for a righteous cause, without protest or complaint, but merely offering himself up as a sacrifice to the Lord and begging the protection of the saints. And, that none of the knights remain guiltless, a second and third struck his head with their swords, cutting it open, throwing the victim to the ground. The fourth, furious with deadly rage and fiendish cruelty, split open his head and bashed in his skull, spilling his brains and blood upon the stone pavement….

In this way, at the beginning of the seventh year of his exile, the martyr Thomas fought up until his very death for the love of God and the liberties of the Church, which had almost entirely perished in England. He did not cower in fear of the words of wicked men, but [stood] firmly upon the rock—that is, upon Christ—for it was on behalf of Christ and Christ's Church that, on the fifth day of the feast of Christmas, the day after the feast of Holy Innocents, this innocent man died.

ST. JOAN OF ARC (1412–1431)

An illiterate nineteen-year-old girl executed for heresy, demonic possession, and cross-dressing might seem an odd candidate for a saint. Modern historians continue to dismiss her as a victim of mental disease and a fanatical French nationalist, but five centuries have done nothing to dim her appeal—even the cynical agnostic Mark Twain admitted that "she is easily and by far the most extraordinary person the human race has ever produced."

Born to an impoverished family in English-occupied France, Joan never learned to read and write. But at the age of thirteen she began to hear voices and see visions of saints and angels summoning her to lead the French armies in defense of her nation.

The Hundred Years' War, which began as an inheritance dispute between the English and French thrones, had by this time led to the utter devastation of the French countryside and dispossession of countless families. Joan's own village was burned by the English during her childhood. The French had lost every major battle for over a generation, and the only great city still standing against the English occupation, Orléans, was under siege.

When she first announced herself to the royal court, Joan's escort was told to take her back to her father for a good whipping. But when she showed a supernatural ability to predict the future, the French prince agreed to put her at the head of his armies, perhaps out of desperation from the failure of every other measure.

Personally leading the French armies into battle, Joan achieved such a sudden series of reversals—beginning with the apparently miraculous lifting of the siege of Orléans—that she put the French on course to recover their nation and drive out the English. During this time she continued to display supernatural abilities, predicting not only the outcome of battles yet to be fought, but also the two wounds she would personally receive in the throes of combat. Ultimately, she was able to escort the French prince to Rheims, the traditional site of his coronation, to see him crowned king.

Unfortunately, a strategic mistake led to Joan's capture by the allies of the English and, having laid their hands on Joan, the English immediately began plotting her death. It was not enough to execute her as an enemy of the state: this divinely appointed heroine must first be humiliated by being convicted of sorcery by a church court, and executed as a heretic.

The resulting inquisitorial trial was illegal on so many counts as to belie description: Joan was imprisoned in despicable conditions, refused access to a legal advocate, and denied access to the sacraments; all of her appeals to the pope suppressed; and the courts were stacked with English partisans, some of them openly coerced into delivering a negative verdict. Nonetheless, weeks of interrogation did nothing to break her spirit. The brilliant tact and wit of this nineteen-year-old girl so shamed her opponents that the courts moved from public to private sessions.

Ironically, her fall was occasioned by the charge of cross-dressing. Joan had repeatedly donned men's garb, including armor and sword, which she deemed more appropriate than a dress for a military general. Further, she claimed that such garb better protected her innocence in environments where she was repeatedly threatened with molestation. Although this practice was defended as upright by every serious contemporary theologian, including St. Thomas Aquinas, the English court considered it worthy of death.

When she was threatened with torture and shown the stake where she would burn, her gentle spirit broke and she was forced to sign a confession whose contents she could not possibly have understood. But her captors didn't want her only humiliated—they wanted her dead. All that was necessary was to trick her into putting on men's clothing again while imprisoned—some reports say they left her no other clothes; others, that she was threatened with molestation and was worried about her modesty.

Once she had been tricked she was accused of a "relapse" into a sin already confessed, a death sentence at the time. She was burned at the same stake, asking only for a crucifix to be held in front of her while she expired, uttering repeatedly the name of her beloved Jesus.

Within only twenty-two years of Joan's death, the English were finally driven out of France. A few years later, the pope himself demanded a retrial, a rehabilitation process that would, even after her death, vindicate her memory. Participants in her original trial presented themselves to admit both the illegality of the proceedings and her untarnished virtue to the end. Beyond being declared innocent of all wrongdoing, she was named a martyr. In the end she had gone to her death not so much for the cause of France but for the cause of the God who had summoned her.

LETTER TO THE KING OF ENGLAND

With her characteristic spunk and audacity, the seventeen-year-old Joan dictated this letter to the King of England in 1429, demanding his unconditional surrender.

JESUS, MARY

King of England, render account to the King of Heaven of your royal blood. Return to the Maid the keys of all the good cities you have seized. She is sent by God to reclaim the royal blood and is fully prepared to make peace if you will give her satisfaction; that is, you must render justice and pay back all that you have taken.

King of England, if you do not do these things, I am the commander of the military; and in whatever place I shall find your men in France, I will make them flee the country, whether they wish to or not; and if they will not obey, the Maid will have them all killed. She comes sent by the King of Heaven, body for body, to take you out of France, and the Maid promises and certifies to you that if you do not leave France she and her troops will raise a mighty outcry as has not been heard in France in a thousand years. And believe that the King of Heaven has sent her so much power that you will not be able to harm her or her brave army.

To you, archers, noble companions in arms, and all people who are before Orléans, I say to you in God's name, go home to your own country; if you do not do so, beware of the Maid, and of the damages you will suffer. Do not attempt to remain, for you have no rights in France from God, the King of Heaven, and the Son of the Virgin Mary.

It is Charles, the rightful heir, to whom God has given France, who will shortly enter Paris in a grand company. If you do not believe the news written of God and the Maid, then in whatever place we may find you, we will soon see who has the better right, God or you....

Duke of Bedford, who call yourself regent of France for the King of England, the Maid asks you not to make her destroy you. If you do not render her satisfaction, she and the French will perform the greatest feat ever done in the name of Christianity.

Done on the Tuesday of Holy Week (March 22, 1429).

HEAR THE WORDS OF GOD AND THE MAID.

THE TRIAL OF JOAN

This English transcript of Joan's trial—on charges of heresy, treason, and cross-dressing—is our only record of Joan's account of her childhood visions. The transcript also reveals her characteristic innocence, piety, and wit.

In the name of the Lord, Amen. Here begin the proceedings in matter of faith against a dead woman, Jeanne [Joan], commonly known as "The Maid."

To all those who shall see these present letters or public instrument, Pierre, by divine mercy Bishop of Beauvais … by apostolic authority Inquisitor of the Faith and of Heretical Error in all the kingdom of France: greeting in the author and consummator of the faith, Our Lord Jesus Christ.

It has pleased divine Providence that a woman of the name of Jeanne, commonly called The Maid, should be taken and apprehended by famous warriors within the boundaries and limits of our diocese and jurisdiction. The reputation of this woman had already gone forth into many parts: how, wholly forgetful of womanly honesty, and having thrown off the bonds of shame, careless of all the modesty of womankind, she wore with an astonishing and monstrous brazenness, immodest garments belonging to the male sex; how moreover, her presumptuousness had grown until she was not afraid to perform, to speak, and to disseminate many things contrary to the Catholic faith and hurtful to the articles of the orthodox belief.…

And first [the inquisitor] exhorted her to answer truly, as she had sworn, what he should ask her. To which she replied: "You may well ask me such things, that to some I shall answer truly, and to others I shall not." And she added, "If you were well informed about me, you would wish me to be out of your hands. I have done nothing except by revelation.".…

Afterwards she declared that at the age of thirteen she had a voice from God to help her and guide her. And the first time she was much afraid. And this voice came towards noon, in summer, in her father's garden: and the said Jeanne had [not] fasted on the preceding day. She heard the voice on her right, in the direction of the church; and she seldom heard it without a light. This light came from the same side as the voice, and generally there was a great light. When she came to France she often heard the voice.

Asked how she could see the light of which she spoke, since it was at the side, she made no reply, and went on to other things. She said that if she was in a wood she easily heard the voices come to her. It seemed to her a worthy voice, and she believed it was sent from God; when she heard the voice a third time she knew that it was the voice of an angel. She said also that this voice always protected her well and that she understood it well.

Asked what instruction this voice gave her for the salvation of her soul: she said it taught her to be good and to go to church often; and it told her that she must come to France [out of English-occupied France]. And, Jeanne added, Beaupère would not learn from her, this time, in what form that voice appeared to her. She further said that this voice told her once or twice a week that she should leave and come to France, and that her father knew nothing of her leaving. She said that the voice told her to come, and she could no longer stay where she was; and the voice told her again that she should raise the siege of the city of Orléans.

She said moreover that the voice told her that she, Jeanne, should go to Robert de Baudricourt, in the town of Vaucouleurs of which he was captain, and he would provide an escort for her. And the said Jeanne answered that she was a poor maid, knowing nothing of riding or fighting.…

After this the said Jeanne told that she went without hindrance to him whom she calls her king. And when she had arrived at Ste. Catherine de Fierbois, then she sent first to Chinon, where he who she calls her king was. She reached Chinon towards noon and lodged at an inn; and after dinner she went to him whom she calls king, who was at the castle. She said that when she entered her king's room she recognized him among many others by the counsel of her voice, which revealed him to her. She told him she wanted to make war on the English….

Then Jeanne said that there is not a day when she does not hear this voice; and she has much need of it. She said she never asked of it any final reward but the salvation of her soul….

Asked whether this voice, which she says appears to her, comes as an angel, or directly from God, or whether it is the voice of one of the saints, she answered: "This voice comes from God; I believe I do not tell you everything about it; and I am more afraid of failing the voices by saying what is displeasing to them, than of answering you."…

Asked if she knows she is in God's grace, she answered: "If I am not, may God put me there; and if I am, may God so keep me. I should be the saddest creature in the world if I knew I were not in His grace." She added, if she were in a state of sin, she did not think that the voice would come to her; and she wished every one could hear the voice as well as she did….

Asked whether the voice which spoke to her was that of an angel, or of a saint, male or female, or straight from God, she answered that the voice was the voice of St. Catherine and of St. Margaret. And their heads were crowned in a rich and precious fashion with beautiful crowns….

Asked how she knew one from the other, she answered she knew them by the greeting they gave her. She said further that a good seven years have passed since they undertook to guide her. She said also she knows the saints because they tell her their names….

Asked which was the first voice which came to her when she was about thirteen, she answered that it was St. Michael whom she saw before her eyes; and he was not alone, but accompanied by many angels from heaven. She said also that she came into France only by the instruction of God.

Asked if she saw St. Michael and these angels corporeally and in reality, she answered: "I saw them with my bodily eyes as well as I see you; and when they left me, I wept; and I wished to have had them take me with them too."…

Asked if God ordered her to wear a man's dress, she answered that the dress is a small, nay, the least thing. Nor did she put on man's dress by the advice of any man whatsoever; she did not put it on, nor did she do anything, but by the command of God and the angels.

Asked whether it seemed to her that this command to assume male attire was lawful, she answered: "Everything I have done is at God's command; and if He had ordered me to assume a different habit, I should have done it, because it would have been His command."…

Asked whether her own party firmly believed her to be sent from God, she answered: "I do not know whether they do, and I refer you to their own opinion; but if they do not, nevertheless I am sent from God." Asked whether she believed that by deeming her to be sent from God they believed rightly, she answered: "If they believe I am sent from God they are not deceived."…

She says that she asked three things of her voices: one was her deliverance; the second was that God should aid the French and keep the towns which were under their control; and the third was the salvation of her soul.…

And then since she had said that we the aforenamed bishop were exposing ourselves to great peril by bringing her to trial, she was asked what that meant, and to what peril or danger we exposed ourselves, we and the others. She answered that she had said to us, the aforesaid bishop: "You say that you are my judge; I do not know if you are; but take good heed not to judge me ill, because you would put yourself in great peril. And I warn you so that if God punish you for it I shall have done my duty in telling you."

Asked what that danger or peril was, she answered that St. Catherine told her she would have aid, and she does not know whether this will be her deliverance from prison, or if, while she is being tried, some tumult might come through which she can be delivered. And she thinks it will be one or the other. And beyond this the voices told her she will be delivered by a great victory; and then they said: "Take everything peacefully: have no care for your martyrdom; in the end you shall come to the Kingdom of Paradise."

And this her voices told her simply and absolutely, that is, without faltering. And her martyrdom she called the pain and adversity which she suffers in prison; and she knows not whether she shall yet suffer greater adversity, but in this she commits herself to God.

Asked whether, since her voices had told her that in the end she should go to Paradise, she has felt assured of her salvation, and of not being damned in hell, she answered that she firmly believed what the voices told her, namely, that she will be saved, as firmly as if she were already there….

Asked if God hated the English, she answered that of God's love or His hatred for the English, or of what He would do to their souls, she knew nothing, but she was certain that, excepting those who died there, they would be driven out of France, and God would send victory to the French and against the English.

Asked if God was for the English when they were prospering in France, she answered that she knew not whether God hated the French, but she believed it was His will to allow them to be beaten for their sins, if they were in a state of sin….

From the tenor of these letters it is manifest that Jeanne has been deceived by evil spirits, and that she has frequently consulted them in her actions; or, to mislead the peoples, she has perniciously and falsely invented such fictions…. The said Jeanne, usurping the office of angels, said and affirmed she was sent from God, even in things tending openly to violence and to the spilling of human blood, which is absolutely contrary to holiness, and horrible and abominable to all pious minds.

To this article on this Tuesday, March 27th, Jeanne answers that she first asked for peace, but if peace was not agreed to, she was quite prepared to fight.

On Saturday, February 24th, she said she came from God and had no business here, in this trial, and asked to be sent back to God from whom she came. On Saturday, March 17th, she said that God sent her to help the kingdom of France….

To the article touching her dress, she answered that she wore her habit and arms at God's bidding; this was true both of the male costume and the arms. When asked to abandon this dress, she answered she would not give it up without Our Lord's permission, not even to save her head, but, please God, it would soon be put off. She added, that if she had not Our Lord's permission she would not wear woman's dress.

The said Jeanne, in and since the time of her youth, has boasted and daily boasts of having had many revelations and visions, and concerning these, in spite of being charitably admonished and lawfully and properly required upon legal oath, she would not and will not swear; further, she refuses to declare them sufficiently by word or sign; but did and still does put off, contradict, and refuse.

And when formally refusing to swear, on many and several occasions, she said and affirmed, in her examination and elsewhere, that she would not discover her visions and revelations, even if her head were cut off or her body were dismembered; that we should not drag from her lips the sign which God showed her, by which she knew she came from God…. Consequently you can and must conclude that these revelations and visions, if Jeanne ever had them, proceed rather from evil and lying spirits than from good.

MEDIEVAL MONASTICS

In some form or another, the monastic vocation has been at the heart of the Church's mission from the first days of her founding. The perennial values of chastity, contemplative prayer, poverty of life, and "undivided devotion to the Lord" (1 Cor 7:35) animated the lives of St. Paul, John the Baptist, the Blessed Virgin Mary, and Jesus himself, and they would remain vitally active in the lives of their followers, often taking on new, imaginative forms in every era.

In the early Church it was precisely these values that had driven the Desert Fathers (and Mothers) into the deserts of Syria and Egypt, fleeing the busyness of life to secure a more intense life of prayer and contemplation. Soon the heroic—and often eccentric—ideal of the isolated hermit gave way to the more organized, stable, and disciplined communities of monks, governed by abbots under the legislation of monastic rules.

In the Middle Ages, these monastic communities would move from the peripheries of society to the very center, often serving as the social, economic, political, and religious hubs of medieval towns and cities. Such vital tasks of the Church such as preaching, education, relief for the poor, and missionary work were often dominated by these vibrant communities of monks and nuns.

Because monastic life was not something Church leaders brainstormed and implemented from above, but rather was a spontaneous, grass-roots movement of the Spirit "from below," it manifests itself in a dizzying variety of forms and structures. Yet at the heart of the monastic vocation lay certain perennial values which these diverse structures sought to preserve and foster: the primacy of the contemplative life over the active (see Lk 10:38–42), a life of chastity (see Mt 19:12), sharing of property in common (see Acts 4:32), and a firm, stable commitment to the consecrated way of life.

The medieval period, however, witnessed a number of creative and innovative ways of living out these perennial values. The formation of the Benedictine communities in the sixth century was the most widely successful attempt to institutionalize the monastic lifestyle in the characteristic framework of a rule of life, an abbot, stability, and a balance of work and prayer.

The twelfth century, however, saw a flurry of new movements, including the Franciscan, Dominican, and Cistercian orders. The Franciscan and Dominican orders, for their part, prized apostolic preaching and a more radical commitment to poverty over the stable, contemplative life so central to Benedictines. The later Middle Ages brought even more innovative experiments, including more informal communities such as the Brethren of the Common Life, whose members lived out monastic values without taking permanent vows.

And while it is the male founders of these great orders who figure most strongly in the historical literature, we should not forget that many more women were typically attracted to the monastic life than men, and the quiet work of female religious in schools, hospitals, poorhouses, orphanages, and chapels fueled the growth of Christian Europe.

All historians now recognize the work of the monastic movements in rebuilding Western civilization after its devastating collapse in the fifth and sixth centuries and in developing and expanding this civilization long afterward. It was the abbeys and monasteries that carried on not only the religious tasks of preaching, catechizing, and Church reform, but also the secular tasks of education, agriculture, relief for the poor, and even civil administration. But at the heart of the monastic vocation, of course, lay nothing more and nothing less than St. Benedict's desire to "prefer nothing whatever to Christ."

ST. BENEDICT OF NURSIA (480–547)

Other than the Bible, the *Rule of St. Benedict* is without a doubt the most influential literary work of the medieval era, directly or indirectly responsible in some way for nearly every major development of the period. It is odd, then, that it is the only document St. Benedict ever wrote—and, in point of fact, it may simply be a revision of an older document by another author—and that we know only the faintest outline of the saint's life.

That we know anything about him at all is thanks to Pope Gregory the Great, who, impressed with the stories of this saintly near-contemporary, interviewed his personal companions and drew up Benedict's biography in his *Dialogues*. From Gregory we learn of Benedict's noble upbringing in Rome with his twin sister, Scholastica, and of his sudden departure from that city in his late teens, driven into the wilderness to find Christians who were serious about living lives of holiness.

Though he lived four years in a cave as a hermit, he eventually adopted a communal form of living, not without some false starts—his first community rebelled against his strict leadership to the point of an assassination attempt! First he lived in the isolated town of Subiaco and then at the busier region of Monte Cassino, where he built an altar on the ruins of a pagan shrine.

Gregory's dialogues give the impression of a serious, quiet man with deep compassion for his monastic brothers. Apparently he was given a privileged vision of God himself shortly before his death, after which he was buried alongside his sister, whom he had assisted in forming a female monastic community.

But it was not for his life that Benedict became famous, but rather for his sole written work, the rule he wrote for his community, a sort of monastic code of conduct which laid out the regulations for daily life, for admission of new members and election of leadership, and so forth. It is important to note that Benedict—unlike later monastic founders—was not responding to any particularly urgent historical crisis of his time, nor did he envision a rigid order of priests committed to some mission in the Church or the world. He simply wanted a common home for those laypersons like himself who desired nothing more than the pursuit of holiness.

Nor did Benedict envision a worldwide religious order. His vision is only for a local community, a compact family of brothers under the rule of a spiritual father (or, of course, sisters under the rule of a spiritual mother). He stresses the priority of prayer and also work—given the many temptations of idleness— as well as stability and permanence, which allow the monk to put down roots in the local community, avoiding the constant pursuit of greener pastures.

Although Benedict does not overly stress absolute poverty, and his monks take no vow of poverty, he emphasizes that all goods are held in common by the family and repudiates all differences of rank or social status. His model of governance prizes social life over individualism, open discussion over despotism: the abbot is freely elected by the community and is himself governed by the community's Rule.

Such an intense concentration of all the values of Christianity was destined for fruitfulness, and as the Christian civilization of Europe collapsed during the invasion of pagan barbarians, the followers of Benedict would emerge from the ruins, planting communities here and there, tilling the soil, teaching children, offering the sacraments, and rebuilding civilization wherever they went. The vast majority of medieval monastics, both men and women, used Benedict's Rule as the framework for their communities (including the later Cistercians), and it remains the most common Rule today, inspiring tens of thousands of religious and untold numbers of laity who have discovered its values.

It was thus no surprise that Pope St. John Paul II named Benedict the co-patron saint of Europe in 1980, nor that he has always been known as the Father of Western Monasticism (St. Basil holds this title in the East).

BENEDICT'S CONVERSION TO MONASTIC LIFE

Pope Gregory the Great, having learned of Benedict's life from interviews with his monks, records the only surviving history of Benedict's embrace of the monastic life. This selection, and those that follow, come from Gregory the Great's Dialogues.

There was a worthy man, blessed both in grace and name, for he was called Benedict [*Benedictus,* Latin for blessed]. Even from his youth he had the soul of an elderly man, for his increase in age lagged behind his increase in virtue. He rejected all empty pleasure, and even though he lived in the world and might freely have enjoyed its riches, he had no desire for either the world or its luxuries.

He was born to noble parents in the province of Nursia and raised in Rome, where he received a good education. But when he saw many people using their good education only to live a lewd and undisciplined life, he drew back the foot he had already placed into the world, afraid that if he walked too far along this path, he would fall into the same dangerous and godless trap.

So he gave up his books, left his father's house and wealth, and with his only desire to serve God, he sought for some new place where he might live the life he wanted. And with this in mind he departed … to lead his life in the wilderness. Only his nurse, who loved him tenderly and refused to abandon him, accompanied him. He came to a place called Enfide and took up residence there in the church of St. Peter in the company of other virtuous men who were living in that place….

But Benedict, preferring the miseries of the world to the praises of men, prizing work in the service of God to any ephemeral admiration, soon left his nurse and went to a deserted region named Subiacum, about forty miles from Rome…. The man of God, Benedict, having come to this place, lived there in a cave, where he spent three years apart from any human companions….

About this time, some shepherds found him in that same cave, and when they first saw him through the bushes in his clothing of animal skins, they actually thought he was a beast himself. But once they met him and got to know him, many of them were converted by him from their own beastly lives to lives of grace, piety, and devotion. And after this he became famous throughout the country, and many people came to visit him. They brought him physical food for his body, and he gave them spiritual food for their souls.

THE FIRST, FAILED ATTEMPT AT COMMUNAL LIFE

Because of his great reputation for living a holy life, he became famous. Nearby the place he was staying there was a monastery whose abbot had died. The whole community came to the holy man Benedict, begging him earnestly to become the head of their abbey. He refused them for a long time, insisting that their standards were different from his, and that they could never agree on things. Yet eventually, worn out with their requests, he agreed.

Once he took charge of the abbey, he began insisting that the rules be followed, with the result that none of them could deviate from the path of monastic life as they were accustomed to before. Once the monks realized this they grew furious, angry that they had ever asked him to be their abbot, realizing that their undisciplined community could never stand his virtuous leadership.

Soon they realized that, as long as he was abbot, they could not live in the way they wished, and they were unwilling to give up their former way of life (it is hard for older minds to consider new things). And because the lives of virtuous men are always offensive to the wicked, some of them began to plot to get rid of him. After some talk they agreed to poison his wine.

Once they had done so they offered the glass of wine to the abbot to bless, as was the custom. But he simply raised his hand and made the Sign of the Cross over the glass, which promptly shattered in pieces, just as though the Sign of the Cross had been a rock thrown against it.

Once this happened, the man of God realized that the glass had been poisoned with death, having been unable to withstand the sign of life. So, standing up calmly and composedly, he summoned all the monks together and said to them: "May Almighty God have mercy upon you and forgive you! Why have you done this to me? Didn't I tell you beforehand that you and I could never agree on things? Go and find some other abbot suitable to your lifestyle, for I have no intention of staying here among you."

After speaking his mind, he returned to the wilderness which he had loved so much and lived alone with his Creator....

COMMUNAL LIFE AT SUBIACO AND MONTE CASSINO

As this servant of God increased daily in virtue and became even more famous for his miracles, he attracted many people in that area to the service of Almighty God, so that with Christ's help he built twelve monasteries there. He appointed twelve monks and an abbot in each one, and he kept a few monks with himself— those he thought would profit by his presence. And soon many noble and virtuous men came to him from Rome, asking for him to raise their children for the service of God....

Yet I would not have you ignorant that this man of God, in addition to all the miracles he worked which brought him so much fame, was also competent in theology. For he wrote a Rule for his monks that is both excellent in wisdom and eloquent in style. In fact, if anyone truly wanted to understand all of Benedict's way of life and discipline, he should consult that Rule, for this holy man could not teach something which he did not himself live.

THE MIRACLE THAT DIDN'T HAPPEN: BENEDICT AND SCHOLASTICA

But I have to tell you about the one miracle which the holy father Benedict could have done, but didn't.

His sister Scholastica, who from her childhood had been dedicated to the Lord, used to come to visit her brother once a year. The man of God came to a place that belonged to the abbey, not far from the gate, to visit with her. And when she came once, as was her custom, her holy brother went to meet her with his monks, and they spent the whole day together speaking spiritually and praising God. And when evening came they ate together, still sitting at the table and speaking of holy things.

But when it grew dark, his sister the holy nun begged him to stay there all night, so they could spend the night talking of the joys of heaven. But he absolutely refused to agree, responding that he could not spend the night outside of his abbey.

Now at that time the sky was absolutely clear, without a cloud to be seen. The nun, hearing her brother's refusal, joined her hands together and laid them on the table. Bowing down her head upon them, she prayed to Almighty God, and when she had lifted her head from the table there suddenly appeared such a storm of lightning, thunder, and pouring rain that neither Benedict nor his monks could even put their head outside....

The man of God, seeing that he could never return to the abbey through that thunder, lightning and pouring rain, began to grumble and complain to his sister. "God forgive you for what you have done," he said. But she answered: "I wanted you to stay and you wouldn't listen. But I asked the Lord and he decided to grant my request. So now, if you really want to go back to your monastery, go ahead, and leave me here all alone."

But the good father, unable to leave, stayed there against his will, in that place where he was previously unwilling to stay. And in this way they spent the whole night, mutually comforting each other by talking of spiritual and heavenly things.

THE RULE OF ST. BENEDICT

These brief selections from St. Benedict's Rule give a sense of the principal values of the monastic community and the kind of lifestyle Benedict envisioned for his monks.

We are about to found a school for the Lord's service, and in organizing it we hope we have not required anything severe or burdensome. But even if the demands of justice have required us to include something a bit troublesome to some, for the purpose of correcting vices or increasing charity, do not from fear flee the way of salvation, which can only be entered through a narrow gate (cf. Mt 7:13–14).

But as one's faith and way of life make progress, the heart is widened, and one advances up the path of the Lord's commandments with the unutterable sweetness of love. Thus, never departing from His guidance, remaining in the monastery in His teaching until death, through patience we participate in Christ's passion, so that we may deserve to be companions in His kingdom.

It is clear that there are four different kinds of monks. The first are the *cenobites*, who live in a monastery serving under a Rule or an abbot. The second are the *anchorites*, or hermits, who—not in the new enthusiasm of conversion but having learned from others through a long preparation of life in a monastery—have learned to fight against the devil. These, well-prepared in the army of brothers for the solitary battle of the hermit, are safe without the assistance of others and are able—with God's help—to fight with their own hand or arm against the vices of the flesh or of their thoughts.

The third are the *sarabites*, who have no Rule and no teacher but their own experience, like gold refined in the furnace. But, softened like lead, their works still worldly, their tonsure is simply a lie to God. Shut up by twos or threes or even alone, without a shepherd—in their own sheepfold, not the Lord's—their only law is the satisfaction of their desires. For they call holy whatever they think is good or preferable, and they call unlawful whatever they don't want.

The fourth kind are the *gyrovagues*. They spent their whole lives as guests in the cells of different monasteries throughout the provinces, for three or four days at a time. Always wandering and never stationary, devoted to satisfying their own pleasures and the joys of their stomach, these are in every way worse than the sarabites. It is better to be silent, rather than to speak of the wretched living of all such monks. Therefore, let us forget about them and proceed, with God's help, to treat of the best kind of monk, the cenobites....

The abbot, if he is worthy to preside over a monastery, should always remember what he is called, and carry out his office with the name of a superior. For we believe him to be Christ's representative, since he shares Christ's name, as the apostle says, "God has sent the Spirit of his Son into our hearts, crying, 'Abba! Father!'" (Gal 4:6). So the abbot should not dare to teach, decree, or order anything apart from the Lord's will; instead, his teaching should be sprinkled with the incitement of divine justice in the minds of his disciples. Let the abbot always remember that, at the great judgment of God, both things will be weighed in the balance: his own teaching and the conduct of his disciples. And let the abbot know that whatever the father of the family finds faulty among the sheep is blamed on their shepherd....

Therefore, if anyone is appointed abbot, he ought to rule over his disciples with a double teaching—that is, let him demonstrate all good and holy things by his deeds more than by words, so that to his earnest disciples he may display the commandments of God in word, but to the hardhearted and simple-minded he may display them by his deeds. But the things that he has taught his disciples to be wrong, he shall show by his deeds that they are not to be done....

He shall make no distinction between persons in the monastery. He should not prefer one to another, unless the one happens to excel in good works or obedience. A free-born man shall not be preferred to one coming out of slavery ... for whether we are slave or free we are all one in Christ (Gal 3:28), and under God we are all equally servants, for God does not make distinctions between persons. The only distinction God makes between us is whether we are humble and surpass others in good works. Therefore, let the abbot have equal love for all, and let him administer the same discipline in every case, only according to merits....

Whenever anything important is to be decided in the monastery, the abbot should call together the whole community to explain the issue to them. And once he has heard the advice of all the brothers, he should think it over himself and do what he considers best….

More than anything else, this particular vice [private property] is to be cut off root and branch from the monastery—that is, that anyone should presume to give or receive anything without the order of the abbot, or should consider anything his own. He should have absolutely nothing at all: no book, no tablet, no pen—nothing at all. For the monks are not even allowed to have their own bodies or wills in their power. Anything they need they should request of the abbot of the monastery, but they may have nothing which the abbot does not give or permit. All things shall be held in common, as it is written: "Let no one consider anything his own" (cf. Acts 4:32)….

Idleness is the enemy of the soul. Therefore, at set times the brothers should be occupied with manual labor and at other set times in holy reading…. One or two elders should be appointed to go around the monastery at the hours when the brothers are engaged in reading and make sure that no troublesome brother is found idling or wasting time, not intent on his reading, of no use to himself and stirring up others….

Let all guests who arrive be received as though they were Christ himself, because He will say, "I was a stranger and you welcomed me" (Mt 25:35). And let appropriate honor be shown to everyone, especially to those of the "household of faith" (Gal 6:10) and to travelers.

ST. ODO OF CLUNY (878–942)

As the Benedictine monks and nuns toiled and prayed, laying the groundwork for a new civilization, they carried on the spirit of their founder. It is, then, no surprise that they felt haunted by his ghost. St. Odo of Cluny reports on frequent visions of St.

Benedict appearing at odd times to check up on his monks, reprimanding them for breaking his Rule and encouraging them in their pursuits. But once or twice, a figure would appear who seemed to be St. Benedict incarnate in flesh and blood, a man and not a "ghost," to rally the sons and daughters of Benedict: such a man was Odo himself.

It has to be admitted that by the tenth century the Benedictine legacy was in tatters. Its very success had precipitated its downfall. The Benedictine reputation for contemplative prayer had led dying nobles to donate large sums of land to the communities, hoping that the prayers of the monks would tip the scales in their favor in the afterlife. Their reputation for holiness had led nobles to "donate" their troublesome sons and daughters to Benedictine houses in the hope of reforming their character.

As a result, after a few centuries these houses were flush with land—in some regions amounting to a fifth of the real estate in a province—and filled with rough characters who had not the slightest inclination to a monastic vocation. The consequences were predictable. Nearby lords, interested in controlling the vast land of the monastic houses, worked hard to manipulate elections of abbots and prioresses, sometimes gaining the power of appointment (this was known as "lay investiture"), after which they could buy and sell the office as they chose, often appointing faraway cronies or blood relatives who would never dream of setting foot in the cloister itself.

Furthermore, many of the monks who grew up in such an environment found numerous loopholes to avoid the requirements of the Rule, or even flaunted it outright. It was not unusual to find monks wearing fashionable clothing and feasting on fine dishes, their mistresses alongside them.

Yet there were always those who cherished the dream of St. Benedict, that the monastic house be a "school for the Lord's service." Young Odo, the son of a noble family, born miraculously (it seemed) to an elderly mother, was offered by his father in prayer to the service of God. When his father later regretted this prayer and sent his son as a page to the court of William of Aquitaine, Odo chafed at the secular environment. Once his father confessed to Odo the prayer he had once made, Odo pledged himself to the monastic life with a companion, the ex-soldier Adhegrinus. But when it came time to pick a house to live in, the companions could not find a single house in France where the Rule was followed and where the brothers preferred nothing whatever to Christ. Finally they met a reforming abbot, Berno (later St. Berno of Cluny), who was intent on returning to the strict discipline of the Rule at his abbey at Baume.

After a few years at Baume, Berno and his new disciple Odo were given a chance to give their reforming impulses a wide field. Odo's former boss, William of Aquitaine, was on his deathbed and wished to give his entire inheritance for the purpose of building a monastery, which he asked Berno to govern as abbot. Berno's conditions were simple: William and his entire family must swear to avoid any interference with the discipline of the monastery, allowing the brothers to choose their own abbot and set their own disciplinary standards.

The Charter of Cluny, signed in 910, was revolutionary. Cutting off the corruption at its source, Berno and Odo were able to enforce the Rule to the letter without fear of being called to task by the donors. In 927, upon Berno's death, Odo was named abbot of Cluny. His success at maintaining high standards of discipline led the pope to send him throughout Europe to reform other monastic houses, and the pope gave a special dispensation that any monk unsatisfied with his monastery could join Cluny.

The so-called Clunaic monasteries sparked a reform movement throughout Europe, aimed at restoring the independence of Church offices from political control and maintaining high moral standards for Christian ministers. It was a monk from Cluny, Pope Gregory VII, who fought the lay-investiture controversy to restore the freedom of the pope to appoint bishops rather than local lords and kings. Another Clunaic monk, Pope Urban II, launched the Crusades to free the lands of Eastern Christians from occupation by Muslim invaders. It seemed that in Odo of Cluny, the spirit of Benedict was alive and well.

CHARTER OF CLUNY

The constitutions of the monastery at Cluny, drawn up by William of Aquitaine and Berno, guaranteed the absolute independence of the monastic community as a protection against corruption and abuse. St. Odo was almost certainly a part of the deliberations, and the document seems to bear his signature.

It is clear to everyone that God's providence has arranged things so that the wealthy, by virtuous use of their earthly possessions, may be able to merit eternal rewards. The Scriptures show this is possible by stating, "The ransom of a man's life is his wealth" (Prv 13:8). I, William, count and duke by God's grace, have diligently considered this. Since I want to provide for my own salvation while I still can, I have seen fit—or rather, have seen it necessary—to give away some of the earthly goods that have been given to me, to gain a little benefit for my soul.

In this way, despite my increase in wealth, no one will be able to accuse me of spending it all on bodily cares. On the contrary, they will rejoice that I have saved something for myself, even when fate will snatch all the rest away. The most suitable way to do this, obeying the command of Christ, to "make friends for yourselves by means of unrighteous mammon" (Lk 16:9), and to be sure that this is permanent and not temporary, is for me to support at my expense a community of monks. And it is my trust and hope that, even though I am personally unable to cast aside all worldly things, by nevertheless supporting righteous men that do so I will share in their righteous reward.

Therefore, be it known to all who live in the unity of the faith and await the mercy of Christ, and to all those who shall succeed them until the end of the world, that for the love of God and our Savior Jesus Christ, I hand over my possessions in the town of Cluny.... I do so with the understanding that in Cluny a monastery will be built in honor of the holy apostles Peter and Paul, that the monks who live there will follow the *Rule of St. Benedict*, and that they will possess and govern these possessions until the end of time.

Also, that this holy house of prayer will be faithfully frequented with vows and prayers, that the heavenly conversation there will be sought with the deepest desire and fervor, and that prayers, petitions, and exhortations will be directed to God for me and for all men, in the fashion already mentioned above.

And let the monks themselves, together with all the possessions mentioned, be under the power and rule of the abbot Berno, who shall preside over them as long as he shall live according to his knowledge and ability. But after his death, those same monks shall have power and permission to elect any one of their order whom they please as abbot and rector, following the will of God and the *Rule of St. Benedict*, and they shall not be impeded from making a purely canonical election by our own will or by any other power….

It is my further intention that, in my own time and in that of my successors, works of mercy toward the poor, needy, strangers, and pilgrims should be carried out there with the greatest zeal, to the extent that circumstances allow.

I have decided to insert into this document a clause that, from this day forward, these monks should not be subjected to my own rule, nor that of my relatives, nor that of the king, nor that of any other power on earth. And I call upon God and the saints, against the awful day of judgment, warning that no secular prince, no count, no bishop, nor the pope himself shall invade the property of these servants of God, or alienate it, diminish it, exchange it, give it as a benefice to anyone, or set any ruler over it against their will.

And in order to ensure that rash and wicked men never succeed in carrying out such a blasphemous act, I call upon the pope himself (and with him Peter and Paul, the holy apostles, and glorious princes of the world) to use the canonical and apostolic authority given to him by God to excommunicate, from the Church and from eternal life, any robbers, invaders, and thieves of these possessions which I am so readily surrendering. I also call upon Peter and Paul to protect and defend the place of Cluny, the servants of God who live there, and all these possessions through the mercy and clemency of the most holy Redeemer.

If anyone—whether a neighbor or a stranger, or whatever his condition or power—should through craftiness attempt to do violence to this charter which I have drawn up out of love for God and reverence for St. Peter and Paul (though heaven forbid it, and I trust the mercy of God and the protection of the apostles will prevent it), may he incur the wrath of almighty God, and may God remove him from the land of the living and wipe out his name from the book of life.

THE MONASTIC VOCATION OF ST. ODO

One of Odo's closest companions, John of Salerno, wrote a biography after Odo's death, part of which was based on an actual interview with the saint. These selections describe the way Odo's father entrusted him to St. Martin as a child, his conversion to monastic life as an adult, his affiliation with the Clunaic reform movement, and some of the disciplines he attempted to instill in his brothers.

"During the time of my infancy," Odo said, "[my father] once picked me up, having entered my bedroom and seeing me in the cradle without a nurse present. Looking around everywhere and seeing no one watching, he raised me up with his hands, gazing upwards and lifting up his heart, and said, 'Receive now this boy, St. Martin, jewel of priests.' Then, lifting the cover and putting me back down, he withdrew and left the room, and he decided to tell no one what he had done."…

[Much later,] a man named Adhegrinus who was with Odo was suddenly struck to the heart. He immediately disposed of his possessions and hastily returned to Odo, laying aside his helmet and military career, and from this time forward he became a soldier for Christ. Next, Odo helped him to gather together all of his worldly goods and distribute them to the poor, just as he himself had done. These two soldiers lived for a time enclosed together in a small cottage. Finally, seeing the great evil in the world, and that those who loved the world and its temptations were being more and more ruined by them, they quickly determined to scale the heights of monastic life.

Yet at the time there was not a single monastery within the borders of France—which they discovered by journeying themselves or sending others in their place—which they could identify as a suitable religious house for them to join, so they returned to their old lodging in great sorrow. They finally decided to send Adhegrinus to Rome. Undertaking the journey, he passed to the borders of Burgundy and arrived at a place called Baume. There he found a monastery recently built by the abbot Berno. And turning aside there, he was received graciously, in the way that St. Benedict had instructed a monastery to welcome guests into the house. And he chose to stay there for some time, not requiring anything of them, but only that he might live there and observe their customs….

Of special note among them is their way of silence. On days when the twelve readings are celebrated, nothing whatsoever is said within the cloister until the time of the chapter, when they hear the office of the day said. And during the octaves of Christmas and Easter there is utter silence both day and night: this brief silence is said to signify the eternal silence. But whenever they need to communicate something urgent, at different times they are able to make signs with their fingers and eyes to make their meanings known. They have so mastered these techniques that, even if they had not the use of speech at all, these various signs would be adequate for communicating the most necessary things….

Truly, Odo confessed that he had more than enough resources to support his brothers and also to lavish gifts on the poor. Indeed, he never withdrew his arms from the poor. For whenever we went somewhere with him, he demanded that we find and bring something to help sustain the poor, and only when we had that would he depart in confidence…. In fact, if anyone ever gave him a gift, and the giver seemed to be poor, Odo would ask him what he needed and give him whatever he lacked. If there were anything he requested, Odo would calculate the value of the gift and give him exactly twice what it was worth. In all honesty, I have seen him do this many times….

He would also assert that, in the future, the blind and the lame would be the gatekeepers of paradise: therefore, no one ought to drive them away from his home, lest the gates of paradise be closed to him. And if anyone in our communities would refuse to put up with the inconveniences of the poor, or answer them harshly and deny them the benefits they were accustomed to, Odo would immediately rebuke him and offer grave threats. He would go speak to the poor man, saying, "Whenever he comes to the gates of paradise, treat him in the same way!" He did this to terrify his brothers, to provoke them to greater generosity and charity….

Also, in those days he began to persuade them to cease from eating meat, to live scarcely, possessing nothing of their own, and to bring forward and present to the community those things they had possessed in secret, as was the habit of the apostles. But on the contrary, the possessions of the monastery were in no way shared in common. Rather, the brothers divided up among themselves whatever they were able, in whatever way pleased them. And when they saw that they would not any longer be able to get hold of these things, they plotted to entrust them to patrons, the lowest profligates, to possess unjustly on their behalf, when they should have simply renounced these things as was the rule. For once the day was fixed when they were no longer allowed to eat meat, they would try as hard as they could to eat all of the stores of fish St. Odo had gathered up, so that once it was all consumed he would be forced to let them eat meat. In this fashion they ate massive amounts of fish….

But in due time, many in the surrounding countryside began to follow in the footsteps of the saint, accepting the way of life which he had taught, and thereby meriting to ascend to heavenly thrones. The fame of his holiness spread so far that not only lay faithful and canons came to him, but even bishops began to leave their sees to associate themselves with him and his congregation.

ST. DOMINIC DE GUZMAN (1170–1221)

St. Dominic has always had something of an image problem. His followers, the Dominicans, are often portrayed in anti-Catholic propaganda as intellectually rigid dogmatists who oversaw the Spanish Inquisition, burning heretics for amusement. (Dominicans were often symbolized as fierce dogs, a play on *Domini canes*, "dogs of the Lord.") You would never imagine that Dominic once sold all of his theology books to benefit the poor: "Would you have me study off these dead skins, when men are dying of hunger?" he asked. And he insisted on living in the French mission field rather than his home diocese in Spain because, as he said, too many people idolized him at home and he preferred to be pelted with mud and spit upon by heretics.

In fact, Dominic's personal holiness is universally attested. His acts of asceticism and self-denial were so severe—he never slept on a bed and usually walked barefoot—that they probably brought on his early death at age fifty-one. Twice he attempted to sell himself into slavery to ransom captives from the Moors. And Dominic probably would have been content to live a life devoted to private acts of charity had it not been for one fateful event in his life. He was tapped as a traveling companion by Bishop Diego of Osma, who had been sent on a diplomatic mission to France to arrange a marriage for the son of Alfonso VIII, king of Castile.

The mission ended as a drastic failure due to the death of the girl in question, yet while lingering in southern France

Dominic was horrified to see that the Christian faith had disappeared from the region, replaced by a heresy. The Albigensians (also known as the Cathars, or "pure ones") were a bizarre sect whose outward resemblance to Christianity was merely superficial. In fact, the Albigensians believed that the world was not the creation of a loving God, but a prison house built by Satan himself, from which imprisoned souls must escape.

Because they believed that earthly things dragged the soul downward, they excelled at fasting, poverty, and sexual restraint. Unfortunately, at that time these were things that most Christian clergy in France were not terribly good at, and the opulence and scandalous behavior of Christian monks were driving French Christians straight into the arms of the Albigensians.

Dominic and his bishop saw immediately that if Europe were not to be lost to the Christian faith, a new and imaginative solution must be found. The traditional orders of monks, at least at that time, would never be suitable as missionaries—they were too tied down to their monasteries, their lifestyles far too lavish and worldly, and their minds too dull from lack of intellectual stimulation. Europe needed a highly mobile organization of preachers, systematically trained in theology and beyond reproach in their simplicity of life. Thus was born the Order of Preachers, committed to theological study and debate on the one hand, and to the twin missionary tasks of poverty and preaching on the other.

Overwhelmed with a flood of new religious orders, the Vatican had temporarily forbidden any new ones, so rather than writing a new rule Dominic accepted a very old one, that of the Augustinian order. The Dominicans naturally gravitated toward the newly emerging universities of Europe and quickly built houses of studies adjacent to each. Within a generation or two they came to dominate the theology faculties, eventually producing the crown jewel of the order, St. Thomas Aquinas. Ironically, Dominic himself left almost no writings behind, leaving that to his disciples.

THE LIFE OF SAINT DOMINIC

Blessed Jordan of Saxony, one of Dominic's first followers and his successor as master general of the order, wrote the earliest biography of Dominic, based mainly on his personal reminiscences and conversations with the saint.

Once while Dominic was a student at Palencia, a severe famine struck throughout almost the whole of Spain. Dominic was moved deeply by the poverty he saw all around him, and struck with compassion he determined to do whatever the Lord willed, doing his best to meet the needs of those dying in poverty. Therefore he sold all that he owned in the town, and even all of his books, to set up a poorhouse for the giving of alms. When he had given everything he had to the poor, his generosity provoked the sympathy of other theology students and their teachers, and so this young man's generosity moved the slothful hearts around him to an abundant supply of charity….

Now, at that time, Alfonso, the king of Castile, wanted a marriage between his son Ferdinand and the daughter of a nobleman of the Marches. To this end, he went to the bishop of Osma, asking him to take charge of this business. The bishop agreed to the king's request, taking a companion suited to his state in life— a man of God in his own right named Dominic, the sub-prior of his church—and set out as far as Toulouse. But they found that the inhabitants of this land had been heretics for some time, and Dominic began to be moved to sympathy for the countless troubled souls who had been so horribly misled.

In fact, that whole night at the house where they were staying, with courage and passion Dominic carried on a prolonged debate with the host of the house, who was a heretic. When the heretic was unable to resist the wisdom and the spirit of Dominic's speech, he returned back to the true faith, thanks to the help of the Holy Spirit.

Soon they left and continued to the place they were headed. After a difficult journey they arrived at the girl's residence:

they explained the reason for their journey, and once the girl had agreed, they were sent on their way back to the king. The bishop enthusiastically informed the king of the success of their mission, and of the girl's consent. The king then called them a second time, sending the bishop and Dominic back with even more generous gifts, so that the girl would think it a great honor to be married to his son.

But when they had finished that toilsome journey once again and arrived at the Marches, they found that the girl had died in the meantime. Yet, as subsequent events were to show, God had arranged their journey for his own beneficial purposes: to bring about a very different wedding, a marriage between God and souls, joined by a bond of eternal salvation between the universal Church and sinners who would be saved from their errors….

For Pope Innocent had chosen twelve abbots of the Cistercian order, each with a companion, to preach the faith against these Albigensian heretics. These abbots, gathering together in council with the archbishops, bishops, and other leaders of the region, debated among themselves which was the most suitable way to deal with the heretics, hoping to be as effective as possible in their task.

While they were debating together, each suggesting what he thought was the best advice, the bishop of Osma arrived. He began to ask them … about the rituals and customs of the heretics, hoping to learn the methods they used to entice others into their treachery through their preaching, arguments, and the pretended example of holiness. And in contrast, he noticed the splendor and opulence of those who had been sent against them, namely the fat purses, the horses, and fancy garments they had prepared. "No, no, brothers," he said,

> this is not the way to go about it. For mere words from such like these will never bring others back to the faith, but a lived example is much more powerful. The heretics have the appearance of pi-

ety, a counterfeit example of frugality and auster-
ity, which convinces the simple people to accept
their way of life. But if you show the opposite, you
will accomplish nothing, and perhaps you even do
more damage, and you will never rest.

Fight fire with fire, as it were. Only true religion
will drive off feigned sanctity, and the pride of these
false apostles will be exposed only by clear humility. Thus Paul played the fool when he enumerated
as his mighty works his austerities and dangers,
thus shaming those who were swollen up with the
merits of their lives (cf. 2 Cor 11:16–33).

They responded, "What is your advice, then, good father?"
"What you see me do," he said, "do likewise." And upon saying
this, the Holy Spirit rose up within him: he called his own men
to his side, sending them back with the horses and equipment,
leaving only a few clerics with him. And he said that his intention
was to remain for some time in order to spread the faith in that
land. He kept also with himself the sub-prior Dominic, whom he
valued immensely, embracing him with great affection and love.
This was the same Dominic who would be the first founder of the
Order of Preachers and Brothers, who from this time after began
to be called not sub-prior, but Brother Dominic….

Having heard this advice and now stimulated by his example, the abbots who had been sent agreed to do the same
thing. Every one of them sent back to their places what they had
brought, retaining for themselves only their breviaries and some
books for study, which they would need for debates when the
need arose. And accepting the bishop of Osma as their head in
the whole business, as it were, they began to proclaim the faith—
on foot, without purses, in voluntary poverty.

Eventually a great debate was held near Fanjeau. A great
number of the faithful gathered together there, along with many
unbelievers. Many of them had written books, putting forward the

arguments and the authorities that supported their faith. Once all of them had been reviewed, the book of the blessed Dominic was the most widely recommended and approved. At this point both his book and a book of the heretics were brought to appointed judges, who had been found mutually agreeable to each side. And they agreed that whichever book was found most reasonable, its faith would be deemed to have surpassed the other.

But the judges could not agree on any outcome to the debate, and at last arrived at an alternative plan, that both books would be thrown into the fire. Whichever one of them was not burned, this one would undoubtedly be concluded to hold the true faith. So a great fire was ignited, and both books were tossed in. The book of the heretics was consumed at once. But the other one, which the man of God Dominic had written, not only remained unharmed, but it also leaped out from the flames a long way off. The fire rejected it a second and third time. The book's leaping back showed the truth of the Faith, and also the holiness of the one whose hand had written it....

Having joined the same bishop when he was attending the Lateran Council [that is, at the Vatican], Dominic submitted his cause to Pope Innocent, begging him to confirm himself and the associates of his order, who were called preachers by name as they would be in fact. Also he begged the pope to confirm the revenues that had been assigned to the brothers by the count and by the bishop. Having heard of this request, the bishop of Rome encouraged Dominic to return to his brothers and spend some time with them. They were to deliberate and all come to agreement on a Rule which had already been approved; then, they were to send someone back to the pope to confirm it for the whole order.

And so, returning from the council, he announced to the brothers the response of the pope. They immediately chose, as the rule of the future preachers, that of the blessed Augustine, who had been an excellent preacher himself. In addition, they decided that they would not have possessions, since the care of earthly things would impede the task of preaching.

ST. FRANCIS OF ASSISI (1181–1226)

It is safe to say that no Christian saint is so universally beloved as the troubadour of God, St. Francis. Nor any so unanimously regarded as a saint even during his own life, as demonstrated by his canonization a mere two years after his death.

Francis was the son of a wealthy Italian cloth merchant, and the way young Francis spent his youth will not sound unfamiliar to many young people today. He showed no inclination for intellectual pursuits and barely finished his education (indeed, he wrote only a few documents during his life, and only out of necessity). Instead he preferred to loaf around with his friends in the city: feasting, drinking, singing, picking fights, and roaming around the city streets in pursuit of entertainment.

His conversion came not in a sudden flash of light, like St. Paul on the road to Damascus, but rather in a series of small but progressively effective inspirations: a night of partying which ended in second thoughts, a moving encounter with a leper, a year spent in prison—which ended his attempt at a military career—a particularly well-timed reading he heard at Mass, and, finally, a voice heard while in prayer.

What made Francis unique, however, was the sheer vivacity of his personality: not one to do anything by halves, if he were to do something he would do it with every shred of his being. Having decided to do away with material possessions, even his underwear was one possession too many, and his biographer records the scene of Francis stripping naked in the city square, to his father's horror and the bishop's bemusement. Hearing of how Christ's followers went out two by two to preach the Gospel among the poor, without a single possession to their name, Francis could not imagine any response but to do likewise.

Such a charismatic figure as Francis was soon joined by a band of followers, leading Francis to draft a formal rule, or way of life, for his new "order." We should not overestimate the radical novelty his order introduced at the time. Until Francis, religious life meant only one thing: stable, contemplative communities devoted to work and prayer in a state of withdrawal from the world. Francis' model—poor, ill-clad beggars wandering through city streets, moving from one town to the next—was nothing short of scandalous to many.

Yet when Francis submitted his rule to Pope Innocent III for approval, the pope recognized in it a reflection of the apostolic life found in the Gospels, and gave Francis his blessing. (A cardinal briefly tried to persuade Francis to enter a monastery like everyone else, but Francis would have none of it.) One legend has it that the pope had seen Francis in a dream the previous night, physically supporting a crumbling church, and was convinced that Francis was divinely sent to revitalize and reform the universal Church.

So the Order of Friars Minor (literally, "little brothers") was born, not a loose federation of independent houses, but a tight-knit, hierarchical organization with Francis as superior general. The Rule mandated that every member take a threefold vow of poverty, chastity, and obedience, with a special emphasis on absolute poverty. Whereas the Benedictines had been content with surrendering *private* property, Francis would have no property *at all* among his poor brothers. With no roof over their head, his brothers would travel two by two, preaching and begging for their daily food.

Francis would later make a Second Order of the Friars Minor for female members, at the request of St. Clare; and, later, a Third Order for laity who remained in their homes but wished to imitate the values of the Franciscan way of life.

THE LIFE OF ST. FRANCIS

Thomas of Celano, one of Francis' companions, wrote two biographies of the saint. The selections below, drawn from both books, describe several significant events that combined to bring about Francis' unique vocation and the formation of the order. The famous account of his preaching to the birds is also included, along with the story of his reception of the stigmata at Mount Alvernia.

Francis had been the chief of a group of young partygoers in Assisi, and they continually invited him to their feasts, which always became excuses for indulgence and foolishness. They had made him their leader because of his reputation for generosity: they could count on him always picking up the tab. They gave him their obedience so that he would fill their bellies, and became his followers in order to become gluttons. He did not turn them down, so as not to appear stingy, and, besides, he knew the value of friendship.

On one occasion he prepared a vast banquet heaped with delicacies, and his guests ate to the point of vomiting, proceeding afterwards to roam the streets singing drunken songs. Francis followed them with his walking staff as "master of the festivities," but gradually he began to withdraw, beginning to sing in his heart to the Lord. Then (as he himself later said) he was filled with such a divine sweetness that he became speechless and was glued to the spot. Then a profound sense of desire came over him, lifting him up to spiritual things, at which point he began to see earthly things as worthless in comparison….

Of all the wretched sights the world has to offer, Francis feared lepers the most. And one day as he was riding near Assisi he met a leper, the sight of whom moved him to disgust and horror. Yet, fearing that a breach of the commandment would mean a lapse from his newfound faith, he dismounted and ran to the leper to kiss him. When the leper held out his hand hopefully, Francis gave him both money and a kiss…. A few days later he got it in his mind to do this again. He went to all the homes of lepers, kissing each one on the hand and mouth as he distributed money. Thus he chose the bitter path over the sweet one….

Having now been changed in heart (and soon to be changed in body, too) he was walking one day by the church of St. Damian, which had been abandoned and was in ruins. Led by the Spirit, he went in to pray: struck with unexpected feeling, he found himself utterly a changed man. And while he was still disoriented, something unheard of occurred: the painted picture of the crucifix moved its lips and addressed him by name: "Francis," it said. "Go repair my house, which as you see is completely falling into ruin." Francis, trembling and amazed, was nearly dumbstruck, but nonetheless he determined to follow these instructions….

From that point onwards, a compassion for the Crucified One was imprinted on his holy soul, and (we may imagine) the stigmata of the Passion were deeply impressed on his heart, though not yet on his flesh….

With this disposition, strengthened by the Holy Spirit, this blessed servant of God let the impulses of his soul lead him onward, trampling worldly things underfoot to attain the highest good. He feared any delay…. So he rose up, strengthening himself with the Sign of the Cross, prepared and mounted his horse, and hurried to the city of Foligno, taking some scarlet cloth with him to sell. He sold all the goods he had brought, and even the horse he was riding, after receiving a fair price. He then wondered what to do with the money. Since he was now utterly devoted to the service of God, it burdened and weighed him down to carry that money even for an hour, and he hastened to get rid of it, considering it as valueless as sand….

But now that he was taking up a life of holiness, his earthly father began to harass him, abusing him with curses, thinking it was sheer madness to serve Christ…. He then brought his son before the bishop of that city…. When brought before the bishop, Francis would not delay or hesitate even for a second. Without even waiting to be spoken to, or even speaking a word, he stripped off all of his clothes and gave them back to his father. He didn't even keep his undergarments, but stripped himself stark naked before all the bystanders. The bishop, amazed at his boldness and passion, took Francis into his arms and covered him with his vestments. For he understood clearly that this action was inspired by God, and that he was witnessing a profound mystery take place before him. From that point on the bishop became his helper and encouraged all of his activities….

One day, when the saint of God was in church, he heard the passage read from the Gospel, how Christ sent His disciples out to preach [cf. Mt 10:5–10]. And once Francis had pondered these words, he waited until Mass was over and asked the priest to explain the passage to him. And once the priest had explained the whole passage, St. Francis understood that Christ's disciples had been forbidden to possess gold, silver, or money, to carry purse, wallet, bread, or staff, to have shoes or more than one tunic.

Instead, they were ordered only to preach the kingdom of God and repentance. Immediately Francis cried out, rejoicing in the Spirit of God: "This is exactly what I want! This is what I have been waiting for! This is what I long with all my heart to do!" From this point on the jubilant holy father hurried to carry out this saving word, nor did he allow any delay in carrying out what he had heard.

Immediately he took off his shoes from his feet, dropped the staff from his hands, and exchanged his leather girdle for a small cord, leaving to himself only one tunic. He put the image of a cross on this tunic to ward off the devil's temptations, and made it of rough material to crucify the flesh with its vices and sins, and made it poor and drab, to avoid greed. And everything else he had heard he strove to carry out with the utmost diligence, for he had not heard the Gospel like a deaf man, but committed it all to memory and strove urgently to fulfill its every letter….

Blessed Francis, seeing that the Lord God was daily increasing the number of brothers around him, decided to write down in a few words a rule or pattern of life for himself and his brothers, using mainly the language of the holy Gospel, for whose perfection he yearned. But he added a few other things he thought would facilitate the attainment of a holy life. So doing, he journeyed to Rome with all of his brothers, hoping desperately that what he had written might be confirmed by the pope, Innocent III….

But first St. Francis went to the bishop of Sabina, John of St. Paul, who seemed to be one of the leaders in the Roman court who loved heavenly things and despised the earthly. This bishop welcomed him kindly and charitably, encouraging his good intentions. But being a temperate and discreet man, he began to second-guess Francis on many points, trying to convince him to become a monk or a hermit instead. But St. Francis, as humbly as he could, refused to give in to the bishop's persuasions, not because he had any dislike for these vocations, but because he had an even higher desire for a different way of life.

The bishop was amazed at his enthusiasm, and was simply afraid that he might have bitten off more than he could chew: for this reason he was suggesting easier ways of life. Eventually he was worn out by Francis' insistence and gave up, trying instead to secure an audience with the pope.

At that time Pope Innocent III ruled over the Church, a glorious man of deep learning and intelligent conversation, burning in zeal for holiness in things that would promote the Christian faith. When he had heard of the desire of these men of God, after first examining their manner, he granted their request and carried it out. Then, encouraging and instructing them in many things, he blessed St. Francis and his followers, saying: "Go, and the Lord be with you, my brothers, and preach repentance to all, just as He inspires you to. And when the Lord Almighty multiplies you, both in number and in grace, come back and report it to me, and I will grant you even more than this, and entrust even greater things to you."...

During the time when (as we have said) many were joining the brothers, the most blessed Francis was journeying to the valley of Spoleto and came to a spot near Bevagna where a great number of different types of birds were gathered together—doves, rooks, and those commonly called daws. When he saw them, Francis—being a most impulsive person, but also very tender and affectionate toward all lower, irrational creatures—left his companions and ran eagerly toward the birds. Once he was close he saw that they were awaiting him, and gave them his normal greeting.

When, to his surprise, they did not fly away (as they normally do) he was filled with joy and humbly begged them to hear the word of God. And after saying many things, he added: "My brother birds, you really ought to praise the Creator, and to love the one who has given you feathers for clothing, wings for flight, and everything else you need. God has made you the noblest of his creatures, for He has given you the pure air to live in, and you neither sow nor reap! He protects and guides you himself, without your slightest worry."

Once this happened (as he himself said, and those with him), those little birds seemed to rejoice in their own way, stretching out their necks, spreading their wings, opening their beaks, and looking at him. And then he went among them, touching their heads and bodies with his tunic. And then he blessed them, making the Sign of the Cross, and permitting them to fly away to another place.

The blessed father rejoined his companions, rejoicing and thanking God whom all creatures humbly acknowledge and worship. Having now become so simple (by grace, for he was not so by nature) he began to complain at himself, blaming himself for not having preached to the birds before, since they listened so reverently to God's word. And from that day forward he diligently preached to all winged creatures, all beasts, all reptiles, and even insensible creatures, to praise and love the Creator....

When he was living in a hermitage known as Alvernia, named for the place nearby, about two years before he gave his soul back to heaven, he saw a vision from God. In this vision he saw a man in the form of a seraph, or angel with six wings, standing over him with hands outstretched and feet together, fixed to a cross. Two wings were raised above his head, two spread out as if in flight, and two veiling his whole body. Now when the blessed servant of the Most High saw this, he was filled with great wonder and could not understand what it meant. But he was overjoyed and delighted at the affectionate look that the seraph, beautiful beyond words, was giving him. But the crucified one, and the bitterness of his suffering, struck him with fear.

Thus he arose, both sorrowful and glad at the same time, as joy and grief alternated in him. He wondered what this vision might mean, and his spirit was struggling to come to grips with it.

And while he was still seeking any understanding of its meaning, and his heart was still perplexed by its strangeness, marks of nails began to appear on his hands and feet, just as he had seen a minute before on the crucified man standing over him. His hands and feet seemed to be pierced through with nails, the heads of the nails appearing on the inside of his hands and the tops of his feet, and the points on the other sides. These marks were round on the inside of the hands and elongated on the other, and bits of flesh could be seen projecting outward like the ends of nails bent and driven back.

The marks of nails were also imprinted in his feet, raised above the rest of his skin. His right side, also, looked like it had been pierced with a spear, and was covered with a scar, and was bleeding so much that his tunic and clothing were covered with the sacred blood. Alas, how few of us were found worthy to see that wound in his side while the crucified servant of the crucified Lord was still alive....

But he was not proud of heart, and would not gratify the curiosity of others out of a desire for glory, but tried in every way he could to hide it, that man's favor might not rob him of the grace bestowed upon him.

THE RULE OF ST. FRANCIS

The Rule that Pope Innocent approved outlines the most essential characteristics of the order: Francis' commitment to absolute poverty, mendicancy (begging), and the simple preaching of repentance for sins.

In the Name of the Lord begins the life of the Friars Minor.

The Rule and life of the Friars Minor is this, namely, to observe the holy Gospel of our Lord Jesus Christ, by living in obedience, without property and in chastity. Brother Francis promises obedience and reverence to the Lord Pope Honorius and to his legally elected successors and to the Roman Church. And let the other brothers be bound to obey Brother Francis and his successors.

Of those who wish to embrace this Life and how they ought to be received.

If any wish to embrace this life and come to our brothers, let [the brothers] send them to their provincial ministers, to whom alone and not to others is given the power of receiving brothers. Then let the ministers diligently examine them regarding the Catholic faith and the Sacraments of the Church. And if they believe all these things, and if they will confess them faithfully and observe them firmly to the end … let the ministers say to them the word of the holy Gospel, that they go and sell all their goods and strive to distribute them to the poor.…

Once a year of probation is finished, they may be received to obedience, promising to observe always this life and rule.…

And let all the brothers be clothed in poor garments, which they may patch with pieces of sackcloth and other things, with the blessing of God. I order and encourage them not to despise or judge men whom they see clothed in fine and showy garments using dainty meats and drinks, but rather let each one judge and despise himself.

Of the Divine Office, and of Fasting; and how the Brothers must go through the world.

Let the ordained clergy perform the Divine Office according to the order of the holy Roman Church, with the exception of the Psalter; for this they may have breviaries. But let the lay brothers say twenty-four Our Fathers in place of Matins; five for Lauds; seven apiece for Prime, Tierce, Sext, and None, twelve for Vespers, and seven for Compline; and let them pray for the dead....

I indeed counsel, warn, and exhort my brothers in the Lord Jesus Christ that when they go through the world they be not argumentative nor argue with words, nor judge others; but that they be gentle, peaceful, and modest, meek and humble, speaking honestly to all as is fitting. And they must not ride on horseback unless compelled by absolute necessity, illness, or weakness.

Into any house they may enter let them first say: Peace be to this house! And, according to the holy Gospel, it is lawful to eat of all foods that are set before them.

That the Brothers must not receive money.

I strictly order all the brothers that in no way they receive coins or money, either themselves or through an intermediary. Nevertheless, for the necessities of the sick and for clothing the other brothers, let the ministers and custodians alone take watchful care through spiritual friends, according to places and times and cold climates, as they shall see expedient in the necessity, saving always that, as has been said, they shall not receive coins or money, ...

That the Brothers shall appropriate nothing to themselves: and of seeking Alms and of the Sick Brothers.

The brothers shall appropriate nothing to themselves, neither a house nor place nor anything. And as pilgrims and strangers in this world, serving the Lord in poverty and humility, let them go confidently in quest of alms, nor ought they to be ashamed, because the Lord made himself poor for us in this world.

This, my dearest brothers, is the height of the most sublime poverty that has made you heirs and kings of the kingdom of heaven: poor in goods, but exalted in virtue. Let that be your portion, for it leads to the land of the living; cleaving to it unreservedly, my best beloved brothers, for the Name of our Lord Jesus Christ, never desire to possess anything else under heaven....

Of Preachers.

The brothers must not preach in the diocese of any bishop when their doing so may be opposed by him. And let no one of the brothers dare to preach in any way to the people, unless he has been examined and approved by the minister general of this brotherhood, and the office of preaching conceded to him by the latter.

I also warn and exhort the same brothers that in the preaching they do their words be brief and pure for the utility and edification of the people, announcing to them vices and virtues, punishment and glory, with brevity of speech because the Lord made His word short upon earth....

CANTICLE OF THE SUN

Francis possessed a profound sense of God's presence in all of His creation, and his biography is filled with stories of his joyful interaction with animals. This song, written late in Francis' life, gives beautiful expression to this aspect of Francis' spirituality.

Most high, omnipotent, good Lord; praise, glory and honor and benediction all are Thine. To Thee alone do they belong, most High, and there is no man fit to mention Thee.

Praise be to Thee, my Lord, with all Thy creatures, especially to my worshipful brother sun, which lights up the day, and through him dost Thou brightness give; and beautiful is he and radiant with splendor great; of Thee, most High, signification gives.

Praised be my Lord, for sister moon and for the stars; in heaven Thou hast formed them clear and precious and fair.

Praised be my Lord for brother wind, and for the air and clouds and fair and every kind of weather, by which Thou gives Thy creatures nourishment.

Praised be my Lord for sister water, which is greatly helpful and humble and precious and pure.

Praised be my Lord for brother fire, by which Thou lightest up the dark. And fair is he, and gay and mighty and strong.

Praised be my Lord for our sister, mother earth, which sustains and keeps us, and brings forth diverse fruits with grass and flowers bright.

Praised be my Lord for those who for Thy love forgive, and weakness bear and tribulation. Blessed those who shall in peace endure, for by Thee, most High, shall they be crowned.

Praised be my Lord for our sister, the bodily death, from which no living man can flee.

Woe to them who die in mortal sin; blessed those who shall find themselves in Thy most holy will, for the second death shall do them no ill.

Praise and bless ye my Lord, and give Him thanks, and be subject unto Him with great humility.

ST. CLARE OF ASSISI (1194–1253)

Many of the more significant male religious movements have a female counterpart, and often the founders of each are closely associated—Sts. Benedict and Scholastica, for example—but rarely are they as intimately associated as Francis and Clare. Indeed, so closely did Clare resemble Francis in her spirituality that she was known as an *alter Franciscus*, another Francis.

Born to a noble Roman family in the town of Assisi, the teenage Clare was all set to enter an arranged marriage and embark on a life of comfort and luxury. Then she heard a sermon by an ill-clad, dirty beggar named Francis, and her life was turned upside down. At age eighteen, Clare renounced her family's wealth and determined to follow this wild-eyed beggar and imitate his love for Christ.

Sneaking away from home, she met Francis and his poor companions late at night, cutting her hair and exchanging her fine garments for a poor habit. Her father apparently hunted her down and attempted to drag her out of the church, but her firm resistance—even to the point of clinging to the altar and refusing to let go—eventually persuaded him.

Francis and his brothers initially did not know what to do with Clare—after all, their order was meant for men, and their life of homelessness, preaching, and begging did not seem to suit women. Initially she was placed in houses of Benedictine nuns, but their comfortable lifestyle did not satisfy Clare, who longed for the absolute poverty and strict asceticism practiced by the friars.

Eventually Francis built a hut at San Damiano, the church affiliated with his order since its beginning, and Clare moved there with several other young women whom she had attracted to the religious life. Before long Francis had drafted a short Rule for Clare and her sisters, and the Order of Poor Ladies was born. (After Clare's death it was renamed the Poor Clares and is generally known by this name today.) Francis led her order personally for a while, but he insisted that Clare take over its leadership after a few years, and she became its first abbess at the age of twenty-two.

From this time on we hear almost nothing of Clare: the scarcity of details only proves the success of her Rule, which imposed a life of silence and withdrawal upon her sisters. The social standards of the time did not permit the kind of wandering and begging that characterized the friars, and formal preaching was out of the question for sisters. Thus Clare's order remained cloistered, or separated from the world, devoted to poverty and prayer.

The absolute poverty that Clare had learned from Francis had to be guarded jealously, as churchmen continued to insist that radical poverty was unsuitable for women, whose weakness and fragility (they said) required at least some modest comforts. Cardinals of Rome pushed Clare to accept the rule of Benedict, which was more moderate in its demands, but Clare consistently refused. When Pope Gregory IX, thinking he was being generous, offered a dispensation from absolute poverty, Clare pointedly responded, "I need to be absolved from my sins, not from the obligation of following Christ." Eventually the pope relented and allowed Clare to write her own Rule, the first ever to be written personally by a female.

In this poverty and silence Clare remained until her dying day, and yet without leaving San Damiano she exercised a tremendous influence in the world about her, attracting hundreds of sisters to her movement, including two of her own biological sisters and her mother (after the death of her husband).

As she had depended so much on Francis earlier in her life, he came to depend on her later, and in his last years—having lost his eyesight, and with his body wracked by sickness—Francis was continually nursed by Clare and her sisters. Like Francis, Clare was canonized within two years of her death, her sainthood never doubted even during her life.

THE FIRST LETTER TO BLESSED AGNES OF PRAGUE

One of only a handful of letters written by St. Clare, this letter is addressed to Agnes of Prague (later known as Agnes of Bohemia), a Czech princess eventually canonized.

To the venerable and most holy virgin, the lady Agnes, daughter of the most excellent and most illustrious king of Bohemia. Clare, unworthy servant of Jesus Christ and useless handmaiden of those cloistered ladies of the monastery of St. Damian, her subject and bondswoman, commends herself in every way to the eternal glory of everlasting happiness….

Therefore, dearest sister, or rather most venerable lady, because you are the spouse, mother, and sister of my Lord Jesus Christ, brilliantly distinguished by the banner of an inviolable virginity and holy poverty, be strengthened in holy service. Form a burning desire for the poor Crucified One, who endured the passion of the cross for all of us, rescuing us from the power of the Prince of Darkness—we who were kept in chains due to the transgression of our first parents—and reconciling us to God the Father.

O blessed poverty, which gives eternal riches to those who love and embrace it! O holy poverty, which gains, for those who desire it and possess it, the promise of a happy life and eternal glory in the kingdom of heaven!

O pious poverty, which the Lord Jesus Christ—who rules and reigns both heaven and earth, who spoke and all things were made—condescended to embrace before all other things! "Foxes have holes," he says, "and birds of the air have nests; but the Son of man (that is, Christ) has nowhere to lay his head" (Mt 8:20), and yet "he bowed his head and gave up his spirit" (Jn 19:30).

If, then, such a great and good Lord, coming into the virgin's womb, has chosen to appear in the world as a contemptible person, poor and needy, so that men who were poor and needy, starving for heavenly food, might be made rich in Him by possessing the kingdom of heaven, then let us be glad and rejoice, filled with great joy and spiritual happiness!

For as the contempt of the world has pleased you more than its honor, its poverty more than great riches, then "lay up for yourselves treasure in heaven, where neither moth nor rust consumes and where thieves do not break in and steal" (Mt 6:20), and "your reward is great in heaven" (Mt 5:12). And this is what you deserve, who have merited to be called the sister, bride and mother of the Son of the most high Father and of the glorious Virgin.

For I am sure that you know that the kingdom of heaven is promised, and is given by the Lord, only to the poor.... For "no one can serve two masters; for either he will hate the one and love the other, or he will be devoted to the one and despise the other" (Mt 6:24). And you know that a clothed man cannot fight a naked man, for his enemy will be able to grasp him, casting him down and throwing him to the ground.

And those who seek glory in this world cannot reign with Christ. And it is easier for a camel to pass through the eye of a needle than for a rich man to enter the kingdom of heaven. For this reason you have disposed of your "clothing," that is, your worldly wealth, striving with your adversary so that, by means of the straight road and the narrow gate, you may enter into the kingdom of heaven.

> What a wonderful and felicitous exchange!
> To give up the temporal for the eternal,
> To merit the heavenly rather than the earthly,
> To receive a hundredfold instead of one,
> And to have a blessed, eternal life!

Farewell in the Lord. And pray for me. Clare of Assisi

THE RULE OF LIFE

The third and final form of the Rule of St. Clare, *drawing from the writings of Francis himself and approved by the pope, firmly secures the order's commitment to absolute poverty. While the basic form reflects Francis' original Rule very closely, note the focus on silence and cloistered life—that is, withdrawal from communication with the outside world.*

This is the form of life of the order founded by blessed Francis called the Order of Poor Sisters, to observe the holy Gospel of our Lord Jesus Christ by living under obedience, without property, and in chastity.

Clare, the unprofitable servant of Christ and the little plant of the most blessed father Francis, does promise obedience and honor to the lord Pope Innocent and his legally elected successors, and to the Roman Church. And just as she promised obedience to blessed Francis together with her sisters in the beginning of her religious life, so she now faithfully promises obedience to his successors. And let the other sisters always be bound to obey the successors of blessed Francis, and they must also be obedient to Sister Clare and the other legally elected abbesses who will come after her.

If anyone, led by divine inspiration, is led to embrace this form of life, the abbess will consult the wishes of every one of the sisters, and if most of them are willing, she may be received, provided that our protector, the lord cardinal, has given the appropriate permission. But the abbess will first examine the postulant, or cause her to be examined, with diligent care about the Catholic faith and the Church's sacraments, to see if she believes these things, confesses them faithfully and intends to practice them until the end of her days ... and if she be deemed worthy, let the words of the holy Gospel be read to her: "Go, sell what you possess and give to the poor" (Mt 19:21)....

And for the love of that most holy and beautiful child who was wrapped in swaddling clothes and laid in a manger, and for the sake of His Most Holy Mother, I exhort, beg and command you, all my sisters, always to dress yourselves in humble clothing....

Let all the sisters except those who are serving outside the convent keep silence from the hour of Compline to the hour of Terce, and let them always refrain from unnecessary conversation in the dormitory, in church and at the table. If they are taking their meals in the infirmary, they may speak with discretion to encourage and console the sick, and whenever necessity demands it they may say whatever they wish, but only briefly and in a quiet voice.

The sisters must not have conversations with anyone in the foyer or at the grille [the window in the door of the convent] except with the permission of the abbess or her vicar. And even if this is the case, no sister should talk to anyone in the foyer except in the hearing of two other sisters....

When the most high heavenly Father saw fit to enlighten my heart by His grace to do penance after the example of our most blessed father St. Francis, shortly after his conversion, my sisters and I promised to obey him of our own free will. And when our blessed father saw that we were not afraid of poverty or work, sorrow or shame, nor the contempt of the world, but rejoiced in these things, he was moved with compassion towards us and wrote for us a form of life.

This began in these words, "Because by divine inspiration you have made yourselves the daughters and handmaids of the most high sovereign King our Father who lives in heaven, and have espoused yourselves to the Holy Spirit by choosing to live according to the perfection of the holy Gospel, I will and promise in my own name and those of my successors to forever have for you the same care and solicitude that I have for my brothers."

He most loyally kept this promise up to the day he died, and he wished that his brothers would keep it forever. And to be sure that we ourselves should never depart from that most holy poverty with which we began, should anyone attempt to dissuade us, he sent us another letter shortly before he died, saying: "I, brother Francis, least of all men, desire to imitate the life and poverty of the most high Lord Jesus Christ and of His most holy Mother. And I counsel and beg you, my ladies, that you too always live this most holy life and poverty, and keep watch over yourselves lest any man ever attempt to lure you away from it by his advice and teaching."

For this reason, I and my sisters have always taken great care to observe that holy poverty which we promised to the Lord God and to blessed Francis. So let the abbesses and sisters who come after me likewise take great care to observe it inviolably to the end. That is, they should not receive or hold possessions, nor have any rights of property or anything that might be construed as such, in any way whatsoever, either directly or indirectly by means of an intermediary.

CLARE MEETS FRANCIS' FUNERAL PROCESSION

Thomas of Celano, Francis' biographer, includes little about Clare in his two accounts of Francis' life, but he could not resist relating the touching incident of Clare's meeting her beloved Francis during the latter's funeral procession, which made its way past her convent.

The brothers came together with all the crowds of people from the neighboring towns, excited at the prospect of being present at such a solemn occasion. The night that the holy father died, they stayed awake the whole night praising God, singing such sweet songs of joy and bearing so many lights that it seemed that a company of angels was keeping vigil.

And in the morning all the clergy and people of Assisi assembled, taking Francis' sacred body from his deathbed and carrying it into the city, the whole while singing hymns and sounding trumpets. Everyone carried olive branches, performing the holy rituals with profound reverence and reciting the prayers with loud voices and many lights. And as the sons carried their father and the flock followed their shepherd, moving forward toward the Shepherd of All, they reached the church of St. Damian, where he had founded both his own order and that of the holy virgins and poor ladies. They laid him in this church, where lived the daughters he had won to the Lord.

The little window was opened, through which these handmaids of Christ ordinarily received holy Communion, and the coffin was also opened, exposing that great treasure of heavenly virtues, who had carried so many himself but was now carried by others. And behold, the lady Clare, properly named due to her brilliance [*clara* means "brilliance" in Latin] in holy merits, the first blossom of this holy order and the mother of the rest, came forward with her daughters. They looked on their father, who would neither speak to them nor return to them, for he was going on to another place. And they sighed repeatedly as they looked at him, and began to cry with choked voices and many tears:

> Father, father, what will we do? How can you leave us behind in such misery and desolation? Why can't you take us, who are left here grieving, with you where you are going? How can you leave us behind, never visiting us again as you used to? Without you we have no comfort, no joy left.
>
> Who can console us in our poverty, both of merits and of material goods? O father of the poor and lover of poverty! Who will strengthen us against temptation other than you, who has endured and overcome so many?
>
> Who will comfort us amid sufferings other than you, who has helped us through so much already? O bitter parting and terrible abandonment! How can death take him away, the father of so many thousands of sons and daughters, who alone was responsible for the success of our projects?

But through modesty they were able to restrain their weeping. In fact, it seemed inappropriate to cry over the one whose passing into eternal life was accompanied by such a large host of angels, and at which the fellow citizens of the saints and of God's household rejoiced so much in heaven.

And so the ladies, wavering between sorrow and joy, kissed his wounded hands, and then the door was shut which never again would be opened to such a desolate scene. But how pitiful was the crying of those ladies! How great was the sorrow of his sons? And everyone else shared their grief, for no one could refrain from crying when those angels of peace were crying so bitterly.

THE TESTAMENT OF ST. CLARE

As the time of St. Clare's death drew near, as was the custom, she wrote a testament—not exactly a last will, but more of a statement of how she wished the order to continue after her death.

In the name of the Lord! Amen.

Among the most significant graces which we have continually received from our benefactor, the Father of Mercies, there is one for which we must above all give him thanks—that is, our vocation, which claims our gratitude insomuch as it is so exalted. And we should remember the example of the first Christians, to whom St. Paul wrote, "Consider your call" (1 Cor 1:26). The Son of God has called us to himself, and the life and teaching of the blessed St. Francis, His true lover and imitator, have led us so far along the straightest path.

Therefore, most beloved sisters, let us never forget the benefits which the Lord has given to us, and especially those He gave us through His great servant, blessed Francis, not only after our conversion, but even while we were still wandering in the turbulence of the world.

After the Most High, our heavenly Father, saw fit by an act of sheer mercy to enlighten my mind and soften my heart, I undertook a life of penance under the instruction and example of the most blessed Francis. Not long after his conversion, I promised him voluntary obedience along with a few companions the Lord had given me, as the Lord himself had led me to do through His grace.

At that time the saint, seeing that despite our fleshly weakness we were not afraid of a life of poverty, suffering, fatigue, humiliation, and the contempt of the world—rather, that we thought these things great joys, just like himself and the other Friars Minor he had sent to us—then the saint rejoiced in the

Lord, and compassionately took us under his wing along with the rest of his religious brothers. And in this way, after a brief stay at another place, we came to live in the monastery of St. Damian, by the will of the Lord and of our blessed father Francis, and in that place the ever-merciful and good Lord multiplied his blessings to us, to fulfill what his servant had predicted.

About that time the saint gave us our rule of life in writing, which is mainly concerned with holy poverty. Not content only to encourage us to practice this precious virtue constantly, by his own example and his instructions, he also left us many written remarks about it so that even after his death it would be impossible for us to leave the path he had marked out for us. And we have kept our promises faithfully, just as the Son of God never departed from holy poverty, and our blessed father St. Francis likewise chose for his inheritance a life of renunciation and abandonment of worldly goods.

However, I, Clare, unworthy servant of Jesus Christ and of the poor servants of the monastery of St. Damian, though only a useless plant in the Lord's field, with all of the sisters in my order, twice voluntarily bound myself to observe our Lady holy poverty, so that after my death no sisters, present or future, may depart from it on any pretense. I made this decision after taking into considering the dignity of our profession, the commands of our Holy Father, and the weakness of human nature, which is most to be feared, especially after the death of the man who was, after God, our only support and consolation.

To be sure that our profession would never be altered, I did everything I could to have it confirmed by our Holy Father Pope Innocent III, who was pope when our order began, so that those who came after him might confirm it with their supreme blessing as well.

I also commend my present and future sisters to the successor of blessed Francis, our father and founder, and to all his religious, that they may help us to serve God better and preserve holy poverty by their instructions and example. And I pray, with all the humility I am capable of, that no matter what weak little plants we may be, we should never waver from our sacred promises.

GERARD GROOTE (1340–1384)

Martin Luther once implied that, had there been more communities like that established by Gerard Groote, there would have been no need for a Reformation. And while it is common to see Groote's movement as sort of a proto-Reformation, an embryonic Lutheranism, it is more accurate to say that Groote and those associated with him represent a genuinely Catholic attempt to reform morals and education within the Church, and that the tragedy of their limited scale of success helped to precipitate the Reformation crisis.

Gerard Groote (sometimes spelled Geert Groote) was at first nothing but an obnoxiously smart Dutch graduate student who found religion dull, which did not stop him from obtaining a luxurious clerical position to cushion his resume. A sudden illness, combined with a well-timed intervention by a concerned friend, led to an unexpected conversion of heart. Gerard retired from his position and abandoned his studies, moving into a monastery to pray and study the Scriptures. Yet the monks, not wanting the high education of Gerard to be put to waste, encouraged him to go out and preach to the people.

Thus Gerard embarked upon a brief career as a missionary preacher, with throngs of people hanging on his every word as he warned them of judgment and the dangers of hell, encouraging them to pray and cultivate good morals. Gerard was a deacon, however, not a priest, and regulations at the time typically restricted preaching to priests, leading Gerard to be silenced by the bishop of Utrecht.

A fateful visit to the famed mystic Jan van Ruysbruck sparked Gerard's next move, the decision to retire from public life and, with his disciple, Radewyns, set up a community of like-minded believers dedicated to the pursuit of holiness.

While part of Gerard's project included a formal order of priests (Augustinian canons), the other part was a more informal community of lay believers, the Brethren of the Common Life. This community, quite unprecedented at the time, did not require formal monastic vows, and yet its members lived a quasi-monastic lifestyle, involving common meals and prayer, listening to Scripture and spiritual readings, wearing simple clothing, and keeping minimal possessions.

Given Gerard's academic background it was inevitable that the Brethren would include an educational mission, especially the copying of books on the spiritual life—making use of the printing press once it was invented—and the establishment of schools to educate young boys, the main one being at Deventer. Nicholas of Cusa, Thomas à Kempis, Erasmus of Rotterdam, the future Pope Adrian VI, and even Martin Luther studied with the Brethren.

The spirituality that was taught, published, and lived by the Brethren of the Common Life is usually called the *devotio moderna* ("modern devotion"). It tends to focus on the cultivation of the interior life through silent contemplation, self-denial or asceticism, and personal meditation on Christ's passion. The Brethren insisted that good morals are more important than a good education, and that even the highest doctrinal orthodoxy was no guarantee of heaven without accompanying holiness of life.

The focus on personal piety, the reading of Scripture, and the love of Christ are often seen as anticipating the ideals of the Reformation, but they are perfectly consistent with medieval Catholic spirituality as well.

Gerard died of the plague, contracted from nursing sick patients, at the age of forty-four, but the Brethren and their schools would spread his ideals to the rest of Christendom.

THE LIFE OF GERARD GROOTE

Thomas à Kempis (1380–1471), a Dutch priest who was closely associated with the Brethren of the Common Life and a fervent admirer of Groote's writings, wrote the only contemporaneous biography of Groote, a testimony to the profound influence of this holy man on the spiritual writers of later centuries.

When he was nearly an adult, Gerard was sent by his parents to the University of Paris. They gave him as much support as he needed, more than most of his companions had, and he busied himself with his studies. At that time he had no interest in the glory of Christ: he cared mainly for a high opinion among his peers, and was wasting his time in pursuit of a great reputation.

Soon, however, once he had finished all of his required courses, he was left wanting something more, so—by virtue of his intelligence—he earned a master of arts degree by the age of eighteen. With this degree in hand, fired up by a natural genius and puffed up with worldly knowledge, he was rewarded with an office in the Church, becoming a priest in the Diocese of Aix. But still, at this point he lived a very uninspired, worldly life, though very soon God's mercy would change him into another man….

In Gelders near the city of Arnheim lived a certain monk who was prior of the Carthusian Monastery in Monichuysen, a well-educated man, profoundly holy, who had been a friend of Gerard's before he joined the monastery. This man—full of compassion and love of neighbor, and earnest for the salvation of souls—began to wonder how he might speak privately to Gerard for the sake of his salvation. He was afraid that such a promising and well-educated man would perish in the world, and hoped that he might be snatched from the devil's snares with God's help and added to the number of God's chosen people.

Now at that particular time the entire world seemed to be given over to evil, so there were few who preached the Word of Life by word and example, and fewer still who followed the rule of chastity. Even worse, those who claimed to be religious and devout lived uninspiring and tepid lives, not following the path set by their fathers before them….

This man approached Gerard and greeted him as a friend, and as his host encouraged him with friendly advice. Mingling kind words with stern ones, he talked to him about the highest good in life, about the rewards of eternal life and the terrors of final judgment. He showed how futile were the ways of the world, since everything under the sun would perish, and spoke highly of the religious life. "Death," he said, "hangs over every man, but we don't know the day or hour of our death. But those who follow Christ are assured of great gifts."

God's grace was present through this whole conversation, which went on for a long time. Gerard's heart was softened, and he believed what was said to him, acknowledging that the prior's words were true. He was convinced by his arguments, attracted by his promises, and encouraged by the examples of the saints. Before long he had decided to change his way of life for a better one, and by the grace of God he renounced the vanities of the world....

Soon afterwards, Gerard began to live out all the resolutions he had made. Once his mind was made up, strengthened by Christ, he resigned all his positions and changed his worldly clothes for a simple habit, more fitting for a humble priest who preferred the world's contempt more than wealth. A rumor spread among the people, and many were curious about this strange news, saying: "Why is he doing this, and what a remarkable change! Has too much education driven him mad? He who used to wear fine clothes is now dressed in rough and drab wool. He used to love feasting on fancy foods, but now he rejects them and seeks only the simplest food. He shuns high positions and loves poverty!"...

But the more this devout and well-educated master increased in virtue, and the more Christ grew sweet to him, to the same extent the world became less and less important in his eyes. And when God's providence had brought him to a suitable state, some wise monks decided that this blazing, shining light should be placed on a candlestick to give light to the whole house of God, so that the voice of his preaching and the example of his holy speech might spark a fire in the hearts of sinners....

For three years he devoted himself to study and prayer before he began to preach. Now equipped with spiritual armor and armed with the Scriptures, the faithful herald began to announce the good news of God's Word in the cities and villages. He had many hearers—priests, laypersons, and religious, small and great, learned and unlearned, men of high degree and councilors, rulers, slaves and free, rich and poor, landed men and foreigners. He blew the trumpet of salvation, not withholding any necessary note from his hearers, but proclaiming openly the plan of God for all men, as was suited to their state, condition, sex, and age. As a result, the many hearts were moved to flee from God's anger, the coming wrath of the last judgment and the fires of hell....

So many people came to hear God's Word that the churches could not hold the crowds that came to hear him. Many left their food, drawn by a greater hunger for holiness, and put aside even urgent business, running to hear his preaching. He often delivered two sermons a day, preaching sometimes for three hours or more, whenever the spirit struck him. He preached in the larger cities in the Dioceses of Utrecht, Deventer, and Zwolle; in Kempen often, and in Utrecht itself before the assembled clergy; in the country of Holland, at Leyden, Delft, and Ghent; in Amsterdam (where he delivered his first sermon in the common language) and in various other towns and well-known villages where he hoped to gather fruit and to bring forth new children for God.

Blessed be God, who, sending His Holy Spirit from above, kindled the hearts of His faithful people and greatly multiplied them. As a result, from the seed of a few converts grew many companies of devout brothers and sisters who served God in chastity; and from these several monasteries of monks and holy nuns were started....

Now Gerard, filled with the Holy Spirit and seeing that the number of his disciples was continually increasing, burning with zeal for spiritual warfare, responded prudently. He arranged that the devout might come together on occasion into one house for mutual encouragement, to deal faithfully with one another regarding spiritual things and the law of charity. He also proposed that if any of them wanted to live together continually, they should earn their own living by the work of their hands, and (as much as possible) live in common under the discipline of the Church. He allowed no one to beg in streets unless they had no other choice, nor to go from house to house to obtain alms: rather, he ordered them to remain at home, and (as St. Paul taught) to be diligent in the labor of their hands.

He ordered them not to engage in any business which might hinder their devotion in the hope of greater gain, or which might give the weak some occasion of falling back into their former, evil ways, at the instigation of the devil….

He was moved to found this religious order mainly by the special love and reverence he had for a holy man named Jan van Ruysbruck, the first prior of Grünthal, and for the other brothers in that place, who lived the religious life so perfectly. He had visited them personally in Brabant, and he had seen in them, and derived from them, a way of life that led to great holiness through deep humility and the wearing of simple clothing.

But although he worked hard and diligently to find a place and a monastery suited for the religious life, he never achieved this, for death took him first. Yet in the sight of God the King immortal, invisible, the Founder of all things, the intention was counted as if it were the completion of his plan. And he left behind him, to those most beloved disciples whom he had converted, a desire to build a religious house, encouraging them not to let so great a plan be forgotten once he was dead, but to come together, and to lend their help and counsel in carrying it out for the greater glory of God.

THE IMITATION OF CHRIST

This classic religious text, The Imitation of Christ, *is usually credited to Thomas à Kempis, Groote's biographer. Many scholars believe the text was originally written by Groote and simply copied by Thomas, the book's copyist somehow being mistaken for its author. At the very least, even if not personally written by Groote, the work closely reflects the principles of his thought.*

"He who follows me will not walk in darkness," says the Lord (Jn 8:12). With these words Christ advises us to imitate His life and habits, if we wish to be truly enlightened and free from all blindness of heart. Let our chief aim, then, be to study the life of Jesus Christ.

The teaching of Christ is more excellent than all the advice of the saints, and whoever has His Spirit will find in it a hidden manna. Now there are many who hear the Gospel often but care little for it, because they have not the Spirit of Christ. But whoever wishes to fully understand the words of Christ must try to pattern his whole life on that of Christ.

What good does it do to speak in an educated way about the Trinity if your lack of humility displeases the Trinity? In fact, it is not education that makes a man holy and just, but a virtuous life makes him pleasing to God. I would rather feel contrition than know how to define it. For what would it profit us to know the whole Bible by heart, and the principles of all the philosophers, if we live without grace and the love of God? Vanity of vanities and all is vanity, except to love God and serve Him alone.

This is the greatest wisdom—to seek the kingdom of heaven through contempt of the world. It is vanity, therefore, to seek and trust in riches that perish. It is vanity also to seek honor and to be puffed up with pride. It is vanity to follow the lusts of the body and to desire things that will someday merit severe punishment. It is vanity to wish for long life and to care little about a well-spent life. It is vanity to be concerned with the present only and not to make provision for things to come. It is vanity to love what passes quickly and not to look ahead where eternal joy abides.

Remember often this proverb: "The eye is not satisfied with seeing nor the ear filled with hearing" [Eccl 1:8]. Try, also, to turn your heart from the love of visible things and bring yourself to invisible things. For those who follow their own evil passions stain their consciences and lose God's grace.

Everyone naturally desires knowledge, but what good is knowledge without fear of God? A humble rustic who serves God is better than a proud intellectual who neglects his soul to study the course of the stars. Whoever knows himself well becomes lowly in his own eyes and is not happy when praised by men. If I knew all things in the world and lacked charity, what would it profit me before God, who will judge me by my deeds?

Shun, too, great desire for knowledge, for there is much fretting and delusion in it. Intellectuals like to appear learned and to be called wise. Yet there are many things whose knowledge does little or no good to the soul, and whoever concerns himself about other things than those which lead to salvation is very unwise. Many words do not satisfy the soul; but a good life eases the mind and a clean conscience inspires great trust in God.

The more you know and the better you understand, the more severely will you be judged, unless your life is also the more holy. Do not be proud, therefore, because of your learning or skill. Rather, fear because of the talent given you. If you think you know many things and understand them well enough, realize at the same time that there is much you do not know. So do not pretend to have wisdom, but admit your ignorance. Why prefer yourself to anyone else when many are more educated, more cultured than you?

If you wish to learn and appreciate something worthwhile, then love to be unknown and considered as nothing. Truly to know and despise oneself is the best and most perfect advice. To think of oneself as nothing, and always to think well and highly of others is the best and most perfect wisdom. Therefore, if you see another sin openly or commit a serious crime, do not consider yourself better, for you do not know how long you can remain in good condition. All men are frail, but you must admit that none is more frail than yourself.

Happy is he who realizes the truth, not in signs and words that fade, but as it actually is. Our opinions, our senses often deceive us and we understand very little. What good is much discussion of profound and obscure matters when our ignorance of them will not be held against us on Judgment Day? Neglect of things that are profitable and necessary and undue concern with those that are irrelevant and harmful are great folly.

We have eyes and do not see. Why, therefore, should we concern ourselves with questions of philosophy? He who listens to the Eternal Word does not theorize. For from this Word are all things, and of Him all things speak—the Beginning who also speaks to us. Without this Word no man understands or judges correctly. He to whom it becomes everything, who traces all things to it and who sees all things in it, may ease his heart and remain at peace with God.

O God, You who are the truth, make me one with You in love everlasting. I am often wearied by the many things I hear and read, but in You is all that I long for. Let the learned be still, let all creatures be silent before You; You alone speak to me.

MEDIEVAL MYSTICS

In a well-known passage of the New Testament, Jesus praises Mary of Bethany, who has chosen to contemplate at Jesus' feet, for having chosen the "better part" over her sister Martha, who was "distracted" over the external business of preparing a meal (see Lk 10:42). Given this precedent, our survey of medieval Christianity would be incomplete if we were only to consider the business of writing books, founding institutions, and carrying out missionary work. Any purportedly Christian society must have at its core the "better part" of those who work quietly to build up the interior life of prayer, contemplation, and conversation with God.

This field is usually known as mysticism, a term that carries with it so many odd connotations that it should probably be avoided entirely. Instead, let's simply define mysticism as the disciplined and methodical activity of cultivating inner union with God. In this sense, a mystic is not necessarily one who has experienced ecstatic raptures, heard voices, or seen visions: although many mystics have done so, they usually advise others that these experiences are atypical and should not be sought for their own sake.

A mystic is simply one who has achieved a certain proficiency in prayer and is willing to show others the ropes. While many Christians are offended that there is any such thing as "proficiency" in prayer, Jesus frequently told stories about some prayers accomplishing more than others (see Lk 18:1–8). As in any other area of life, then, it makes sense to heed the guidance of those who have achieved a mastery of the skill we want to perfect.

No period in Christian history boasts as many mystics, in the sense we are defining the term, as the Middle Ages. These came from all walks of life—religious and laity, men and women, poor and wealthy, and from every nation and culture. Because the Spirit "blows where it wills" (Jn 3:8), we should not be surprised that He filled the hearts of many believers—including, for example, a disproportionate number of illiterate, lower-class young women—who otherwise would have attracted the interest of few historians.

Some of the mystics, such as Julian of Norwich, lived quietly and avoided public affairs. Others, such as Bernard of Clairvaux and Hildegard of Bingen, found themselves drawn into the great controversies of their age. The fact that some, like Julian, came to be known only because they left books behind, should alert us to the fact that many thousands of others, having left no books behind, will always remain unknown to all but God.

Whatever the differences in the lives of the great mystics, the maps they draw of the inner life usually look surprisingly similar upon close examination. All of them stress the need for Christians to detach themselves from earthly things, the necessity of cultivating an interior silence in order to hear better the voice of God, and the supreme goal of complete and unreserved union with God in Christ.

It should not surprise us that some of these mystics use occasional expressions or describe experiences which seem odd, eccentric, or exaggerated to us. After all, we would probably be similarly bewildered by a highly technical discussion among experts in any field—astrophysics or biochemistry, for example. But the same mystics, often in the same sentences, will stress the importance of the "everyday" Catholic regimen of sacraments, Scripture reading, love of neighbor, and attendance at Mass. The great mystics of the Middle Ages have something to teach any Christian who is humble enough to recognize that he or she has something to learn.

ST. BERNARD OF CLAIRVAUX
(1090–1153)

Bernard's whole life was a series of paradoxes, and his critics could perhaps be forgiven for wondering if there were two Bernards inhabiting the same body. He is known to posterity as the "honey-tongued doctor" for his sweetness of speech, yet a critic in the papal court called him a "noisy, troublesome frog," emerging from its marshy hole to annoy the world with its croaking.

One moment he was calling upon crowds of soldiers to spill the blood of infidels in the Second Crusade, and the next he was preaching to his monks from the Song of Songs about the intimate nature of the love between God and the soul.

Born into a family of French nobility, Bernard entered religious life during an age of turmoil. The continuous corruption of Benedictine monastic houses—even those of the reformed order of Cluny—had led a small band of renegade monks to found a new monastic settlement at Cîteaux, thereafter known as the Cistercians, committed to a literal and uncompromising observance of the *Rule of St. Benedict*. Bernard arrived at Cîteaux only fifteen years after its foundation. It is a mark of his deep charisma that he was accompanied by thirty of his friends and family members.

Impressed with Bernard's character and running out of space, the abbot of Cîteaux sent him to plant a new monastery in a nearby region called the Valley of Bitterness, which Bernard promptly renamed the Valley of Beauty (*Clairvaux*). Here Bernard formed a community marked by such intense religious observance that he soon damaged his health through excessive fasting, yet he attracted so many thousands of new monks that he was forced to plant new houses. By his death he had personally founded 163 monasteries; if you count those monasteries that sprang up from these, the number reaches 343. Although technically he arrived in the third generation of Cistercians, he is usually credited as their founder due to the enormity of his influence.

Bernard's administrative skill and impartial judgment soon gained him an international reputation, such that he was called upon by statesmen and churchmen alike to preside over councils and synods. When two papal claimants (Anacletus II and Innocent II) asserted their identity as the true pope, the bishops summoned Bernard to Rome to choose between them. When Peter Abelard, a proponent of the new scholastic method being taught in the universities, protested his papal condemnation as a heretic, Bernard was summoned to investigate the case. Though not a bishop, Bernard was summoned to the Second Lateran Council to assist in reforming the Church.

And when Pope Eugene II (a Cistercian monk from Bernard's own monastery, who had taken the monastic name Berno to honor his abbot) announced a new, Second Crusade to free the Holy Land from its occupation by the Turks, he called upon Bernard to drum up international support. Bernard reportedly tore up his own habit to make crosses for those who wished to sew them onto their clothing, the traditional way of making a vow to fight. He not only generated a massive international response to the Crusade, but he also recruited members for a new monastic order to aid the cause.

This order, the Knights Templar, combined the traditional vows of a monk with the military discipline of a soldier. Bernard's support for this movement was so strong that the Knights claimed him for their patron. (The Crusade ended in humiliating failure, causing Bernard, who felt personally responsible, to send a letter of apology to the pope.)

While known to his contemporaries mostly as a larger-than-life international celebrity involved in nearly every significant historical event of his era, Bernard was known to subsequent generations of Cistercians as a quiet, pious, and profoundly humble abbot, who left behind him a large corpus of writings which focused on personal, heartfelt faith, deep trust in the love of Christ and the help of the blessed Virgin, and the value of intimate meditation on the Scriptures.

A VISITOR'S DESCRIPTION OF CLAIRVAUX

One of Bernard's lifelong friends, a Benedictine monk named William of St. Thierry, gave this description of his visit to St. Bernard's monastery.

At the first glance as you entered Clairvaux by descending the hill you could see that it was a temple of God; and the still, silent valley, in the modest simplicity of its buildings, spoke of the sincere humility of Christ's poor. Moreover, in this valley full of men, where no one was permitted to be idle, where one and all were occupied with their allotted tasks, a silence deep as that of night prevailed. The sounds of labor, or the chants of the brethren in the choral service, were the only exceptions. The orderliness of this silence, and the report that went forth concerning it struck such a reverence even into secular persons that they dreaded breaking it, not only by idle or wicked conversation, but also even by proper remarks.

The solitude, also, of the place, between dense forests in a narrow gorge of neighboring hills, in a certain sense recalled the cave of our father St. Benedict, so that while they strove to imitate his life, they also had some similarity to him in their habitation and loneliness….

Although the monastery is situated in a valley, it has its foundations on the holy hills, whose gates the Lord loves more than all the dwellings of Jacob. Glorious things are spoken of it (cf. Ps 87:2–3), because the glorious and wonderful God works great marvels there. There the insane recover their reason, and although their outward man is worn away, inwardly they are born again. There the proud are humbled, the rich are made poor, and the poor have the Gospel preached to them, and the darkness of sinners is changed into light (cf. Lk 7:22).

A large multitude of blessed poor from the ends of the earth have there assembled, yet they have one heart and one mind; justly, therefore, do all who dwell there rejoice with no empty joy. They have the certain hope of perennial joy, of their ascension heavenward already begun. In Clairvaux, they have found Jacob's ladder, with angels upon it; some descending, who so provide for their bodies that they faint not on the way; others ascending, who so rule their souls that their bodies may be glorified afterwards with them.

For my part, the more attentively I watch them day by day, the more do I believe that they are perfect followers of Christ in all things. When they pray and speak to God in spirit and in truth, by their friendly and quiet speech to Him, as well as by their humbleness of demeanor, they are plainly seen to be God's companions and friends. When, on the other hand, they openly praise God with psalms, how pure and fervent are their minds is shown by their posture of body in holy fear and reverence, while by their careful pronunciation and modulation of the psalms is shown how sweet to their lips are the words of God—sweeter than honey to their mouths.

As I watch them, therefore, singing without fatigue from before midnight to the dawn of day, with only a brief interval, they appear a little less than the angels, but much more than men….

As regards their manual labor, so patiently and peacefully, with such quiet faces, in such sweet and holy order, do they perform all things, that although they exercise themselves at many works, they never seem moved or burdened in anything, whatever the labor may be. Therefore it is clear that that Holy Spirit works in them who disposes of all things with sweetness, in whom they are refreshed, so that they rest even in their toil.

Many of them, I hear, are bishops and earls, and many illustrious through their birth or knowledge; but now, by God's grace, all distinction of persons being dead among them, the greater anyone thought himself in the world, the more in this flock does he regard himself as less than the least. I see them in the garden with hoes, in the meadows with forks or rakes, in the fields with scythes, in the forest with axes.

To judge from their outward appearance, their tools, their bad and disordered clothes, they appear a race of fools, without speech or sense. But a true thought in my mind tells me that their life in Christ is hidden in the heavens.

ON THE LOVE OF GOD

This tract of St. Bernard's, On the Love of God, *lays out the gradual progression of human love of God in four stages.*

Love is one of the four natural affections, which it is needless to name since everyone knows them. And because love is natural, it is only right to love the Author of nature first of all. Hence comes the first and great commandment, "Thou shalt love the Lord thy God" (Lk 10:27). But nature is so frail and weak that necessity compels it to love itself first; and this is fleshly love, by which *man loves himself for his own sake*, as it is written, "It is not the spiritual which is first but the physical, and then the spiritual" (1 Cor 15:46). This is not what the law commands but what nature requires: "No man ever hates his own flesh" (Eph 5:29)....

Yet God has decided in His profound wisdom that we should be subject to tribulations, and when man's strength fails and God comes to his aid, it is right and just that man, rescued by God's hand, should praise Him, as it is written, "Call upon me in the day of trouble; I will deliver you, and you shall glorify me" (Ps 50:15). In this way man, beastly and fleshly by nature, and loving only himself, begins to love God because of that very self-love; since he learns that in God he can do all good things, and that without God he can do nothing. So then, finally, *man loves God, not for God's sake, but for his own sake*....

But when tribulations, recurring again and again, force him to turn to God for unfailing help, would not even a heart as hard as iron, as cold as marble, be softened by the goodness of such a Savior, so that he would love God not altogether selfishly, but just because He is God? Let frequent troubles drive us to frequent requests; and certainly, after tasting, we must see how gracious the Lord is (cf. Ps 34:8).

Then His goodness, once we realize it, draws us to love Him unselfishly, even more than our own needs draw us to love Him selfishly. In the same way the Samaritans told the woman who announced that it was Christ who was at the well: "It is no longer because of your words that we believe, for we have heard for ourselves, and we know that this is indeed the Savior of the world" (Jn 4:42). We too proclaim the same testimony to our own fleshly nature, saying, "No longer do we love God because of our necessity, but because we have tasted and seen how gracious the Lord is."… The third degree of love, we now see, is *to love God for His own sake,* solely because He is God.

But how blessed is he who reaches the fourth degree of love, in which *man loves himself only for the sake of God!*… When shall this flesh and blood, this earthen vessel which is my soul's tabernacle, attain to this? When shall my soul, rapt with divine love and altogether self-forgetting, become like a broken vessel, yearn wholly for God and, joined unto the Lord, be one spirit with Him?… I would count him blessed and holy to whom such rapture has been granted in this mortal life, even for an instant, to lose himself, as if he were emptied and lost and swallowed up in God, for this is no human love; it is heavenly!

But if some poor mortal feels that heavenly joy for even one rapturous moment, then this wretched life envies his happiness, the malice of daily trifles disturbs him, this body of death weighs him down, the needs of the flesh make demands of him, the weakness of corruption fails him, and, above all, brotherly love calls him back to duty. Alas! That voice summons him to reenter his own round of existence; and he must ever cry out lamentably, "O Lord, I am oppressed; be my security!" (Is 38:14); and again, "Wretched man that I am! Who will deliver me from this body of death?" (Rom 7:24).

But seeing that, as Scripture says, God made all things for His own glory (Is 43:7), surely His creatures should conform themselves to His will as much as possible. All our affections should center on Him, so that in all things we seek only to do

His will and not to please ourselves. And our real happiness will come not from gratifying our desires or gaining passing pleasures, but in carrying out God's will for us, as we pray, "Thy will be done on earth as it is in heaven" (Mt 6:10).

O chaste and holy love! O sweet and gracious affection! O pure and refined purpose, thoroughly washed and purged from any mixture of selfishness, sweetened by contact with the divine will! To reach this state is to become godlike. As a drop of water poured into wine loses itself and takes on the color and taste of wine, or as a bar of iron when heated red-hot forgets its own nature and becomes like fire itself, or as the air when shot through with sunbeams seems not so much to be lit as to be light itself: so in the saints all human affections melt away by some unspeakable transformation into the will of God….

I think that, in this life, we cannot fully and perfectly obey that commandment, "You shall love the Lord your God with all your heart, and with all your soul, and with all your strength, and with all your mind" (Lk 10:27). For here the heart must think of the body, the soul must energize the flesh, the strength must guard itself from harm, and even increase by God's favor. It is therefore impossible to offer our whole being to God, to yearn entirely for His face, as long as we have to compromise our purposes and hopes with these fragile, sickly bodies of ours.

Therefore the soul may hope to possess the fourth degree of love (or rather, to be possessed by it) only when it has been clothed with that spiritual and immortal body, which will be perfect, peaceful, beautiful, and in every way entirely subject to the spirit. And no human effort can achieve this degree: it is in God's power to give it to whomever He wills.

HOMILIES ON THE SONG OF SONGS

Bernard's most famous work is his series of homilies, presumably given to his monks, on the Song of Songs, a love poem between King Solomon and his queen. Using the allegorical method, Bernard encourages the spiritually mature to see the poem as a song of the love between Christ and the Church, or between the soul and the divine Word.

Sermon 1, On the title of the book, the Song of Songs, written by Solomon.

To you, brothers, I will speak of different truths than I would speak to those in the world—or at least, I will speak in a different way. To them, if a preacher wishes to follow the order prescribed by the apostle, then milk, not solid food is to be given (1 Cor 3:2).… But "among the mature we do impart wisdom" (1 Cor 2:6), and I trust you are such, my brothers, unless it is in vain that you have so long occupied yourself with the study of heavenly things, in meditating on the law of God day and night, and trained yourselves to arrive at a knowledge of the truth.

Prepare, then, to be nourished, not with milk, but with bread. For there is bread in these words of Solomon called the "Song of Songs," bread pure and sweet. Let us set it before us and break it according to our needs.…

For here is a song that surpasses all others in its excellence and incomparable sweetness, and thus it is rightly called the "Song of Songs," seeing that it is the fruit of all others. Only the anointing of grace can teach us to sing this song; only experience makes our soul familiar with its tune. Those who have experienced it know it well; those who have not yet had this happiness earnestly desire it—not to know it, but to experience it.

It is not a cry from the mouth but gladness of the heart; not a noise from the lips but the impulse and emotion of interior joy; not a concert of words but of wills moving in harmony. It is not heard without, nor does it make a sound in public. Only she who sings, and He in whose honor it is sung—that is, the Bridegroom and the Bride—hear the accents of this song. It is a marriage song, expressing the chaste and sweet emotions of souls, the entire conformity of character, the blending of affections in mutual charity.

But as for everyone else, this song cannot be sung or even understood by a soul that is yet a novice in the infancy of virtue, and newly converted from the world. It belongs to the mature and well-instructed soul, which has grown to full adulthood through progress in grace through God's power, such as to become marriageable (remember, I am speaking not of years but of virtues), fit for nuptials with its heavenly spouse….

Sermon 2, On the Incarnation of Christ, which was announced by the patriarchs and prophets, and eagerly awaited by them, on the text, "Kiss me with the kisses of your mouth" (Sgs 1:2).

I think frequently of the deep sincerity and fervor with which the Israelites desired the presence of Christ in the flesh, and I am struck with a feeling of extreme grief and shame, and am barely able even now to restrain my tears, so ashamed am I of the coldness and apathy of the unhappy times we live in. Who is there among us who feels such joy at the actual appearance of this wonder of grace, as the ancient Israelites felt through the mere desire and longing for so great a thing?…

For each of these saintly souls say, as it were: "Why am I hearing all these wordy speeches from the mouths of prophets? Let Him who is 'fairest of the sons of men' (Ps 45:2) come to me with the touch of His lips. I have no wish to listen to Moses, who is 'slow of speech and of tongue' to me (Ex 4:10). The lips of Isaiah are impure (cf. Is 6:5), and Jeremiah does not even know how to speak, as a mere child (cf. Jer 1:6). Indeed, all the prophets are speechless.

"Let Him of whom they speak, speak to me himself. Let Him speak no longer through them or by means of them, for their words are like a cloud darkening the light of heaven, but let Him whose presence is full of grace, and whose teaching shall become a fountain of water springing up to eternal life in me (cf. Jn 4:14), come to me with the touch of His lips….

"I want neither visions nor dreams, and I turn away from parables and metaphors: I disdain even angelic glories. For my

Jesus surpasses even these by His fairness and beauty to my soul. I make my request, then, neither of angel nor to man, but of Him alone. Yet I would not presume to ask the kiss of His mouth. That is the unique privilege and incomparable happiness of the Man whom the Word assumed to himself in the Incarnation. My request is far more humble, a privilege common to all those who can say, 'from his fullness have we all received' (Jn 1:16).

"Observe the Word who becomes flesh: it is He who is the Mouth who gives the kiss. It is the human nature which is assumed who receives this kiss. The kiss, brought to perfection equally by Him who gives and Him who receives it, is that Person constituted by each nature, the Mediator between God and man, the man Christ Jesus….

"Happy the sign, wonderful and amazing the condescension in which no lip is pressed to lip, but God is united to man. If the pressure of the lip signifies the union of souls, here the union of natures joins that which is Divine and that which is Human, reconciling all things which are on earth to those things which are in heaven. 'For He is our peace, who has made the two one' (Eph 2:14)."

It was for this, then, that every ancient saint longed, because they felt the assurance beforehand that joy and gladness were abundantly poured on Him, and in Him were hidden all the treasures of wisdom and knowledge (Col 2:3), and they earnestly desired to share in Him and His fullness….

Sermon 3, On what it means to kiss the feet, the hands and the mouth of the Lord.

We shall read today the book of experience. Each of you turn your minds inwardly upon yourselves, and examine your own conscience about these things we mention. I would like to ask whether any of you have been able to speak the words of the text we are considering. It is not the privilege of all men to speak these words sincerely. Only the one who has received, even once, the spiritual kiss from the lips of Christ, is able to do so, as this experience constantly drives him to renew again what he found so full of sweetness....

Thus, let not a soul burdened with sin and still subject to fleshly passions, a soul which has not yet tasted the delights of the Holy Spirit, wholly ignorant of and inexperienced in interior joys—in short, a soul like mine—even dare to pretend to such a degree of grace.

I will point out to a soul like this, though, his most suitable position with respect to this saving grace. Let him not be so rash as to lift himself as high as the lips of the Divine Bridegroom, but let him with holy fear lie with me at the feet of that great Lord. Let him, like the tax collector, not dare to lift his eyes to heaven (Lk 18:13) for fear that his eyes, which are accustomed only to earthly gloom, would be dazzled by the light of heaven and blinded by its glory, plunged into an even deeper darkness by the unexpected splendor of that majesty.

Do not, O sinful soul, whoever you may be, view this position and posture—the one adopted by the woman who had been sinful yet became a saint, laying down her sins and putting on the robe of holiness—as too lowly and humble for yourself.... This woman wept bitterly and sighed remorsefully from the depths of her soul, her body shaken by sobs, thus casting out the deadly poison from within her....

Follow the example of this happy penitent, O unhappy soul; kneel down that you may cease to be unhappy; kneel down in the dirt, embrace His feet, cover them with kisses and wet them with your tears—not to wash them but to wash yourself—and you may join the flock of newly shorn sheep coming up from the cleansing bath (Sgs 4:2). And do not dare to lift up your face, covered with tears of shame ... until you hear the words of absolution, "Your sins are forgiven" (Lk 7:48), until you hear, "Shake yourself from the dust, arise, O captive Jerusalem" (Is 52:2).

Now that you have placed your first kiss upon His feet, do not presume immediately to lift yourself up to the kiss of the mouth, but let the kiss of his hand be a middle point or second step on the way to the higher state. Note the reason for this: If Jesus has said to me, "Your sins are forgiven," how can this benefit me if I do not stop sinning? If I have taken off my cloak and then put it on again, how does it help me? Or if I wash my feet and then dirty them again, what is the good of having washed them at all?

I have long lain down in the filthy mud, wallowing in every kind of vice: but having escaped from it, if I now fall back into it, I will certainly be even worse off than at first. For I remember how the one who healed me said, "You are well! Sin no more, that nothing worse befall you" (Jn 5:14). What I need, then, is that the one who helped me to repent for my past sins add a second gift of grace to help me avoid sin in the future, so I can avoid committing crime after crime, ending up in an even worse state than the first....

This is what I ask, then, before I presume to approach the higher and more sacred degrees of blessedness. I do not desire to reach the highest point immediately, but to proceed by gradual steps.... From the foot to the mouth the distance is long and difficult, and it would be disrespectful to pass from the one straight to the other. What? Will you, still stained with dust, dare to touch those sacred lips? And having been only yesterday drawn out of the muck, will you now hope to look Him straight in the face?

For you there must be a middle stage of preparation, and this is His hand, which will cleanse you from your stains and lift you up. How? By giving you the means of rising higher—the grace of chastity, the fruits worthy of repentance, which are works of piety. These will lift you up from the dung heap and give you hope of higher things....

Once you have made those two kisses, a double proof of God's condescension, perhaps you may be so bold as to begin to climb to higher and more sacred things. For as you grow in grace, your confidence will also grow, you will love more fervently, you will knock on the door with more assurance of success, and to seek out what you lack, for the door will be opened to whoever knocks. And I believe that you—once you have this disposition of mind and soul—will not be refused that kiss, the highest and most sacred of all, which contains in itself a supreme condescension and an ineffable sweetness.

This is the way and the order that must be followed. First, we fall at the feet of the Lord and beg for mercy from our Maker for the faults and sins we have committed.

Second, we ask him for His helping hand to lift us up and strengthen our feeble knees so that we can stand upright.

Third, when we have with prayers and tears obtained these two former graces, then finally we may perhaps dare to lift our eyes to that Face full of glory and majesty, not only so that we might adore, but so that we might—I say it with fear and trembling—kiss, because the spirit before us is Christ the Lord, with whom we are made one spirit by being united in a holy kiss through His marvelous condescension.

IN PRAISE OF THE NEW KNIGHTHOOD

St. Bernard wrote this letter to define the scope and mission of the Knights Templar, and to encourage them in their task of restoring the sites of the Holy Land through prayer and warfare. The medieval doctrine of just war permitted the taking up of arms in self-defense or in defense of innocent parties. Latin writers understood the Crusades not as wars of aggression, but as attempts to assist Greek Christians in repelling the unprovoked invasions of Turks.

Once, twice, and three times, if I am not mistaken, you have begged me, dearest Hugh, to write to you and your fellow soldiers a word of encouragement. And because it is not permitted that I should brandish a spear in my hands against the tyranny of the enemy, but only a pen, I thought it would be of some little use to you if I should rouse you a bit with my words, if not by force of arms....

This, I say, is indeed a new kind of knighthood, as of yet untried in history, which fights tirelessly the double conflict, both against flesh and blood, and against the evil spirits in the heavenly places (cf. Eph 6:12). For I do not think it is a rare occurrence, and would hardly think it worth remarking, when a bodily enemy is resisted boldly, merely by means of bodily strength. Neither is it terribly rare when war is proclaimed against vices and devils, overcome by the powers of the soul (even though this is highly to be praised), since the world is full of monks doing exactly this.

But when we see a man boldly taking up *both* swords, and placing both into his belt, who would suggest that this is not worthy of the admiration of all, which—I submit—is so completely unheard of? How fearless a soldier, and how safe from all sides, who bears on his body a breastplate of iron, and on his soul a breastplate of faith! He is protected in both cases, and fears neither demon nor man! And how can he be afraid of death, who desires death? For indeed, how can one fear living or dying, when "to live is Christ, and to die is gain" (Phil 1:21)? To remain gladly and faithfully for Christ, but to desire to depart and be with Christ, for this is far better (cf. Phil 1:22–23).

Go forth, then, soldiers of Christ, secure and fearless in mind, to turn back the enemies of Christ, persuaded that neither death nor life will separate you from the love of God which is in Christ Jesus (Rom 8:38), fearless of every danger, for "whether we live or whether we die, we are the Lord's" (Rom 14:8). How glorious will be your return from this battle! For you are more than happy to die as martyrs in this battle. So rejoice, strongest of athletes, for if you win you will live in the Lord, and shout for joy, for if you die you will be gathered to the Lord. A sacred death is to be preferred even to fruitful life or glorious victory. For if those who die in the Lord are blessed (Rv 14:13), how much more those who die for the Lord?....

What then? Shall it be forbidden to Christians to strike with the sword? Why, then, did the herald of the Savior [that is, John the Baptist] instruct soldiers to be content with their pay (Lk 3:14) and not prohibit them entirely from being in the military? If, however (which is true), this is allowed for those who are called to this purpose by His divine providence, unless they are called to some higher calling, who is more capable of this than those whose hands and strength are holding all the fortifications of Zion, the city of our strength?

ST. HILDEGARD OF BINGEN (1098–1179)

It is not hard to explain the sudden burst of popularity that Hildegard has enjoyed in the last thirty years, after languishing in obscurity for eight centuries. As a woman who routinely denounced the moral corruption in the male hierarchy, and who was called upon by popes and emperors alike for her wisdom, she has become a hero to modern feminists. As an author of nine books on wildlife, herbal medicine, and natural remedies, she has become a hero to modern naturalists. As a visionary who could portray the most profound elements of the spiritual life in a highly dramatic, vivid, and picturesque fashion, she has become a hero to modern spiritual seekers.

Yet as a child, Hildegard gave no particular signs of her future greatness. So weak and sickly as a girl that her family chose not to invest in an education in her, she remained barely literate through her entire life. Sent to be brought up in a Benedictine monastery at the age of eight, Hildegard made her monastic profession ten years later and was chosen as the head of the community twenty years after that. Only then did the world discover her hidden secret, the mystical visions she had been receiving since the age of five and which increased in intensity after she turned fifteen.

She was never able to explain why God had chosen her for these, calling herself His "most ignorant servant." Perhaps her constant sickness as a child—partially blind and often unable to leave her bed—predisposed her to a vivid interior life. As a child she once asked her nurse if she, too, received such visions, and when told no, Hildegard was struck with terror. She chose to keep them to herself until, at the age of forty, she was commanded by God to publicize them, transcribing them with the aid of her lifelong associate, a monk named Volmar.

They were submitted, as was the custom, to the local bishop, who after reviewing them pronounced them doctrinally sound and likely divine in origin. As her reputation spread, the visions were then submitted to Pope Eugenius III, who gave the same verdict and sent her his apostolic blessing.

Word spread of this "Sibyl of the Rhine" (a phrase which compared her to the ancient oracles among the Greeks), and visitors and letters poured in. Nearly four hundred of her letters survive, to and from bishops, nobles, emperors, and popes. Hildegard was summoned before the emperor and invited to speak to councils of bishops, where she unfailingly called for a moral reform in the Church, denouncing especially corruption among the clergy.

Her works include three large transcriptions of her visionary experiences, nine books on natural medicine—these do not come from her visions, but from her ordinary experience practicing medicine within her community—and seventy-two musical compositions she wrote for liturgical use. She made use of recently invented musical notation to transcribe these, and thus her music is widely produced and performed today. Perhaps most oddly of all, she wrote a dictionary of nine hundred words using a language that she invented herself (*lingua ignota*).

Hildegard died shortly after the process of canonizing saints had become much more formalized, with very strict requirements overseen by the Vatican. She was never quite able to make it through the process, for whatever reason, and after four unsuccessful attempts her canonization process was dropped. But no one ever doubted her sainthood. She was perpetually known as St. Hildegard, her feast day was established and placed on the universal calendar, and Pope Benedict XVI named her a Doctor of the Church in 2012.

THE FIRST RECORDED VISION AND ITS MEANING

Hildegard's most comprehensive mystical work is her Scivias *(in Latin, "Know the ways!"). The prologue to this work describes the process by which she received her visions and began to make a written record of them. Also included is her first vision, of God and His relationship with the human race. Her writings follow the style of the biblical prophets like Daniel: a narrative of her calling, the depiction of a vision (often rather bizarre), and then an explanation of its significance.*

When I was forty-three years old, I beheld a heavenly vision on which I fixed my gaze with great fear and a trembling effort: a dazzling light and a voice from heaven said:

> O fragile human, ashes of ashes and dust of dust, say and write what you see and hear. But because you are bashful of speech, timid in conversation and uneducated in writing, do not say and write them in human ways of speaking, thinking and willing, but in just the heavenly way that you now see and hear these wonderful things of God.
>
> When you explain these things, do so as though you were relating the precise words of a teacher, and let them be welcomed and published in exactly the way they were spoken. Therefore, O human, relate what you hear and see, and do not write your own thoughts, or another man's: relate only the secret of these mysteries which you see and hear.

And again I heard a voice from heaven saying to me, "Tell and write these wonderful things, and do so in exactly this way."

In the year 1141, when I was forty-two years and seven months old, a dazzling, fiery light shone from heaven, poured into my brain, and sparked a fire in my heart and my breast, which warmed but did not burn, just as the sun's rays heat everything they touch. And suddenly I knew and understood the true meaning of the Psalms, the Gospels, and all the books of the Old and New Testaments, even though I did not yet know the interpretation of the text, the words, the syllables, the case, or the tenses.

But ever since I was a fifteen-year-old girl I had received wonderful visions like this and was given the ability to understand deep mysteries. Yet I told no one about these things, except a few religious who lived as I did. In the meantime, until God wanted me to speak about these privileges, I kept them quietly to myself. But these visions did not come to me in dreams, while sleeping; and I did not see them with my physical eyes or hear them with my physical ears. They did not come to me in private but in public places. Rather, I saw and heard them with my inner eyes and ears, as God willed it. It is difficult to explain this in natural, human terms.

But when I was no longer a girl [and] had reached the more mature age I just mentioned, I heard a voice from heaven saying:

> I am the living and hidden light, enlightening the one I have chosen, whom I sought because of her wonderful gifts, excelling even the ancient visionaries, but I humbled her to the dust so that she would not become proud. The world saw no joy, pleasure or playfulness in her, and I kept her from obstinate pride through the fear and trembling of her sufferings. For she ached, in the marrow of her bones and the veins of her flesh, her mind and judgment paralyzed, so that she lost all her confidence and saw herself as blameworthy in all things. For I guarded her heart from danger, to keep her from becoming proud and arrogant: she felt only fear and grief, not frivolity and childishness.

Then she wondered where she could find someone who loved me and could show her the path of salvation. And she found him [that is, the monk Volmar] and loved him, recognizing his faithfulness and his similarity to herself. And clinging closely to him, she worked with him in all these ways, to ensure that my hidden miracles would finally be revealed.

And this man did not attempt to rule her, but with a good will submitted to her in humility. Therefore, O human, who receives these things not with guile and trickery, but with purity and simplicity of heart, write what you see and hear, so that hidden things may be revealed.

But although I had heard these things, I still refused for a long time to write them down, out of fear that men would doubt me and form bad opinions about me—not out of stubbornness, but out of humility. Eventually I fell sick, as a punishment from God, until finally I was forced in my weakness to write. With the help of a certain noble girl of good morals, and of the man I mentioned before that I had found, I began to write. While I did this, I received the profound understanding of the books I mentioned above, and my strength was restored, and yet with great difficulty I finished writing this work after ten years.

I completed them in the days of Henry, Archbishop of Mainz, and Conrad the Roman emperor, and Kuno the Abbot of Mount St. Disibode, and Pope Eugenius III. And I wrote them not from my own thoughts or ideas, or of any other man's, but only what I saw, heard, and understood from heaven through the secret mysteries of God. And again I heard a voice from heaven saying to me, "Go cry aloud, and write this."

Vision 1. I saw a great mountain, the color of iron, and above it was seated One who shone so brightly that I was blinded by the brilliance. And from both sides of Him extended a soft shadow, like a vast pair of wings. And some other form sat before Him, at the foot of the mountain, so completely covered with eyes that I could not make out what it was. And standing before this form was a child in dull clothing and white shoes, whose head reflected so much light from the One standing above that I could not look directly on his face. And living sparks floated down all about these forms, and many small windows could be seen in the mountain, through which men's heads could be seen, both dull and white.

And the One sitting atop the mountain called out, in a strong and striking voice:

> O human, fragile dust of the earth and ashes of ashes, cry aloud and speak about the entrance to eternal salvation. For those who are wise enough to see the inner meaning of the Scriptures are too blind and indifferent to preach it to others, so it is up to you to unlock these mysteries, which these cowards wish to keep buried in a barren field. So you must write abundantly, as from a bursting fountain, overflowing with such mystical wisdom that those who dismissed you as a woman (blaming you for Eve's sin) may be overwhelmed by the abundant stream that flows forth from you. But remember that you did not receive this wisdom from humans, but from the great and heavenly Judge who sits above, emitting the brilliant light which reflects from the radiant ones below.

> Arise, therefore, and say that these things were revealed to you by divine power, by the One who oversees all of His creatures with power and kindness. Tell them that He has poured forth His light of heaven upon those who fear Him and walk humbly in His love, leading to the joy of eternal vision those who persevere in the path of holiness.

See now, the iron color of this mountain signifies the strength, stability, and eternity of the kingdom of God, which no change or decay can overcome. And the One seated on it, whose brilliant light blinded you, signifies He who governs the whole world in the glory of His serenity, incomprehensible to men on account of His heavenly divinity. The soft shadows extending from each side of Him, appearing like a pair of vast wings, signify His stern discipline, on the one hand, and His sweet and gentle protection, on the other, a perfect balance of justice and love.

And the form covered with eyes which sits below Him signifies those who, with humility, fear of the Lord, and the clarity of good and just intention, gaze at the kingdom of God, strengthened by God himself. You could not see any human form behind the eyes because He has so thoroughly suppressed the weakness of human nature which would otherwise restrain and limit that heavenly gaze.

The child in a dull tunic and white shoes below this form signifies those who are poor in spirit and fear the Lord. These, holding fast to that blessed poverty of spirit, desire neither glory nor ambition but rather love, simplicity, and clarity of mind, attributing all of their good works to God rather than to themselves, and therefore appear both dull and white as they follow the innocent footsteps of the Son of God.

The brightness from above which his head reflected signified the power and strength which God infuses into the creatures which He oversees from the serenity of His heavenly home, so that your weak and mortal vision could not grasp its fullness, even though He who has the fullness has abased himself to share your poverty. And the living sparks which floated down from Him who sits on the mountain signify the many virtues which shine down from Almighty God, gently and comfortably landing on those who fear God and live faithfully in poverty of spirit, surrounded by His help and guidance.

At the same time, the windows opening from the mountain, showing both dull and white faces, signify that no human act is hidden or concealed from the sight of the kingdom of God, and that he sees both good acts and evil. For sometimes men languish in idleness, and at other times they are roused to act nobly, as Solomon said, "A slack hand causes poverty, but the hand of the diligent makes rich" (Prv 10:4).

For a man who is unwilling to do justice, to remove sinfulness or forgive debts, remaining careless of good works, is said to make himself poor and weak. But the man who performs good works and runs in the way of truth obtains a fountain of glory, preparing for himself great riches both in heaven and on earth. And whoever has the knowledge of the Holy Spirit and the wings of faith will not violate my command, but will understand it and embrace it in the joy of his soul.

MEISTER ECKHART (1260–1327)

Though little is known of Eckhart's personal background, his brilliant academic and professional career reveals him to be one of the most profound thinkers of his era. It seems that Eckhart lived two lives at once. On the one hand, he appears as a standout student and popular lecturer in theology at Paris and Cologne, capable of writing weighty tomes of scholastic theology in Latin, which nearly equal those of the great Aquinas and Albert: in fact, *Meister* is not a first name, but German for "Master," the equivalent of "Professor."

On the other hand, Eckhart was a Dominican pastor, a shepherd of souls who spent much of his career as spiritual director to convents full of nuns and wrote rich, poetic sermons in the common German language. Thus historians may speak of Eckhart the theologian or Eckhart the mystic, depending on whether one is speaking of his theological treatises or the spirituality found in his sermons.

The trouble, of course, is keeping the two together. Eckhart's spirituality strongly emphasized the self-emptying of the soul, its detachment from external things, and its complete unification with God. Some of his hearers complained that this sounded like pantheism (the denial of a difference between God and creation). Eckhart's religious superiors ordered an investigation of his writings and found nothing unorthodox. Yet the complaints continued to pour in, eventually finding their way to the pope himself. To the end Eckhart protested his utter rejection of pantheism and insisted on his willingness to submit unconditionally to the will of the pope.

Sadly, he died before the papal investigation was complete. Normally this would bring an end to such a process, but the pope ordered it to continue. Several statements of Eckhart, removed from their larger context—and especially considered apart from his undeniably orthodox theological treatises—were identified as problematic and condemned as heretical. Eckhart was not, of course, condemned by name—only statements drawn from his writings, as was the custom—but he was not able to clarify his meaning or qualify the statements. The rather odd nature of this procedure showed that the papacy was less interested in Eckhart himself and more interested in sending a signal to other, openly pantheistic theologians and pastors who were found throughout Germany.

In any case, Eckhart's writings lapsed into obscurity for several centuries, a shadow cast over their author's reputation. Interest in Eckhart exploded, however, in the nineteenth and early twentieth centuries, but not always for the right reasons. Many modernists and New Age pantheists, or those eager to forge a synthesis with Eastern philosophy, have embraced Eckhart as their champion. But recently a more accurate consensus has begun to emerge: When the high spirituality of Eckhart's sermons is synthesized with the highly traditional dogma of his theological treatises, he is revealed to be a dynamic and profound Catholic thinker.

Popes St. John Paul II and Benedict XVI quoted him frequently, and the great Meister has perhaps taken a step toward regaining his place at the podium.

ON THE RELATIONSHIP BETWEEN THE ACTIVE LIFE AND CONTEMPLATIVE LIFE

In this sermon, Eckhart applies technical concepts from scholastic philosophy (free will, grace, good works, the faculties of the soul) in a practical, down-to-earth pastoral approach to cultivating the interior life.

1 Corinthians 15:10, "By the grace of God … "

Grace is from God, and works in the depths of the soul whose powers it employs. It is a light that issues forth to do service under the guidance of the Spirit. The Divine Light permeates the soul, and lifts it above the turmoil of temporal things to rest in God. The soul cannot progress except with the light that God has given it as a nuptial gift; love works the likeness of God into the soul.

The peace, freedom, and happiness of all souls consist in their remaining in God's will. The soul strives perpetually toward this union with God for which it is created. Fire converts wood into its own likeness, and the stronger the wind blows, the greater grows the fire. Now the fire stands for love, and the wind for the Holy Spirit. The stronger the influence of the Holy Spirit, the brighter grows the fire of love; but not all at once, rather gradually as the soul grows. Light causes flowers and plants to grow and bear fruit; in animals it produces life, but in men happiness. This comes from the grace of God, who lifts up the soul, for if the soul is to grow godlike it must be lifted above itself.

To produce real moral freedom, God's grace and man's will must cooperate. As God is the Prime Mover of nature, so also He creates free impulses towards himself and to all good things. Grace renders the will free that it may do everything with God's help, working with grace as with an instrument which belongs to it. So the will arrives at freedom through love, or rather, it *becomes* love, for love unites with God. All true morality, inward and outward, is comprehended in love, for love is the foundation of all the commandments.

All outward morality must be built upon this basis, not on self-interest. As long as man loves something other than God, or outside of God, he is not free, because he has not love. Therefore there is no inner freedom that does not manifest itself in works of love. True freedom is the government of nature in and outside man through God; freedom is essential existence unaffected by creatures. But love often begins with fear; fear is the approach to love: fear is like the awl that draws the shoemaker's thread through the leather.

As for outward works, they are intended for this purpose, that the outward man may be directed to God. But the inner work, the work of God in the soul, is the chief matter; when a man finds this within himself, he can let go of externals. No law is given to the righteous, because he fulfills the law inwardly and bears it in himself, for the least thing done by God is better than all the work of creatures. But this is intended for those who are enlightened by God and the Holy Scriptures.

But here on earth man never attains to a state of being un-affected by external things. There never was a saint so great as to be immovable. I can never arrive at a state when discord shall be as pleasing to my ears as harmony. Some people wish to do without good works. I say, "This cannot be." As soon as the disciples received the Holy Spirit, they began to work. When Mary sat at the feet of Our Lord, that was her school time. But afterwards, when Christ went to heaven and she received the Holy Spirit, she began to serve and was a handmaid of the disciples.

When saints become saints, they begin to work, and so gather to the refuge of everlasting safety.

How can a man abide in love, when he does not keep God's commands that issue forth from love? How can the inner man be born in God, when the outer man does not abide in the following of Christ, in self-denial and in suffering, for there is no being born of God except through Christ. Love is the fulfilling of all commands; therefore, however much man strives to reach this freedom, the body can never quite attain it and must be ever in conflict. Seeing that good works are the witness of the Holy Spirit, man can never do without them. The aim of man is not outward holiness by works, but life in God, yet this life expresses itself in works of love.

Outward as well as inward morality helps to form the idea of true Christian freedom. We are right to lay stress on inwardness, but in this world there is no inwardness without an outward expression. If we regard the soul as the formative principle of the body, and God as the formative principle of the soul, we have a profounder principle of ethics than is found in pantheism. The fundamental thought of this system is the real distinction between God and the world, together with their real inseparability, for only really distinct elements can interpen-etrate each other.

The inner work is first of all the work of God's grace in the depth of the soul, which subsequently distributes itself among the faculties of the soul, in that of Reason appearing as Belief, in that of Will as Love, and in that of Desire as Hope. When the Divine Light penetrates the soul, it is united with God as light with light. This is the light of faith. Faith bears the soul to heights unreachable by her natural senses and faculties.

As the peculiar faculty of the eye is to see form and color, and of the ear to hear sweet tones and voices, so is desire peculiar to the soul. To relax from ceaseless desire is sin. This energy of desire directed to and grasping at God, as far as is possible for the creature, is called Hope, which is also a divine virtue. Through this faculty the soul acquires such great confidence that she deems nothing in the Divine Nature beyond her reach.

The third faculty is the inward Will, which, always turned to God like a face, absorbs to itself love from God. According to the different directions in which redemptive Grace through the Holy Spirit is imparted to the different faculties of men, it finds corresponding expression as one of the Spirit's seven gifts. This impartation constitutes man's spiritual birth, which brings him out of sin into a state of grace, while natural birth makes him a sinner.

As God can only be seen by His own light, so He can only be loved by His own love. The merely natural man is incapable of this, because nature by itself is incapable of responding to the Divine Love and is confined within its own circle. Therefore it is necessary for Grace, which is a simple supernatural power, to elevate the natural faculties to union in God above the merely temporal objects of existence. The possibility of love to God is grounded in the relative likeness between man and God. If the soul is to reach its moral goal, that is, godlikeness, it must become inwardly like God through grace, and a spiritual birth which is the spring of true morality.

The inner work that man has to do is the practical realization of Grace—without this, all outward work is ineffectual for salvation. Virtue is never mere virtue; it is either from God, or through God, or in God. All the soul's works that are to inherit an everlasting reward must be carried on in God. They are rewarded by Him in proportion as they are carried on in Him, for the soul is an instrument of God by which He carries on His work.

The essence of morality is inwardness, the intensity of will from which it springs, and the nobleness of the aim for which it is practiced. When a good work is done by a man, he is free of it, and through that freedom is liker and nearer to his Original than he was before.

The moral task of man is a process of spiritualization. All creatures are go-betweens, and we are placed in time that by diligence in spiritual business we may grow liker and nearer to God. The aim of man is beyond the temporal—in the serene region of the everlasting Present.

In this sense the New Birth of man is the focus towards which all creation strives, because man is the image of God after the likeness of which the world is created. All time strives towards eternity or the timeless Now, out of which it issued at creation. The merely temporal life in itself is a negation of real being, because it depends on itself and not on the deepest foundation of life; therefore also natural love is cramped, finite, and defective. It must, through grace, be lifted to the highest sphere of existence and attain to freedom outside the narrow confines of the natural.

Thereby love becomes real love, because only that is real which is comprehended and loved in its essence. Only by grace man comes from the temporal and transitory to be one with God. This lifting of plurality to unity is the supreme aim of ethics; by thus the divine birth is completed on the side of man.

This passage from nothingness to real being, this departure from oneself is a birth accompanied by pain, for by it natural love is excluded. All grief except grief for sin comes from love of the world. In God is neither sorrow, nor grief, nor trouble. Would that you would be free from all grief and trouble, abide and walk in God, and to God alone. As long as love of the creature is in us, pain cannot cease.

This is the chief significance of the suffering of Christ for us, that we cast all our grief into the ocean of His suffering. If you suffer only regarding yourself, from whatever cause it may be, that suffering causes grief to thee, and is hard to bear. But if you suffer regarding God and Him alone, that suffering is not grievous, nor hard to bear, because God bears the load. The love of the Cross must swallow up our personal grief. Whoever does not suffer from love, for him sorrow is sorrow and grievous to bear; but whoever suffers from love does not sorrow, and his suffering is fruitful in God.

Therefore, is sorrow so noble; he who sorrows most is the noblest. Now no mortal's sorrow was like the sorrow Christ bore; therefore he is far nobler than any man. If there were anything nobler than sorrow, God would have redeemed man by that instead. Sorrow is the root of all virtue.

Through the higher love the whole life of man is to be elevated from temporal selfishness to the spring of all love, to God. Man will again be master over nature by abiding in God and lifting her up to God.

BLESSED JAN VAN RUYSBRUCK (1293–1381)

Blessed Jan van Ruysbruck (many alternate spellings of his name exist), whom some have called the greatest of Christian mystics, has remained largely unknown outside of the small circle of those predisposed to study mystical literature. Even his life is somewhat unremarkable, apart from the collection of writings he left behind. Raised by a devout mother, he left home unexpectedly at the age of eleven to be raised by his uncle, a priest in Brussels.

He was ordained in his twenties and served for twenty-five years as a parish priest, until—driven by a desire for greater isolation and quietness—he moved to a small hermitage in a forest by the name of Groendaal. So many disciples flocked to him, however, that he eventually established an order of priests. He received many visitors seeking spiritual direction, including the great Gerard Groote, founder of the Brethren of the Common Life. He spent most of his days wandering in the forests in quiet prayer, scribbling notes on a wax tablet as inspirations came to him.

This scribbling was eventually collected into a body of writings: twelve complete books, not a systematic body of theology, but more of a collection of moral and spiritual exhortations, personal descriptions of the interior life of prayer by which the soul communes with God. Uninterested in academic scholarship, Ruysbruck wrote in common Dutch rather than Latin—quite unusual at the time—to reach a wider audience. His writings have the same emphasis as the broader school of "Flemish Mysticism" of which he forms the leading figure—inner union with God, the need to cultivate an "emptiness" of outward works of virtue (which are a necessary prerequisite to a spiritual life, but are no substitute for it), and the search for a "formless silence" of the soul which moves beyond images and words to contemplate the divine essence itself.

His writings contain many shocking expressions that have provoked the accusation of pantheism—his emphasis on the unmediated union with God sometimes seems to imply that the mystic is no longer distinct from God, but identical to Him—but his defenders have always insisted on his orthodoxy on this point. Indeed, in other places in his writings, Ruysbruck makes clear that his teachings utterly exclude pantheism, and during his lifetime he incurred much trouble due to his relentless condemnation of a heretical group of preachers in the Low Countries known as the Brethren of the Free Spirit, whom he accused of pantheism.

The countless other mystical writers after Ruysbruck who have voiced their indebtedness to his teachings generally reply that those who protest against these descriptions of union with God have simply not experienced such union, or they would not find them so strange. Pope Pius X beatified Ruysbruck in 1909, dispelling all doubts about his orthodoxy.

THE SPIRITUAL MARRIAGE

In The Adornment of the Spiritual Marriage, *perhaps his best-known work, Ruysbruck charts the path by which the contemplative, having reached the highest stages of the spiritual life, enters into the most intimate form of union with the Blessed Trinity.*

The ardent lover of God—possessing God in love, possessing himself in a constant and active love, and possessing his whole life in holy virtue—will by means of these three things, along with the help of God's mysterious revelation, enter upon the contemplative life. Indeed, God in His freedom will be pleased to choose and lift up this ardent and holy lover into supernatural contemplation of himself, in His divine light, and by His own divine way.

This contemplation will establish us in unimaginable purity and clarity, for it is both a unique adornment and a heavenly crown, and the eternal reward of all virtues and for our entire life. And no one can attain this through his own knowledge or skill, or through any exercise at all. Only the one whom God chooses to unite in His Spirit, whom He chooses to enlighten by Himself, can see God, and no one else.

For the mysterious divine nature is eternally and actively contemplating and loving in its personal relations, and has everlasting happiness in the mutual embrace of the persons in the one divine essence. All contemplative spirits are immersed in this love and enter this embrace within the essential unity of God, becoming one with this essence itself through the mode of eternal bliss. And in this highest unity of the divine essence, the heavenly Father is the beginning and source of all things that happen, both in heaven and earth. And in these profound and hidden depths He says to the spirit, "*Behold, the Bridegroom comes. Go out to meet Him*" (see Mt 25:6).

We will now explain these words and their relationship to that supernatural contemplation which is the source of all holiness and all perfection of life that is possible for us. Few can attain to this contemplation, both because of their own incapacity and because of the mysterious nature of the light that is seen. Therefore, no one may grasp its meaning by any of his own learning or investigation, for all words and all forms of creaturely knowledge are foreign to, and far below, the truth which I am talking about.

But the one who is united with God and enlightened to this truth will be able to understand this truth. For to be able to comprehend and understand God above all things, God as He is in himself, is to be God with God, without any intermediary, without any distinction which would amount to a hindrance or obstacle.

Therefore, I beg everyone who cannot understand this, or cannot feel it in the fruitful depths of his spirit, to not be offended at this, and to accept it for what it is. For what I am saying is true, and Christ the Eternal Truth has said it himself in His teaching in many places, if we could only show and explain it adequately. Therefore, whoever wishes to understand this must have died to himself and must live in God; he must turn his gaze to the eternal light in the depths of his spirit, where the hidden truth reveals itself without intermediary.

"Behold": For our heavenly Father wishes us to see, for He is the Father of Light, and this is why He utters—eternally, without intermediary and without interruption, in the hiddenness of our spirit—one singular and profound word, and no other. And in this word He utters himself and all things; and this word is none other than *"Behold."* And this is the generation and birth of the Son of Eternal Light, in whom all blessedness is known and seen.

Now if the soul wishes to see God with God in this divine light without intermediary, three things are required on the part of man. First, he must be outwardly formed perfectly in all the virtues, and yet inwardly he must be oblivious to them, as though he did not have them at all, for if his interior emptiness is disturbed by some image like this, he is not truly empty, and he will be unable to contemplate.

Second, he must inwardly cleave to God with constant intention and love, just like a burning and unquenchable fire: as long as he feels he is in such a state, he will be able to contemplate.

Third, he must lose himself in formlessness and darkness, a state in which all contemplative men wander happily, never again able to find their way back to creaturely things.

For in this darkness there shines and is born an incomprehensible Light, which is the Son of God, in whom we find eternal life. And in this Light one can see, and this divine Light is given to the simple in the depths of their spirit, which receives the brightness that is God himself, above and beyond all gifts and all creatures. The soul receives this brightness of God, without intermediary, when it is in a state of rest and inner emptiness, having lost itself through blissful love, and is changed ceaselessly into the same brightness which it receives.

So great is this mysterious brightness—in which, through the emptiness of one's spirit, one sees everything one can possibly desire—that the loving contemplative senses nothing in the depths of his spirit but an incomprehensible Light. And through that simple emptiness which enfolds all things, he finds and feels himself to be that same Light by which he sees, and nothing else. And this is the first point as regards seeing in the divine Light. Blessed are the eyes that see in this way, for they possess eternal life.

"*The Bridegroom comes*": Once we can see in this way, we can behold in joy the eternal coming of our Bridegroom, and this is the second point I would like to speak about. What is the eternal coming of our Bridegroom? It is the new birth and new, uninterrupted enlightenment, for the inner source from which the Light shines forth, which is the Light itself, is happy and life-giving, and therefore the manifestation of the Eternal Light is renewed unceasingly in the hiddenness of the spirit.

Behold, all exercise of virtue, and every creaturely work, must here cease, for here God alone works in the heights of the

spirit. And here there is nothing but an eternal staring and gazing at that Light, by that Light, in that Light. And the coming of
the Bridegroom is so swift that He is perpetually coming, and
yet dwelling within with unfathomable riches, and yet ever coming anew, in His own person and without interruption, with such
new brightness that it seems as though He had never come before. For His coming consists in an eternal *Now*, beyond time,
which is ever received with new longing and new joy.

Behold, the delight and the joy which this Bridegroom
brings with Him in His coming are boundless and without measure, for they are His very Self. And this is why the eyes with
which the soul sees and gazes upon the Bridegroom have opened
so wide that they can never close again. For the spirit continues
forever to see and to gaze at the secret manifestation of God. And
the capacity of the spirit is expanded so much for the coming of
the Bridegroom that the spirit itself becomes the very breadth
that it widens to admit.

And so God is admitted and beheld through God, and in
this lies all our blessedness. This is the second point: in which we
receive, without interruption, the eternal coming of the Bridegroom in our spirit.

"*Go out*": Now, in the hidden depths of our spirit, the
Spirit of God says, "Go out" in the way of God, through eternal
contemplation and happiness. All the riches which are in God
by nature we may possess by way of love of God, through God's
dwelling in us through the immeasurable love which is in the
Holy Spirit, for in this love one tastes everything one might possibly desire.

And therefore in this very love we die to ourselves and go
forth in loving immersion in formlessness and darkness. There
the soul is embraced by the Holy Trinity and dwells forever within that supernatural Unity, in rest and happiness. And in that
same Unity, in supreme happiness, the Father dwells in the Son,
and the Son in the Father, and all creatures dwell in both. And
this is above and beyond the distinction between the Persons,

for we understand Fatherhood and Sonship to be the life-giving overflowing of the divine nature itself.

Here there begins an eternal procession and an eternal activity that has no beginning, for here there is a beginning without beginning. For once the Almighty Father had understood himself in His own divine being, so the Son—the eternal Word of the Father—came forth as the second Person in the Godhead. And through this eternal Birth, all creatures came to exist in eternity, before their creation in time. So God has seen and known all things in himself, as distinct, living ideas, both distinct from himself and yet not entirely other than himself, for all that is in God is God.

This eternal procession and life, which we eternally have and are within God himself, is the cause of our creation in time. And our created being abides in the eternal Essence and is one with it in its essential existence. And this eternal life and being, which we have and are in the eternal Wisdom of God, is godlike. For it eternally remains in the divine essence, without distinction, and through the birth of the Son it has an eternal procession as something distinct and other than the divine Idea.

And between these two states it is so godlike that He knows and reflects himself eternally in this likeness, both in Essence and in Persons. For though even here the intellect can discern distinction and otherness, it remains a likeness of the same image of the Holy Trinity whereby the wisdom and self-understanding of God proceeds in an eternal Now, without before or after. In a single vision He sees both himself and all things. And this is the Image and Likeness of God, and the image and likeness of ourselves, for through it God reflects himself and all things.

In this divine Image all creatures have an eternal existence outside of themselves in their eternal Archetype, and we have been made by the Holy Trinity in *this* eternal Image and Likeness. And therefore God wills that we "go out" from ourselves in this divine Light, to reunite ourselves supernaturally with this Image, which is our true and proper life, and to possess it with Him, in all activity, happiness, and eternal bliss.

For we all know well that the bosom of the Father is our beginning and source, in which our life and being had their beginning. And from our proper source—from the Father and all that lives in Him—there shines an eternal brightness, which is the birth of the Son. And in this brightness (that is, the Son) the Father knows Himself and all that lives in Him: for all that He has and is He gives to the Son, all except the property of Fatherhood, which remains in himself. And this is why all that lives in the Father, remaining hidden in the Unity, is also poured forth clearly in the Son.

Thus the origin of our eternal Image remains in formlessness and darkness, while at the same time the infinite brightness streaming forth from it clearly reveals the hidden things of God. And all those who are lifted up above their created being into a contemplative life are united with this divine brightness, and become this brightness itself. Thus they see, feel, and find, by means of this divine Light, that they are one in essence with the origin of the brightness which shines forth from it and remains eternally one and formless within the simplicity of the essence.

And this is why contemplative, interior souls will proceed through contemplation, beyond reason, distinction, and created being itself, through an eternal, intuitive vision. By means of this inner light they are transfigured and made one with the same light they see and by which they see. And thus contemplatives arrive at the Eternal Image in which they were made, and in the divine Brightness they see God and all things in Him, in one simple vision without distinction.

And this is the highest and most profitable form of contemplation one can attain in this life, for in this contemplation one remains both free and master of himself. And at each loving vision he may increase in holiness beyond all understanding, for he remains free and master of himself in both interior life and virtue. And this vision of the divine Light raises him above all interior life and all virtue and all merit, for it is the crown and reward we are striving for, and which we now possess, for a contemplative life is a heavenly life.

But if we were only freed from this misery and exile, we would have in our created being a greater capacity to receive this brightness, and the glory of God would shine through us in a greater and higher way. This is the highest way of proceeding through divine contemplation and eternal, intuitive vision, by which one is transfigured and transformed into the divine Brightness.

This elevation of the contemplative man is also done in love, for through the happiness of love he rises above his created being and finds and tastes the riches and delights which are in God himself, which He causes to pour forth eternally in the hiddenness of the spirit, where the spirit is utterly godlike.

"… *to meet Him*": Once the interior contemplative soul has attained to his Eternal Image, and in this brightness, through the Son has entered into the bosom of the Father, then he is enlightened by divine truth and receives, anew and constantly, the eternal Birth, shining forth like light in divine contemplation. And here is the last point: a loving union that is our highest blessedness.

You should know that our heavenly Father, as living source, is actively turned toward the Son in everything that is in Him, as toward His own eternal Wisdom. And that same Wisdom is actively turned back toward the Father in everything that is in Him, as toward His own eternal source. And from this meeting proceeds the third Person, between the Father and the Son: the Holy Spirit, their mutual Love, who is one with both of them in the same essence. And He enfolds and infuses both the Father and the Son, and all that lives in them, in activity and happiness, with such profound riches and joy that all creatures must fall silent, for the incomprehensible wonder of this love eternally transcends the understanding of all creatures.

But wherever this wonder is understood and tasted without being overwhelmed, the spirit transcends itself and becomes one with God's Spirit, and tastes and sees infinitely, as God himself, these riches which are the Spirit itself, in the unity of the living source where it possesses itself in the uncreated essence.

Now this exalted union is eternally and actively renewed in us in a divine way, for the Father gives himself in the Son, and the Son gives himself in the Father, in an eternally happy and loving embrace, which renews itself constantly in the bond of love. For as the Father perpetually knows all things in the birth of His Son, so all things are loved perpetually by the Father and Son in the outpouring of the Holy Spirit. And this is the active union of Father and Son, in which we are lovingly embraced by the Holy Spirit in eternal love.

Now this active union and loving embrace are both formless and blissful. Formless, because the profound formlessness of God is so dark and unfathomable that it swallows up in itself every divine action and operation, and all the attributes of the Persons, within the depths of its essential unity, bringing about a divine happiness in the ineffable hiddenness.

And here one dissolves in happiness, collapsing into the essential emptiness, where all the divine names, conditions, and images (which are reflected in the mirror of divine truth) collapse together in the Ineffable Oneness, without form and without reason. For in this unfathomable depth of simplicity, all things are enwrapped in joyful bliss, and the depth itself is incomprehensible except through the essential Unity. To this Unity the divine Persons, and all that lives in God, must give way, for here there is nothing else but an eternal rest in the happy embrace of an outpouring love.

And this is that very formlessness that all contemplative souls have chosen above all other things. This is the dark silence in which all lovers lose themselves. But if we wished to prepare ourselves by means of the virtues, we would strip ourselves of all but our very bodies and flee into the wild Sea, from which no created thing could draw us back again. May we possess this happiness in the essential Unity, and clearly behold Unity within the Trinity. May divine Love, which turns no beggar away, bestow this upon us. Amen.

JULIAN OF NORWICH (c.1342–1423)

It is quite fitting that Blessed Julian, one of the most famous of medieval mystics, is such an enigma to us that we don't even know her name. We know only that this anonymous hermit lived alongside the church of St. Julian in Norwich, England—hence the name she is assigned for convenience.

Other than this we know practically nothing. This "simple, illiterate creature," as she calls herself, fell deathly ill at the age of thirty—apparently she prayed for the sickness herself, in the hope that it would make her more meek and humble—and the priest who came to give her last rites held a crucifix before her eyes to comfort her. Gazing at this crucifix, she received sixteen miraculous visions in the space of a few hours.

Sometime after her sickness passed, "Julian" became an anchoress. A fairly widespread urban phenomenon in the Middle Ages, anchoresses were something like urban hermits, who would build monastic cells in the middle of cities to isolate themselves for the purposes of fasting, prayer, and penance. Sometimes, they would literally build three walls to enclose themselves against the exterior wall of a church, leaving no door but only a window for the passage of food.

Julian lived like this for the rest of her life, spending her time meditating on the visions she had received and eventually having her reflections transcribed in a book, *Revelations of Divine Love*. (Historians tell us this made her the first woman to write in the English language.)

At the heart of the *Revelations* is Julian's own mystical experience, when in those brilliant moments the entire mystery of creation, sin, and redemption was made clear, their hidden meaning unfolding before her eyes. Whereas much medieval spirituality focuses on the misery and sinfulness of the human condition, emphasizes the wrath such sin evokes from God, and implies that human suffering is simply God's punishment for sins, Julian's vision is much more optimistic. Human sins and mistakes appear as part of the inevitable process of human learning and spiritual maturation, and they inspire in God not anger but pity, causing Him to use such sins as opportunities for merciful correction and growth. Suffering and pain thus appear, ironically, as signs of divine love.

As Julian remarkably concludes, "All shall be well, and all shall be well, and all manner of things shall be well." In her later visions she describes God as not only a Father, but also a kind Mother, gently but firmly guiding her children homeward.

JULIAN RECEIVES HER VISIONS

The following selections are from Revelations of Divine Love, *Julian's autobiographical account of the form and content of her mystical experiences.*

These revelations were shown to a simple, illiterate creature on May 13, 1373. This creature had desired three gifts from God: an understanding of His passion; bodily sickness at the young age of thirty; and God's gift of three wounds.

In regard to the first, I thought I had some sense of Christ's passion, but I desired more through God's grace. I wished to be there with Mary Magdalene and the other lovers of Christ; therefore I wanted to see Him visibly, so as to gain a greater sense of our Savior's bodily pains, our Lady's compassion, and the pains that His true lovers saw. For I wanted to be one of them also, and to suffer with Him. I wanted no other sight or revelation, until my soul should leave my body. The reason for my petition was that, afterwards, I would have a true understanding of Christ's passion.

The second desire arose from contrition: I wanted a nearly mortal sickness, which would require last rites, since both I and others would expect my death; for I had no wish for a comfortable life. Rather, through this sickness I desired all the physical and spiritual sufferings that accompanied death, and even the devil's temptation, so long as my soul did not leave my body. I hoped that this would purge me of sin, through God's mercy and this sickness, to help me worship God more effectively afterwards. But I made these first two requests with a condition attached, saying: "Lord, you know what I desire. If it is your will that I have it, please grant it. If it is not your will, good Lord, do not be displeased with me, for I only want your will to be done."

The third petition, by God's grace and the teaching of the holy Church, was to grant my desire to receive three wounds in my life—that is, the wounds of true contrition, of kind compassion, and of a constant longing for God. And I made this last petition without any condition attached to it.

When I was thirty years old, God sent me a bodily sickness which left me in bed for three days and nights. On the fourth night I received last rites and did not expect to live until the morning. But I lingered on two more days and nights, though on the third night I expected to die, and those who were with me shared this expectation.

Being still young, I was sad to face death. Yet there was nothing on earth that I wanted to live for, and I feared no pain, trusting God's mercy. I only wanted to live longer to learn to love God more, so that I might know and love Him even still more in the joy of heaven. For I thought that my own life had been so short, virtually nothing at all, in comparison with that endless joy. So I thought, "Good Lord, please let me live no longer in worship!" Through reflection and through the pain I felt I expected to die, so I submitted fully with all my heart to God's will.

I bore this until the morning, and by then I could not feel the lower half of my body. Then I asked for help to sit upright and lean back, which would help free my heart to grasp God's will, and to think of God as long as my life lasted. My priest was sent for to be present at my death, and by the time he arrived I had lost the power of speech, yet was still staring. The priest put a crucifix before my eyes, saying, "I have brought an image of your Master and Savior: look at it and take comfort."

For my part, I preferred to stare up into heaven, where I hoped to go through God's mercy. But I agreed to set my eyes on the crucifix, for it was easier for me to look straight ahead than upwards. At this point my sight began to fail, and darkness seemed to fill the room as if it were night, except for a strange light that shone from the cross. Everything that was away from the cross was horrible to me, as though occupied by demons.

At this point I lost feeling in the upper part of my body and could barely breathe; I expected immediately to die. But at this moment all pain dissipated, and feeling and health returned to my body. I was amazed at this sudden change, and decided it was a miracle of God, not from natural causes. Yet despite this, I did not expect to live, and the change did not relieve me, for I had expected to be delivered from this world.

Then the thought entered my mind, that I should desire the second wound as Our Lord's gracious gift, and that I might come to know a true understanding of His blessed passion. For, out of compassion and longing for God, I wished that His pains were my pains. I had no desire for any revelation or vision, but only for a sharing in the passion and suffering of Christ.

At that moment I saw red blood trickle down from the crown of thorns [of the crucifix]—warm, fresh, and plentiful—just as it did at the time of His passion, when the crown of thorns was pressed on the blessed head of He who was both God and man, He who suffered this for me. And I understood truly that it was He himself who was showing this to me, with no intermediary.

And in this same vision, the Trinity suddenly filled my heart with joy, and I understood that all who go to heaven will feel such joy without end....

HOW EVEN SIN FITS INTO GOD'S PLAN

And after this, in my mind I saw God as the center-point of all things, and understood how He is present in all things. And as I saw this I considered, with some dread, thinking, "What is sin?" For I saw with certainty that all things, no matter how small, are done by God through His foreseeing wisdom, and nothing is by accident or happenstance. When things appear so to us, it is through our blindness and lack of foresight. For all things are foreknown by God in His wisdom, so that He rightly and blessedly brings them to their best end, yet they seem to us to happen suddenly and unexpectedly, and so they seem to our blindness and lack of foresight to be accidents or happenstance. But they are not so to our Lord God.

For this reason I realized that all things that were done were done well, simply because our Lord God did them all. At this time the actions of creatures were not shown to me, but only the actions of our Lord God in and through creatures, for He is the center-point of all things, and all things are done by Him. But I was also certain that He did not sin. Thus I concluded that no action is truly sin, for in all that was done I saw no sin. And I no longer wondered at this but simply beheld what our Lord showed me….

And all this He happily showed me, in such a way as to say: "See! I am God. See! I am in all things. See! I do all things. See! I never remove my hand from my works, nor shall I do so for eternity. See! I lead all things to the end I have ordained for them from the beginning, by the same might, wisdom, and love by which I made them. How could anything be amiss?"…

After this the Lord brought my mind back to the longing I had for Him; and nothing hindered me except sin. So I looked out upon all of us and thought, "If there had been no sin, we would all be clean and like the Lord, just as He made us." And before this, in my foolishness I had often wondered why God's foreseeing wisdom had not prevented sin, for then I thought all would have been well. Later, I would leave behind this worry, but at this time I was left mourning and sorrowful, without understanding this matter.

But Jesus informed me in this vision of all I needed to know, answering me in this way: "It was fitting that there should be sin. But all shall be well, and all shall be well, and all manner of things shall be well." And Our Lord showed me that this simple word "sin" contained all the evil, all the shame, and all the suffering and dying that He bore for us in this life, including all of the passions and pains of His creatures, both physical and spiritual, and all the suffering that ever was or will be, all of which was borne in His passion…. All this was shown to me quickly, after which I was immediately comforted, for our good Lord did not wish me to be afraid of this horrible sight.

But yet I saw no sin, for I believe it did not have any substance or being; thus it could not be known except for the pain it causes. Thus pain, it seemed to me, was indeed something, for it purges us and makes us know ourselves and ask for mercy. For Our Lord's passion is a comfort to us against all this, with His blessed will. And our good Lord comforts those who will be saved, readily and sweetly, with His tender love, as if to say: "Sin is the cause of all this pain. But all shall be well, and all shall be well, and all manner of things shall be well." He said these words tenderly, not implying any blame toward myself or any others.

Then I knew it would be unkind to blame God for my sin, since He does not blame me for sin. And I knew the deep mystery hidden in God, which will be made known to us in heaven, when we will see the reason why He suffered for sin; and seeing this, we will rejoice endlessly in our Lord God….

For I saw no wrath, except on man's part, and He forgives this in us. For wrath is only a resistance to, and a defiance of, peace and love, arising from a lack of strength, of wisdom or of goodness. And none of these are lacking in God, but only in us. For we resist peace and love through our sin and wretchedness. Yet He looked upon us lovingly with pity. For love is the ground of mercy, and it is the work of mercy to keep us in love. And He showed this to me in such a way that I could not perceive mercy except in and alongside love.

Mercy is a sweet work of love, mingled with abundant pity, for mercy works to keep us and turn all things into good. Mercy, through love, allows us to fail a little, and whenever we fail we fall, and whenever we fall we die, for it is death to fall from the God who is our life. Our failing is dreadful, our falling is shameful and our dying is sorrowful, but in all this His sweet look of pity and love never leaves us, nor does His work of mercy cease.

For I saw the properties both of mercy and of grace, which are different outworkings of the same love. Mercy is a kind of pity that belongs to the tender love of a mother, and grace is what we find in the love of a royal lord. Mercy works to keep, to suffer, to enliven, and to heal, all through the tenderness of love. Grace works to raise, to reward, to pass over what our works deserve, dispensing the bounty of the royal lord in his marvelous generosity, all through the abundance of love….

As truly as God is our Father, so truly God is our Mother, which He showed me in those sweet words which He said, "I am." That is: "I am the Might and Goodness of a Father. I am the Wisdom of a Mother. I am the Light and Grace of blessed Love. I am Trinity. I am Unity. I am the supreme Goodness of all things. I am He who makes you love. I am He who makes you desire. I am the eternal fulfillment of all true desire."…

And after this, He allows some of us to fall, harder and more hurtfully than we think we ever did before. And then we foolishly think that all we have done is for nothing. But this is not so. For indeed it is necessary for us to fall, and it is necessary for us to see our fall. For if we never fell, we would never know how feeble and wretched we are in ourselves, and further, we would not fully know the wonderful love of our Maker. When we are in heaven we will see, for all eternity, all of our grievous sins in this life; and yet we will nonetheless see that His love for us was never any less, that we never lost any value in His sight.

And through our falling we will gain insight into God's endless love. For how strong and overwhelming is that love which is not destroyed—and cannot be—by sins. And we will profit by this understanding, and also by the humility and meekness that we will get by seeing our fallings. And this will raise us high in heaven, higher than we ever had gotten without such meekness. This is why we need to see it: if we do not see it, our falling would not profit us. Thus both our falling and our later seeing it are both from God's mercy.

A mother may let her child fall sometimes, and even be hurt in some ways, for the child's own benefit. But through her love she will never let her child enter into any danger. And even if an earthly mother might let her child perish, our heavenly Mother, Jesus, would never let His children perish. For He is Almighty, All-Wisdom, and All-love, He and He alone—blessed may He be!

But often when He shows us our falling and our wretchedness, we are so horrified and ashamed of ourselves that we do not know what to do. But our gentle Mother does not want us to flee away—indeed, He wants nothing less. He wants, instead, for us to act like a child, for when a child is hurt or afraid, it runs quickly to its mother for help, as fast as it can. He wants us to do the same, as a meek child saying, "My kind, gracious and loving Mother, have mercy on me. I have made myself foul and unlike you, and I cannot make it right without your help and grace."

And if we are not immediately aided, we are confident that it is because of our Mother's wisdom. For if He sees that it will benefit us more to mourn and weep, He allows it, with mercy, pity, and love, as long as it is beneficial. And He wants us to act like a child, who by nature constantly trusts the love of his mother, both in good times and bad.

And He wants us to embrace the faith of the holy Church and to find in her a loving Mother, the comfort of a true understanding, with the whole communion. For a single person may often be broken, as he himself recognizes, but the whole body of the holy Church has never been broken, and never will be for all eternity. And so it is a sure, good, and gracious thing to be fastened closely and strongly, with a meek will, to our Mother, the holy Church—that is, to Christ Jesus.

For the merciful food that is His precious blood and water is abundant to make us fair and clean; our Savior's blessed wounds are open and ready to heal us; our Mother's sweet and gracious hands are ready and diligent to embrace us. For in all this He acts like a kind nurse that has no other intention than the salvation of her child. It is His task to save us; it is His desire to help us; it is His will that we should know it, for He wants us to love Him sweetly and trust in Him meekly and mightily.

THE JOY OF GOD IN OUR SALVATION

For it is God's will that we share His joy in our salvation, and for this reason He wants us to be comforted and strengthened, and our souls to be joyfully filled with His grace. All that He has done for us, all He now does, and all He will ever do costs Him nothing, and could not possibly cost Him anything. But in our human nature He took on—from the beginning of the sweet Incarnation to the blessed Resurrection on Easter morning—He endured the cost of our redemption, and yet He endured this with great and endless joy.

And Jesus wants us to understand the great bliss that the blessed Trinity enjoys in carrying out our salvation, and He wants us to share this great bliss through His grace—that is, that our joy in our salvation, even while we are still here on earth, would be the same joy that Christ has in our salvation. For the whole Trinity was at work in Christ's passion, pouring out abundant virtues and grace to us through Him. Though only the Virgin's Son suffered, the whole Trinity shared His joy.

All this Christ showed me through these words, "Are you happy?" And again, "If you are happy, then I am happy." His meaning was, "It is a great joy to me, and I ask for nothing more for all my suffering than that I might make you happy."

And this made me realize the qualities of a glad giver. A glad giver does not care for the thing he gives, for his whole desire and intent is to please and give consolation to the receiver. And if the receiver is grateful for the gift, then the glad giver cares nothing for his cost and his work, but takes joy and delight that he has pleased and brought consolation to the one he loves….

Then with great joy Our Lord looked at His wounded side and rejoiced. For by looking into His side in this way, He led my mind into that same side. And there He showed me a fair, delightful place, large enough for all of mankind who are to be saved to rest in peace and love. And from there He brought my mind to the precious blood and water which He let pour from His side out of love. And looking further, He showed me His blessed heart, cloven in two.

And rejoicing in this way, He led my mind to think of the blessed Godhead, helping me to understand and think upon the endless love, which is without beginning and without end. And our good Lord said, blissfully, "Look how I have loved you," as if to say: "My darling, look and see your Lord, your God, your Maker, your endless joy. See what joy and bliss I have in your salvation, and rejoice with me in my love."

And, to help me understand even more, He said, "How I have loved you! Look and see that I loved you so much, even before I died for you, that I was willing to die for you in this way. And now I have suffered and died willingly for you, and all my sorrows are turned to endless joy and bliss, both to me and to you. How could you now ask for anything, and I would not grant it to you? For I delight only in your endless joy and bliss with me."…

ST. CATHERINE OF SIENA (1347–1380)

It is one of the typical enigmas of medieval history that a sickly, middle-class woman who rarely left her monastic cell was one of the primary forces in shaping fourteenth-century Europe.

Catherine was the twenty-fourth of twenty-five children—more than half of whom died in childbirth or infancy—born to the family of a middle-class Italian cloth dyer. While still in her infancy she received her first mystical visions, and at seven she had irrevocably consecrated her chastity to Christ. (When her father attempted to force her to marry her deceased sister's husband, she cut her own beautiful hair in protest.)

At sixteen her father permitted her to join the Dominican tertiaries, a Third Order whose members were permitted to remain at home rather than share a common residence. Moving into a quiet cell in her father's home, her visions—often accompanied by terrible pain and illness—increased in frequency and intensity, culminating in a mystical marriage to Jesus at the age of twenty-one.

Two years later Catherine was instructed by God to enter public life. When not feeding the hungry and nursing the sick, Catherine, who was illiterate, began dictating to secretaries letters to kings, popes, princes, and bishops all over the world. Over four hundred of her letters survive, masterpieces of diction and public policy.

Her reputation for holiness preceded her, and Catherine began to be summoned to royal and ecclesiastical courts and sent on diplomatic missions. She functioned as the formal ambassador between Rome and the neighboring Italian states for the decade before her death, working to negotiate an end to the civil wars which wracked Italy. She was once nearly assassinated for her trouble.

The greatest crisis of Catherine's day was the scandal of the Avignon Papacy. Beginning in 1309 the popes, all of whom were Frenchmen, had lived in Avignon, France, rather than Rome. They were motivated both by the constant warfare in Italy and the political opportunities made possible by the French royal court, but the absence of the popes from the city of Rome had brought shame to the papal office. Catherine wrote at least six letters to Pope Gregory XI, urging him—and even at times, it seems, bullying him—to return to Rome, which he finally did in 1378. Though it will never be known what role Catherine's influence played, there is no denying that her letters were a factor in ending the nearly seventy-year scandal.

Unfortunately, Pope Gregory's death was followed by a disputed papal election, and one of the claimants—the correct one, as it turned out—summoned Catherine to Rome to help cement the support for his claims. In the meantime, Catherine worked tirelessly to promote the cause of the moral discipline of the clergy and—in the face of aggressive attacks of Ottoman Turks, which eventually culminated in the collapse of the Eastern Christian Empire in 1453—a new Crusade.

Catherine died at the age of thirty-three, sickened by illness and malnutrition caused by her extreme regimen of fasting. Her *The Dialogue*, transcribed conversations between herself and God that she dictated to secretaries during her visions, was widely read as a theological treatise, often compared to Dante's *Divine Comedy*. She was canonized in 1461 and named a Doctor of the Church in 1970 with Teresa of Ávila, the first two women to be so named.

THE DIALOGUE

The only book left by St. Catherine is this one, written in the form of a conversation between herself and God the Father, which, at least in its initial form, was dictated to her secretaries during a series of mystical visions Catherine experienced. This section, in which God speaks about the path of salvation using the metaphor of a bridge, is a brilliant theological exposition. ("The soul," who occasionally responds, is, of course, Catherine.)

> It is true, as I have told you, that I have made a Bridge out of my Word, my only-begotten Son. You, my children, should know that the road was broken by the sin and disobedience of Adam, so that no one could ever arrive at eternal life....
>
> And the flesh immediately began to war against the Spirit and, losing the state of innocence, became a foul animal, and all created things rebelled against man, whereas they would have been obedient to him had he remained in the state in which I had placed him. Not remaining there, he failed to obey, and merited eternal death in soul and body.
>
> And as soon as he had sinned, a violent flood arose, which continually crushes him with its waves, bringing him weariness and trouble from himself, the devil, and the world. Everyone was drowned in the flood, because no one, by his own righteousness alone, could arrive at eternal life. And so, wishing to remedy your great evils, I have given you the Bridge of my Son, so that you will not be drowned passing across this flood, which is the tumultuous sea of this dark life. See, therefore, what all creatures owe to me, and how foolish they are if they do not accept the remedy I have offered, but are willing to drown instead.
>
> My daughter, open the eye of your mind, and you will see the accepted and the ignorant, the imperfect and the perfect who follow me in truth, so that you may mourn the damnation of the foolish, and rejoice in the perfection of my beloved servants.

You will also see how those who walk in the light conduct themselves, in contrast to those who walk in darkness. I also want you to look at the Bridge of my only-begotten Son and notice its greatness, for it reaches from heaven to earth—that is, the earth of your humanity is joined to the greatness of the Deity. I say, then, that this Bridge reaches from heaven to earth, and constitutes the union I have made with man.

This was necessary in order to fix the road which was broken, as I said, so that man could pass through the bitterness of the world and arrive at life. But if the Bridge were made of earth it could never be large enough to cross the flood and give you eternal life, because the earth of human nature was not adequate to satisfy for guilt and to remove the stain of Adam's sin. This stain corrupted the whole human race and gave out a stench, as I said earlier. It was, therefore, necessary to join human nature with the height of My nature, the eternal Deity, so that it might be adequate to satisfy for the whole human race, so that human nature could sustain the punishment, and that the divine nature, united with the human, could make acceptable the sacrifice of My only Son, offered to Me to take death from you and to give life to you.

So the height of the Divinity, humbled to the earth and joined with your humanity, made the Bridge and fixed the road. Why was this done? So that man might come to his true happiness with the angels. And notice that, if you wish to have life, it is not enough that my Son should have made you this Bridge: you must also walk across it.

Then the soul exclaimed with profound love:

O immeasurable Love, sweet beyond all sweetness! Who would not be inflamed by such great love? What heart can help breaking at such tenderness? It seems, O Depth of Charity, as if you were mad with love for your creature, as if you could not live without him, and yet you are our God who has no need of us; your greatness does not increase through our good, for you are unchangeable, and our evil causes you no harm, for you are the supreme and eternal Goodness.

What moves you to do us such mercy through pure love, and on account of no debt that you owed us, or need that you had of us? We are simply your guilty and spiteful debtors. Therefore, if I understand correctly, O supreme and eternal Truth, I am the thief and you have been punished for me. For I see your Word, your Son, fastened and nailed to the Cross, out of which you have made for me a Bridge, as You have explained to me, your miserable servant.

And for this reason, my heart is bursting, and yet cannot burst because of the hunger and the desire which it has developed for you. My Lord, I remember that you were going to show me who walks across the Bridge and who does not; should it please your goodness to show this to me, I would gladly see and hear it.

Then the eternal God, to inflame and excite that soul even more for the salvation of souls, replied to her, saying:

First, just as I have already shown you what you wished to see, so now I will explain to you the nature of this Bridge. I have told you, my daughter, that the Bridge reaches from heaven to earth; this is through the union which I have made with man, whom I formed of the clay of the earth. Now learn that this Bridge, my only-begotten Son, has three steps, two of which were made with the wood of the most Holy Cross, and the third still retains the great bitterness He tasted when He was given gall and vinegar to drink. In these three steps you will recognize three states of the soul, which I will now explain to you.

The first step is the feet of the soul, which signifies its affection, for the feet carry the body as the affection carries the soul. So these pierced feet are steps by which you can arrive at his Side, which reveals to you the secret of His Heart.

Second, the soul, rising on the steps of its affection, begins to taste the love of His Heart, gazing into that open Heart of my Son with the eye of the mind, and finds it consumed with ineffable love. I say "consumed," because He does not love you for His own profit, because you cannot possibly profit Him, who is consubstantial with me. Then the soul is filled with love, seeing how much it is loved.

Having passed the second step, the soul reaches out to the third, that is, the Mouth, where it finds peace from the terrible war it has been waging with its own sin. In summary, on the first step, lifting its feet from the earthly affections, the soul strips itself of vice; on the second it fills itself with love and virtue; and on the third it tastes peace. So the Bridge has three steps, so that, climbing past the first and the second, you may reach the last which is so elevated that the water which runs underneath may not touch it; for in my Son there was no poison of sin.

This Bridge is elevated, and yet at the same time it is joined to the earth. Do you know when it was elevated? When My Son was lifted up on the wood of the most holy Cross, the divine nature being joined to the lowliness of the earth of your humanity.

This is why I told you that, when He was lifted on high, He was not lifted off of the earth, for the divine nature is united and made consubstantial with it. And no one could go on the Bridge until it had been lifted on high, which is why He said, "If I am lifted on high I will draw all things to myself" (see Jn 12:32). In my goodness, seeing that there was no other way that you could be drawn to me, I sent Him so that He should be lifted on high on the wood of the Cross, making of it an anvil on which my Son, born of human generation, should be remade, in order to free you from death and restore you to the life of grace.

This is why He drew everything to Himself by this means—to show the ineffable love with which I love you, since the heart of man is always attracted by love. I could not have shown you any greater love than this, to lay down my life for you. So you see that my Son was treated in this way because of love, so that ignorant man should be unable to resist being drawn to me.

LETTER TO POPE GREGORY XI

In this letter Catherine presents to the pope her threefold program for the renewal of the Catholic Church: (a) moral reform of the clergy, (b) the pope's return to Rome, and (c) a new Crusade against the Muslims who have invaded the Holy Land.

In the Name of Jesus Christ crucified and of sweet Mary:

Most holy and dear and sweet father in Christ sweet Jesus: I, your unworthy daughter Catherine, servant and slave of the servants of Jesus Christ, write to you in His precious Blood. With fervor I have desired to see in you the fullness of divine grace in such a way that you might be the means, through divine grace, of pacifying the whole world.

Therefore, I beg you, my sweet father, to use the means of your power and virtue—with zeal and burning desire—for peace, the honor of God, and the salvation of souls. And should you say to me, father, "The world is so ravaged! How can I bring about peace?" I tell you, on behalf of Christ crucified, it is necessary for you to achieve three chief things through your power.

First, you must uproot from the garden of Holy Church the foul-smelling flowers, full of impurity and greed, swollen with pride—that is, the bad priests and rulers who poison and rot that garden. O you, our Ruler, use your power to pluck out those flowers! Throw them away, that they may have no rule! Insist that they work to discipline themselves in a holy and good life.

Plant in this garden fragrant flowers, priests and rulers who are true servants of Jesus Christ, and care for nothing but the honor of God and the salvation of souls, and are fathers of the poor. Alas, what confusion is this, to see those who ought to be a mirror of voluntary poverty, meek as lambs, distributing the possessions of Holy Church to the poor; and they appear in such luxury and state and pomp and worldly vanity, more than if they had turned to the world a thousand times! For many laypersons put them to shame by living a good and holy life.

But it seems that highest and eternal Goodness is allowing to happen by force which should have been done by love; it seems that He is permitting dignities and luxuries to be taken away from His Bride, as if to show that Holy Church should return to her first condition, poor, humble, and meek as she was in that holy time when men took note of nothing but the honor of God and the salvation of souls, caring for spiritual things and not for temporal. For ever since she has aimed more at temporal than at spiritual, things have gone from bad to worse.

See therefore that God, in judgment, has allowed much persecution and tribulation to happen to her. But take comfort, father, and fear not for anything that could happen, which God does to make her state perfect once more, in order that lambs may feed in that garden, and not wolves who devour the honor that should belong to God, which they steal and give to themselves.

Take comfort in sweet Jesus Christ; for I hope that His aid will be near you, fullness of divine grace, divine aid, and support in the way that I said before. Out of war you will attain the greatest peace; out of persecution, the greatest unity; not by human power, but by holy virtue, you will overcome those visible demons, wicked men, and those invisible demons who never sleep around us.

But reflect, sweet father, that you could not do this easily unless you accomplished the other two things which must precede the other—that is, your return to Rome, and the raising of the standard of the most holy Cross. Let not your holy desire fail on account of any scandal or rebellion of cities which you might see or hear. Instead, let the flame of holy desire be more kindled to wish to do so swiftly. Do not delay, then, your coming. Do not believe the devil, who perceives his own loss, and so works to rob you of your possessions in order that you may lose your love and charity, and our coming be hindered.

I tell you, father in Christ Jesus, come swiftly like a gentle lamb. Respond to the Holy Spirit who calls you. I tell you, come, come, come, and do not wait for time, since time does not wait for you. Then you will do like the slain Lamb whose place you hold, who without weapons in His hand slew our foes, coming in gentleness, using only the weapons of the strength of love, aiming only at care of spiritual things, and restoring grace to man who had lost it through sin.

Alas, sweet my father, with this sweet hand I pray you, and tell you to come to overcome our enemies. On behalf of Christ crucified I tell it you: refuse to believe the counsels of the devil, who would hinder your holy and good resolution. Be manly in my sight, and not afraid. Answer God, who calls you to hold and possess the seat of the glorious shepherd St. Peter, whose vicar you have been.

And raise the standard of the holy Cross; for as we were freed by the Cross—so Paul says—thus raising this standard, which seems to me the help of Christians, we shall be freed—we from our wars and divisions and many sins, the infidel people from their infidelity.

In this way you will come and bring about a reformation, giving good priests to Holy Church. Fill her heart with the deep love that she has lost; for she has been so drained of blood by the iniquitous men who have devoured her that she is wholly weak. But take comfort and come, father, and no longer make the servants of God wait, who are tortured by desire. And I, poor, miserable woman, can wait no more; living, I seem to die in my pain, seeing God thus dishonored....

Give me your blessing. Remain in the holy and sweet grace of God. Sweet Jesus, Jesus Love.

THE SPIRITUAL MARRIAGE OF CATHERINE

Blessed Raymond of Capua, Catherine's spiritual director, recorded her primary biography. In this selection he describes the apex of her spiritual life, her mystical marriage to Christ.

The soul of Catherine became daily more enriched with the grace of the Savior. She flew rather than walked in the paths of virtue, and she conceived the holy desire of arriving at so perfect a degree of faith that nothing would ever be capable of separating her from her divine Spouse, whom alone her heart desired to please. She therefore begged God to increase her faith, and make it strong enough to resist any and every enemy. Our Blessed Lord answered her, "I will espouse you in faithfulness" (Hos 2:20). And each time Catherine repeated her prayer, Jesus Christ repeated the same answer.

One day, at the approach of the holy season of Lent, when Christians celebrate the Carnival (a foolish goodbye to the delicacies which the Church is on the eve of prohibiting), Catherine withdrew into her cell to enjoy her Spouse more intimately by fasting and prayer. She repeated her request with more fervor than ever, and Our Lord answered her: "Because you have shunned the vanities of the world and forbidden pleasures, and have set all the desires of your heart on me alone, I intend, while your family members are rejoicing in irreverent feasts and festivals, to celebrate the wedding which is to unite me to your soul. I am going, according to my promise, to betroth you to me in faithfulness."

Jesus Christ then spoke once more, when the Blessed Virgin appeared; and with his glorious mother, St. John the Evangelist, the apostle St. Paul, St. Dominic, founder of her order, and with them the prophet David who plucked from his harp tones of heavenly sweetness. The Mother of God took the right hand of Catherine in her holy hand, in order to present it to her Son, asking Him to betroth her in faithfulness.

The Savior consented to it with love, and offered her a golden ring, set with four precious stones, in the center of which blazed a magnificent diamond. He placed it himself on Catherine's finger, saying to her: "I, your Creator and Redeemer, betroth you in faithfulness, and you will preserve it intact, until we celebrate together in heaven the eternal wedding feast of the Lamb. Daughter, now be courageous; carry out without fear the things that my Providence will show to you; you are armed with faith and will triumph over all your enemies."

The vision disappeared, but the ring remained on the finger of Catherine. She saw it, but it was invisible to others. She told me about it, while blushes colored her cheek, saying that it never left her, and that she never tired of admiring it.

MEDIEVAL THINKERS

Christianity is unique among world religions in the privileged role that it gives to intellectual reflection on the contents of its faith. The discipline of theology has always been center stage in the Christian intellectual tradition, but Christians have always shown a strong interest in other intellectual disciplines as well—such as science and philosophy—driven by the belief that a deeper knowledge of the created world will yield a deeper knowledge of its Creator (cf. Rom 1:20).

In the Middle Ages, so often derided as the Dark Ages in popular opinion, this intellectual reflection reached its high point. After all, it was in the thirteenth century that the great universities of Europe were erected, and the philosophical framework for the later Scientific Revolution was established.

In the earlier, patristic period it was the great, foundational dogmas of Christianity that were being hammered out, and the great controversies over the Trinity and the Incarnation overshadow that entire period. It is understandable, then, that the greatest patristic theologians are almost all bishops, given that the bishop was the figure chiefly responsible for over-seeing the creeds and their interpretation.

By the dawn of the Middle Ages most of the great controversies over central Christian beliefs had settled, and medieval debates typically involved more peripheral, secondary questions, such as how to explain the transformation of bread and wine into Christ's Body and Blood (transubstantiation? con-substantiation?). They were typically fought not in grand, international councils but in the lecture halls of universities, not by bishops but by minor clerics or monks. (Higher education was rare among laity and virtually nonexistent among women, so we have to wait for the modern period for the emergence of a class of lay theologians of both sexes.)

The roots of Western education lay in the Greek system of the liberal arts, which at the height of the Roman Empire had crystallized into a formal curriculum that included philosophy, grammar, logic, literature, mathematics, and numerous subordinate disciplines. This system had virtually collapsed with the demise of the Roman Empire in the West in the fifth century, St. Augustine being one of its last great beneficiaries. No system of formal education existed until it was pieced back together under Charlemagne's cultural renaissance in the eighth century.

At the height of the Middle Ages theology was fully incorporated into this system, often seen as its culminating discipline, so that students would begin the study of Christian doctrine already fully equipped with a well-rounded background in subjects includ-ing philosophy, logic, and grammar. This develop-ment accompanied the rise of the universities, which added faculties of natural science, law, and medicine.

The scholars of the universities, known as schoolmen or scholastics, approached their subjects from a highly disciplined, logical perspective that valued precise terms and logical distinctions, exploring both sides of every question and synthesizing and harmonizing all the data into a single, comprehensive answer. The logical and metaphysical teachings of the ancient philosopher Aristotle, reintroduced to Latin speakers from the East during the Crusades, provided the most helpful tools for this method.

Some, like St. Bonaventure, worried that theology was being reduced to a mere classroom exercise in logic-chopping rather than a reverent, prayerful practice of contemplation, whereas others, like St. Thomas Aquinas, relished the abundant fruit that the new system seemed to be producing. Nor were the other disciplines neglected: the medieval universities produced a large crop of pioneers in the fields of law (Gratian), philosophy (St. Anselm, Duns Scotus) and natural science (Robert Grosseteste, Roger Bacon).

By the end of the medieval period, the Catholic Church passed into the modern age with a fully developed, mature system of theological, philosophical, and scientific thought that would shape the future of Western Europe.

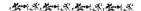

ST. AUGUSTINE OF HIPPO
(354–430)

At age thirty, from the looks of things, no one would have thought Augustine had the makings of a saint. His father was a Roman pagan, his mother an African Christian, and Augustine had long abandoned the Christianity of his mother for a heretical cult, Manichaeism. He fathered a child out of wedlock, and tells us in his autobiography that at one point he prayed, "Lord, give me chastity, but not yet!"

Having left his native Africa for the buzzing metropolitan cities of Rome and Milan, Augustine had attained a high position in the imperial court and had nothing but scorn for Christianity, whose Scriptures he found crude and barbaric and whose moral code he found impracticable. But between the prayers of his mother and the preaching of St. Ambrose, then bishop of Milan, he found his way into the Church. After returning to Africa he was ordained a bishop.

Augustine's written works number over a hundred, and he is perhaps the most influential of all Christian writers in history. His *Confessions* are a tell-all autobiography of his spiritual journey, detailing how the grace of God brought him through even the darkest moments of his life. As a bishop he wrote numerous tracts directed to his former Manichaeans, trying to convince them that humans are created good and sin only through free will, rather than, as they thought, being created evil. Against the African sect known as the Donatists, he tried to articulate how the Church should be a "school for sinners" (like himself), rather than the small company of saints that they pretended to be.

His later years were spent arguing with the Pelagians, who believed humans were good enough to obey God's commandments and merit eternal life by their own powers. Augustine's emphasis on the damage done to human nature by original sin—

which he understood personally—and man's need for divine grace were enough to make him known to later thinkers as the "doctor of grace."

Although most of the fierce Trinitarian debates of the early Church were over by his day, Augustine made his own contributions to Trinitarian theology, suggesting that the Holy Spirit's relation to the Father and Son was somewhat analagous to a bond of love that unites two human persons. This meant that the Holy Spirit proceeded not from the Father *alone*, but from the Father *and the Son*, a position that would later cause much disagreement with the Greek Christians of the East.

Overall there are very few areas of theology to which Augustine did not make some contribution, and the basic worldview he puts forward in his writing did more than anything else to shape the worldview of the later Middle Ages.

After the city of Rome was sacked by barbarians in AD 410, Augustine wrote *City of God* to comfort his fellow Christians, assuring them that the end of the empire did not mean the end of the Church: Christians are merely pilgrims here, making use of earthly goods to speed them on their journey toward their final destination in the next life. It was not for nothing that Emperor Charlemagne would later have the *City of God* read to him every evening—it was a charter for a Christian civilization.

AUGUSTINE'S CONVERSION

Augustine's biography, Confessions, *tells of his conversion, which up to that point was hindered by his inability to live chastely. This scene occurs after he and his friend Alypius hear the story of the conversion of Anthony of Egypt, which puts them to shame.*

In the middle of this great conflict of my inner self, which flared up in my soul within the chamber of my heart, both my mind and face were troubled. I seized Alypius, crying: "What is wrong with us? What is this? Didn't you hear? The uneducated rise up and seize heaven (cf. Mt 11:12) while we, with all our education, wallow in flesh and blood, merely because we lack courage! Because others have preceded us, are we ashamed to follow? Shouldn't we be more ashamed *not* to follow?"

I said something like this, and in my excitement tore myself from him, while he stared at me blankly in astonishment. For I didn't speak in my normal tone—my face, cheeks, eyes, color, and tone of voice all expressed my emotion more than words did. Our lodging had a little garden we were allowed to use, for our landlord did not live there. The storm within my heart carried me there, where no one would interrupt the fiery struggle in which I was engaged with myself…. I was greatly upset in spirit, impatient with myself that I did not enter into your will and covenant, O my God, which all my bones cried out for me to enter….

Thus I was sick and tormented, accusing myself even more severely than usually, tossing and turning to free myself from the chain that held me, though now only loosely. And you, Lord, pressed upon my heart with your severe mercy, increasing your lashes of fear and shame in case I should give up again, and that last remaining tie, not being cut, might strengthen and bind me all over again. For I said to myself, "Let it be done now, let it be done now." And as I spoke, I almost came to a decision. I almost did it, but I did not do it. But I didn't fall back into my old condition, either, but simply drew up for breath. And I tried again, and very nearly reached it, almost, then nearly touching and grasping it….

And the very moment I was about to become a new man, the nearer this approached me, the more this very thing horrified me, yet it did not drive me back or turn me aside, but kept me in suspense.

"Vanity of vanities" (Eccl 1:2): My old lovers still captivated me; they tugged at my flesh, whispering softly: "Are you leaving us? From now on will we never be with you again? And from this moment will you never be allowed to do this or that again?" And what did they suggest by "this or that"?… What impurities did they suggest! What shame!

But now I could barely hear them, as though they were muttering behind my back, not daring to show themselves openly, but pulling at me as I was departing, urging me to look back at them. Yet they did delay me, so that I hesitated, unwilling to shake myself free of them to leap over to where I was being called. My unruly habits kept saying to me, "Do you really think you can live without them?"

But now this was very faint, for in the direction I had turned, and to which I trembled to go, the innocent dignity of Chastity appeared to me, cheerful but not foolish, honestly drawing me to come and doubt nothing. She opened her arms, full of countless good examples, to receive and embrace me. In her arms were so many young men and women, a multitude of youth and every other age, solemn widows and elderly virgins, and Chastity herself in each one of them, not barren but a fruitful mother of joyful children, all by you, O Lord, her husband.

And she smiled at me with a teasing look, as if to say: "Can't you do what these young men and women can do? Or perhaps they can't do it by themselves, but only through the Lord their God? For God gave me to them. Why are you relying on your own strength, and so failing? Cast yourself upon Him: He will not let you fall. Cast yourself upon Him without fear, for He will accept you and heal you."...

And as I was weeping with bitter sorrow in my heart, I suddenly heard the voice of a boy or girl (I don't know which), coming from a neighboring house, chanting repeatedly, "Pick up and read! Pick up and read!" Immediately my face changed, and I began seriously to wonder whether these were the words to some common game, but I could never remember hearing anything like it before. So, restraining my tears, I stood up, interpreting it as a command from heaven to open the book and read the first thing I saw....

So, quickly, I returned to the place where Alypius was sitting, for I had left there the book of the apostles when I got up.

I grabbed it, opened it, and in silence read the first thing I saw: "Not in reveling and drunkenness, not in debauchery and licentiousness, not in quarreling and jealousy. But put on the Lord Jesus Christ, and make no provision for the flesh, to gratify its desires" (Rom 13:13–14).

I read no further, nor did I need to, for instantly, as the sentence ended, as if by a light of confidence infused into my heart—all the gloom of doubt vanished away.…

THE HUMAN PERSON AS AN IMAGE OF THE TRINITY

Augustine's main contribution to Trinitarian theology, especially in his book On the Trinity, *was to see a reflection of the Trinity in the human person, whose soul is a "triad" of mind, knowledge, and love. Thus, whenever you see human persons loving one another, you see a picture of the Trinity.*

In this connection, let us hold that the Father, Son, and Holy Spirit are one God, the Creator and Ruler of all creation, and that the Father is not the Son, nor is the Holy Spirit either the Father or the Son. Rather, they are a Trinity of persons mutually interrelated, and a unity of an equal essence. And let us seek to understand this, praying for help from himself, the very one we wish to understand.…

This being the case, let us focus on the three things that we think we have found. We are not speaking of heavenly things yet, of God the Father, Son, or Holy Spirit, but of that faint image, which is still yet an image—that is, man himself. For our feeble mind can gaze upon this more comfortably and more easily.

Well, then, when I, the one making this inquiry, love anything, there are three things involved: myself, that which I love, and the love itself. For I can't love unless I have a lover, for there is no love where no one is loved. Therefore there are three things: he who loves, the one who is loved, and the love itself … and these three are yet one, and when they are perfect, they are also equal.

ON OUR NEED FOR GRACE

Augustine's toughest battle was against Pelagius, a British monk who felt that human nature was so well-made that it did not need any additional help from God to live rightly, but could avoid sin and keep the commandments by its own powers. Augustine knew from personal experience that our human effort requires God's help to overcome sin. (From On Nature and Grace*)*

No doubt, we also do our part in the work, but we are mere fellow workers with He who does the work, because His mercy goes before us. He goes before us, however, so that we may be healed. But then He also follows after us, so that being healed we may grow healthy and strong. He goes before us that we may be called, and follows after us so that we may be glorified.

He goes before us that we may lead godly lives; He follows us so that we may always live with Him, because "without Him we can do nothing" (see Jn 15:5). Now the Scriptures describe both of these actions as operations of grace: "My God in his mercy will meet me" (Ps 59:10) and "mercy shall follow me all the days of my life" (Ps 23:6). Therefore, let us not praise our life by defending it; rather, let us submit it to Him by confessing.

Further, he [that is, Pelagius] flatters himself by saying he is taking God's side by defending human nature, which God made. But in doing so he forgets that by pretending that this nature is perfectly healthy, he rejects the help of the physician. But the one who created him is also his Savior. We should not, therefore, praise the Creator so much that we are forced to say (or rather, should dare to admit) that we do not need a Savior! Indeed, we should honor our human nature with suitable praise, and attribute that praise to the glory of its Creator. But at the same time that we are showing our gratitude to Him for creating us, we should not be ungrateful to Him for healing us.

Now, undoubtedly, we must not blame God for the sins which He heals. These come only from human willfulness, and we should submit them to God for His just punishment. Since, however, we admit that we were able to avoid them if we chose, let us admit that only His mercy can heal them, and not our power. But the mercy and beneficial help of the Savior, according to this writer [Pelagius] consists only in forgiving past sins, not in helping us to avoid sins in the future. Here he is dreadfully mistaken, even if it is by mistake. If we listen to him, who says that it is entirely in our own power to avoid sin, we will not be watchful and pray that we will not enter into temptation (cf. Mt 6:13).

HAPPINESS AND HOW TO FIND IT

Augustine's greatest work, City of God, *is a reflection on the true meaning of happiness and how we should live in order to obtain it. Its vision of life as a pilgrimage toward heaven deeply influenced the medieval worldview.*

If we are asked what *City of God* has to say in answer to these questions, especially what its opinion is about the supreme good and evil, it will reply that eternal life is the supreme good and eternal death the supreme evil, and that we must live rightly to obtain the one and avoid the other. Rightly then, is it written, "The righteous shall live by his faith" (Hb 2:4), for we do not yet see this good, and must therefore live by faith. We also lack the power by ourselves to live rightly, but can only do so if He who gave us faith to believe in His help also helps us when we believe and pray. As for those who imagined that the supreme good and evil are to be found in this life (either in the soul, the body, or both; either in pleasure, rest, bodily goods, or virtue, or some combination of these), all these have, with incredible shallowness, sought to find their happiness in this life and in themselves....

For what flow of words is adequate to describe all the miseries of this life?... For when, where, and how in this life can these bodily goods be possessed in such a way that they are safe from being lost by unexpected accidents? Is the wise man's body safe from pain that may drive away pleasure, from anxiety which may drive away rest? The amputation or decay of the body's limbs destroys its integrity, deformity blights its beauty, weakness ruins health, lethargy eats away at its energy, sluggishness or sleepiness at its activity, and from which of these is the wise man safe?…

What shall I say about the blessings of the soul, sensation and intelligence, one for perception and the other for understanding truth? But where is the sense in a man who becomes deaf and blind? And where is intelligence when disease makes a man delirious?…

Granted, virtue itself, which is not something we are born with but is acquired as a result of careful formation, is the best of all human goods. But what is its main occupation but to wage perpetual war with vices, not only outside ourselves but also especially within, and not the vices of others but our own. And the primary virtue we need is what we call temperance (what the Greeks call *sophrosyne*), which restrains fleshly lusts and prevents them from gaining the soul's consent to wicked deeds? For we must not imagine that there is no vice within us when, as the apostle says, "The desires of the flesh are against the Spirit" (Gal 5:17)….

But what do we want in desiring the supreme good, except that the flesh should cease lusting against the spirit, so that there will be no vice in us for the spirit to fight? And since we cannot attain this in the present life, no matter how much we want it, let us with God's help at least do this, to keep the soul safe from surrendering and succumbing to the flesh that lusts against it, and to deny our consent to sinful acts.

Far be it from us, then, so long as we are engaged in this civil war, to imagine that we have already found the happiness that we hope to gain by winning the war. And who is there so virtuous that he has no need to struggle against his vices?… Therefore, so long as we are stricken by this weakness, this plague, this disease, how shall we dare to say that we are safe? And if we are not safe, then how can we be already enjoying our eternal happiness?…

For we are saved by hope: now hope which is seen is not hope; for how can a man hope for what he can see? But if we hope for what we do not see, then we patiently wait for it (cf. Rom 8:24). Therefore, as we are saved by hope, so we are made happy by hope. And since we do not yet possess salvation at present, but look for it in the future, so it is the same with our happiness. And we do so with patience, for we are surrounded by evils we must patiently endure, until we come to the ineffable enjoyment of unadulterated goodness. For then there will be nothing left to endure. Salvation, such as it will exist in the world to come, shall itself be our final happiness….

But those who do not live by faith seek their peace in the earthly advantages of this life, while those who live by faith look for those eternal blessings that are promised. As though they were pilgrims here, they make use of those advantages offered by this time on earth, so long as they do not fascinate and divert them from God, but rather aid them in enduring more easily the burdens of the corruptible body which weigh the soul down.

Thus those things that are necessary for this mortal life are used by both kinds of person, but each has its own very specific and distinct aim in using them. The earthly city, which does not live by faith, seeks only an earthly peace, with its goal of an orderly agreement to live under obedience to laws, to coordinate the wills of citizens in attaining the necessaries of life. The heavenly city, or rather that part of it which is still on its earthly pilgrimage and lives by faith, makes use of this peace only because it must, until the mortal condition which makes it necessary shall pass away.

Therefore, so long as it lives like a captive and a stranger in the earthly city, even though it has received the promise of redemption and the gift of the Spirit as its down payment, it has no problem obeying the laws of the earthly city, so as to help provide for the maintenance of this mortal life. Thus, inasmuch as this mortal life is common to both cities, there will be an agreement between both of them.

ON USE AND ENJOYMENT

This selection from Augustine's On Christian Doctrine *articulates the way Christians must live in the earthly city while traveling toward the heavenly city—namely, by living as pilgrims, not as permanent residents.*

Some things are meant to be enjoyed, others are meant to be used, and others to be enjoyed *and* used. We should enjoy only those things that make us perfectly happy. We should use those things that assist and support us in our efforts to obtain happiness, so that we can enjoy these and rest content in them. When we are placed among both kinds of objects, and if we try to enjoy those things which we ought to be using, we will be prevented from reaching our goal and sometimes led away from it. We will become entangled in the love of lower pleasures, lagging behind and even turning back from the pursuit of the real and proper objects of enjoyment.

For enjoying a thing means resting content, satisfied with it for its own sake. To use a thing, on the other hand, is to use whatever means are at one's disposal to obtain what one desires, so long as it is an appropriate thing to desire (for an inappropriate use of something should be called an abuse).

Suppose, then, we were wanderers in a foreign country, and could not live happily so far away from our homeland, and feeling wretched from wandering, we wished to put an end to our wandering and return home. Let's say, then, we found some means of travel, either by land or water, to reach that homeland where our enjoyment could finally begin. But we might become charmed by the beauty of the countryside we traveled through, and the pleasant sensation of the vehicle's motion, and we might begin to enjoy things we should merely be using. Then, we might become unwilling to hurry to our destination, and we might become bogged down in a false delight, our mind distracted from that homeland whose delights would make us truly happy.

This is a picture of our condition in this mortal life. We have wandered far from God, and if we wish to return to our Father's home, the things of this world must be used and not enjoyed, so that "his invisible nature, namely, his eternal power and deity, has been clearly perceived in the things that have been made" (Rom 1:20)—that is, by means of what is material and temporary we may grasp hold of the things that are spiritual and eternal.

ST. ANSELM OF CANTERBURY (d. 1109)

It is beyond ironic that a bookish monk who spent the first half of his life scribbling proofs for God's existence in a dark monastic library should spend the second half as an international careerist and statesman, intervening in political and ecclesiastical disputes across Europe and the world. Known in his own day for the provocative stances he took concerning English politics, Anselm is known today almost exclusively for the unpretentious proofs he drafted as a young monk in France.

Born in Burgundy (in what is today considered part of Italy) to a family of dispossessed nobility, Anselm was denied permission to enter a monastery at the age of fifteen. His father disapproved. He left home and spent three years wandering around Europe until he arrived at the monastic school of Bec in France, where he enrolled as a student of the legendary teacher Lanfranc, finally replacing him as abbot himself.

While visiting England in his forties, Anselm was literally pressed into becoming Archbishop of Canterbury—the crosier was pushed into his hand and he was physically carried to the church. Such desperate measures were necessary: it was a dangerous office to fill. Europe was in the heat of the investiture controversy—a debate over the right of the king to invest, or choose, those who would fill Church offices. King William II of England and his successors vigorously defended this right and threatened to punish those who disputed it, and Anselm was well known to defend the freedom of the Church to choose her own leaders.

Anselm would suffer bitterly for his refusal to cooperate with the king's demands over investiture and would undergo two long exiles from England before the controversy was settled. While in exile in Europe, Anselm used his influence to settle a dispute over the papacy—supporting the true claimant, Urban II, against the antipope, or false claimant, Clement III—and to help reconcile a group of Greek bishops to communion with the Latin Church.

Anselm is best known today for his attempt to provide rational proofs for Christian beliefs, a part of the overall project of showing the harmony of faith and reason that would characterize the later scholastic theologians of the universities. His writings always assume that theology is an exercise in "faith seeking understanding," an attempt of believers to better understand by reason what they already hold to be true by faith. In particular, his ontological argument for God's existence and his attempt to prove the necessity of the Incarnation to satisfy the debt of man's sin have exercised a strong influence on the Western theological tradition.

His writings have the form of personal meditations or dialogues rather than the rationalistic, encyclopedic form of the later scholastics, and yet his foundational work in philosophy and theology led to his reputation as the Father of Scholasticism.

THE GREATEST ARGUMENT FOR GOD'S EXISTENCE … EVER

Anselm is best known for advancing the so-called ontological argument for God's existence, which has vexed philosophers for centuries. Not everyone has found it convincing (Aquinas himself did not), but it has always found its defenders. (From Proslogion*)*

I began to wonder whether it was possible to discover a single argument, requiring nothing else for its proof than itself alone, which all alone might be enough to demonstrate beyond a doubt that God truly exists…. Although I often and earnestly devoted my mind to discovering such a proof, and at times it seemed just beyond my reach, and at other times entirely beyond my mind's powers, I was on the point of giving it up in despair, admitting that such an argument simply did not exist…. Yet one day, when I was exhausted with the task, my mind a cluttered mess of thoughts, the proof I had searched for suddenly appeared in my mind.

Lord, let me look up to your light, even from far off, even from the depths. Teach me to seek you, and reveal yourself to me when I am seeking you, for I cannot even seek you unless you teach me, or find you unless you reveal yourself to me. Let me seek you in longing for you; and let me long for you in seeking you; let me find you in love, and love you in finding you….

I have no desire to penetrate your mysteriousness, for I know I am not wise enough for that; but I long to gain even a little degree of understanding of your truth, which my heart believes and loves. For I do not seek to understand in order to believe, but I believe in order to understand. For I believe this, that unless I believe first, I will never understand.

Indeed, I believe that you are the Greatest Possible Being. Or is there no such being, since the fool says in his heart, "There is no God" (Ps 14:1)? But even this fool, when he hears me speaking about this Greatest Possible Being, understands what I am talking about, and the Greatest Possible Being exists in his mind, even though he does not think it exists in reality.

Because it is one thing to exist in the mind, and quite another to exist in reality. When a painter first imagines what he will paint, he has that painting in his mind, but knows it does not yet exist in reality, since he has not yet painted it. But once he has painted it, it exists both in his mind and in reality, and he knows it exists in reality, since he has painted it.

Thus even the fool knows that the Greatest Possible Being exists in his mind, at least, if not in reality. We know this because, when he hears about it, he understands what we are talking about. And what he understands must therefore exist in his mind.

But the Greatest Possible Being simply *cannot* exist in the mind alone, for if it did, we would have to theoretically grant that it might also exist in reality, and then *that* would be the greater being. So if the Greatest Possible Being existed in the mind alone, it would not be the Greatest Possible Being, since we could imagine a greater one! But obviously this is impossible, for we would be imagining the Greatest Possible Being while simultaneously admitting that it is not the greatest, but could be greater. Thus there must also exist a Greatest Possible Being which exists both in the mind *and* in reality, and thus truly is the Greatest Possible Being.

I thank you, gracious Lord, I thank you, because what I formerly believed through your gift, I now understand by your enlightenment, such that even if I were unwilling to believe that you existed, I nonetheless could not rationally deny that you did.

WHY GOD BECAME MAN

The most significant contribution Anselm made to theology was his theology of the atonement. His attempt to "prove" the necessity of the Incarnation by reason alone (putting aside faith, for the sake of the argument), relying heavily on understanding Christ's death as a payment for man's infinite debt of sin, vastly influenced Western theology. (From Cur deus homo, *framed as a dialogue between Anselm and one of his fellow monks, Boso)*

I have been often and earnestly asked by many people to write down proofs of a certain doctrine of our faith, which I am accustomed to give to those who ask, for they say that these proofs gratify them, and satisfy their curiosity. They do not ask for these proofs in order to be argued into believing, but rather to take delight in understanding and meditating on things which they already believe, and also so that, if possible, they can "always be prepared to make a defense to any one who calls you to account for the hope that is in you" (1 Pt 3:15)....

Boso: Although the proper order is for us to believe the deep things of Christian faith before we undertake to discuss them by reason, yet it would be a shame if, once we were well-established in the faith, we did not seek to understand what we believed. Now, I consider myself to have such a firm faith in our salvation, by the grace of God, that even if I could not understand what I believed, yet nothing would shake my belief in it.

Therefore, I ask you to explain to me what I and others have asked for, that is, why the omnipotent God would have assumed the smallness and weakness of human nature for the sake of its salvation.

Anselm: In this investigation, you should play the role of those who are unwilling to believe anything unless it has been proven by reason.

Boso: In this matter, there is nothing I would do more willingly than to preserve this agreement.

Anselm: Let us imagine, then, that the Incarnation of God, and all the things we believe about him as man, had never taken place. Let us merely agree that man was made for happiness, which cannot be attained in this life, that no man can attain happiness except by being freed from sin, and that no man lives his life entirely without sin.

Boso: I grant these things, for none of them seem inappropriate to God.

Anselm: Therefore, in order for man to attain happiness, he must have his sins remitted.

Boso: We all hold this to be true.

Anselm: We must ask, then, how God remits man's sins. Just to clarify things, let us first ask what it means to sin in the first place, and what it means to make satisfaction for sin.

Boso: If you explain, I will listen.

Anselm: If a man or angel always gave God what He deserved, he would never sin.

Boso: I cannot deny that.

Anselm: Therefore to sin is nothing else than not to give God what He deserves.

Boso: But what *does* God deserve?

Anselm: It is justice, or uprightness of will…. This is the sole and complete debt of honor which we owe to God, and which God requires of us…. Whoever does not give this honor which is due to God robs God of what is His and dishonors him, and this is sin.

Even more, as long as he does not restore what he has taken away, he remains in fault, and it will not be enough merely to restore what has been taken away, but, given the gravity of the offense, he ought to restore more than he took away. For example, if you endanger another person's life, it is not enough merely to restore him to safety: you must make some compensation for the anguish you put him through, and if you violate someone's honor it is not enough to begin honoring him again, but must do something to make restitution to the person you have dishonored.

And when you pay back what you have unjustly stolen from someone, you cannot merely give what you owed that person anyway, and which might have been rightly demanded from you even if you had not stolen something new. Therefore, everyone who sins must pay back the honor which he has robbed from God. This is the satisfaction every sinner owes to God.

Boso: Since we have agreed to stick to reason in all of these things, I cannot object to anything you say, although you somewhat frighten me.

Anselm: Let us return to the question, then, and ask whether it is appropriate for God to simply forgive our sins out of mercy alone, without any repayment of the honor we took from him.

Boso: I don't see why it's not appropriate for Him to do so.

Anselm: To forgive our sins in this manner is nothing but failing to demand satisfaction for them, and since it is not right to forgive sin without demanding satisfaction, if satisfaction is not demanded, then the sin is not dealt with.

Boso: What you say is reasonable.

Anselm: It is therefore not proper for God to forgive sin without demanding satisfaction. Besides, there is another problem with sins not receiving satisfaction: the guilty will be treated the same as the innocent, and this is unbecoming of God.

Boso: I cannot deny it.

Anselm: Therefore, consider it settled, that without satisfaction, that is, without voluntary repayment of the debt, God cannot forgive the sin unpunished, nor can the sinner attain happiness.

Boso: Your reply with regard to this matter suffices me for the present….

Anselm: Neither, I think, will you doubt this, that degree of satisfaction should be proportionate to the degree of guilt.

Boso: Right. Otherwise, there would be something disorderly about how sin is treated, and nothing is disordered in God's kingdom.

Anselm: Tell me, then, what payment you make God for your sin.

Boso: Repentance, a broken and contrite heart, self-denial, various bodily sufferings, pity in giving and forgiving, and obedience.

Anselm: What do you give to God in all these?… When you give God things you already owed Him anyway, even had you not sinned, you should not count these things as satisfaction for the debt you incurred when you sinned. But you already owe to God every one of the things you just mentioned.

Boso: Now I would not dare to say that I repay any portion of my debt to God in those things.

Anselm: How, then, will you repay Him for your transgression?

Boso: If in justice I already owed to God my being and all my powers, even had I not sinned, then I have nothing left to give Him for my sin.

Anselm: What will become of you then? How will you be saved?

Boso: Merely looking at your arguments, I see no way of escape.

Anselm: Therefore you cannot make satisfaction for sins unless you restore something greater than you owed in the first place.... But this cannot be done, unless the sin of man were repaid by something greater than everything in the universe besides God.

Boso: So it appears.

Anselm: Further, the one who can give God something of his which is more valuable than all the things already possessed by God must be greater than everything in the universe but God.

Boso: I cannot deny it.

Anselm: Therefore no one but God can make this satisfaction.

Boso: So it appears.

Anselm: But no one but a man ought to do this, or else man will not be the one who makes the satisfaction.

Boso: Nothing seems more just.

Anselm: If it is necessary, therefore … that the appropriate satisfaction be made, and none but God can make it and only man ought to make it, it is necessary for a "God-man" to make it.

Boso: Blessed be God! We have made a great discovery with regard to our question. Go on, therefore, as you have begun, and may God assist you.

Anselm: But the divine and human natures cannot alternate, the divine becoming human or the human becoming divine. Nor can they be mixed together so that a third nature is produced from the two, neither divine nor human, for in these cases the resulting being would be God or man, but not both, or ... neither God nor man.

Moreover, if these two natures were joined in such a way that one were human and one were divine, and yet they were not in the same being, it would be impossible for the two to collaborate in doing the work necessary of them. For God could not do it, because He has no debt to pay, and man could not do it, because he cannot. Therefore, in order that the God-man may perform this task, it is necessary that the same being should be perfect God and perfect man, in order to make this atonement....

Since, then, it is necessary that the God-man preserve the completeness of each nature, it is also necessary that both natures be united entirely in one person ... for otherwise it is impossible that the same being should be true God and true man.

Boso: All that you say is satisfactory to me.

Anselm: And do you not think that so great a good, so lovely in itself, can suffice to pay what is due for the sins of the whole world?

Boso: Yes! For it has even infinite value.

Anselm: Do you see, then, how this life conquers all sins, if it is given in satisfaction for them?... Now we have discovered the compassion of God, which seemed absent earlier when we were considering God's holiness and man's sin. We have discovered it, I say, so great and yet so consistent with His holiness as to be beyond anything we can conceive.

For what compassion is greater than the words of the Father, saying to the sinner doomed to eternal torment and having no way of escape, "Take my only begotten Son and make him an offering for yourself," or these words of the Son, "Take me, and ransom your souls." For these are the things they say when inviting us and leading us to faith in the Gospel.

Boso: All things you have said seem to me reasonable and undeniable. And by the solution of the single question proposed I see the truth of all that is contained in the Old and New Testaments. For, in proving that God became man by necessity, leaving out what was taken from the Bible … you convince both Jews and pagans by the mere force of reason.

A PRAYER FOR MY ENEMIES

Anselm likely spent a great deal of time praying for his enemies. This prayer, found in his collected Prayers and Meditations, *embodies his spirit of forgiveness and charity.*

Lord Jesus Christ, Lord of all power and goodness, I pray that you will be gracious to my friends. You already know what my heart desires for my enemies. For … you know the secrets of my heart within me, which is not hidden from you…. And if at any point I ask for my enemies something which goes against your rule of love, whether through ignorance or weakness or wickedness, do not do that to them, and leave my prayer unanswered.

You who are "the true light" (Jn 1:9), enlighten their blindness. You who are the supreme Truth, correct their errors. You who are the true Life, revive their souls. For you have said through your beloved disciple, "He who does not love remains in death" (1 Jn 3:14). I pray, therefore, O Lord, that you grant to them as much love of yourself and of their neighbor as you command us to have, so that they will have no sin before you regarding their brother.

Forbid it, good Lord, forbid it that I should be an occasion of death to my brothers, that I should be to them "a stone that will make men stumble, a rock that will make them fall" (1 Pt 2:8). For it is enough and more than enough that I should be an offense to myself; my own sin is more than enough for me. Your servant begs you, on behalf of his fellow servants, that they should not offend so great and so good a Master, but be reconciled to you, and agree with me for your sake according to your will.

This is the vengeance my inmost heart desires to ask of you upon my fellow servants, my enemies, and fellow sinners. This is the punishment that my soul asks upon my fellow servants and enemies, that they should love you and one another according to your will. That they should thereby satisfy our common Master, both in regard to ourselves and in regard to one another, and to serve our common Lord in unity by the teaching of charity to the common good.

I, your sinful servant, pray that you may give this vengeance to all those who wish me evil and do me evil. Give it also to me, most merciful Lord, your sinful servant. Amen.

ROBERT GROSSETESTE (1175–1253)

It is fitting that Robert became known to posterity by the name *Grosseteste*, or Big-Head. After all, his student, the famous medieval scientist Roger Bacon, compared him to Solomon himself in his possession of wisdom, and his scientific savvy was so remarkable that he was popularly described as a magician.

Born to an obscure and poor family, Robert began lecturing at Oxford University in his forties, but mainly as a tutor to the students of the Franciscan order, which he admired and at one time contemplated joining. His reputation for brilliance led to his being named bishop of the Lincoln diocese, in which Oxford was located, allowing him to retain a close connection with the university throughout his life.

His appointment came at the height of the English Church-reform movement, whose figurehead, St. Thomas Becket, had been martyred five years before Robert's birth. Robert immediately announced a plan to visit every institution in his diocese, the largest in England, to eradicate corruption and vice. The main problem in England was simony, the buying and selling of Church offices (and the incomes that went with them), with the accompanying problems of pluralism—holding multiple offices simultaneously—and absenteeism, holding an office while living in a different region.

Robert sought to root these vices out of England and was even willing to criticize the bishop of Rome for collaborating with the practice. The popes had frequently increased their own revenues by appointing Italians to English offices abroad, drawing English money into Italian coffers. When the pope gave his own nephew a Church office in Robert's diocese, Robert visited Rome personally to complain.

But apart from his work of reform, Robert was best known to his contemporaries as a scientist. A polyglot (he knew Latin, Greek, and Hebrew), he wrote more than sixty treatises on scientific subjects. He prized mathematics over the other natural sciences because, as he pointed out and as all modern scientists acknowledge, mathematics is foundational for all others, which build upon its principles. It was Robert who pointed out the mathematical defects in the Julian calendar, helping point the way to the modern Gregorian calendar we use today.

He wrote on topics as diverse as animal breeding, estate management, and music, but his favorite topic was light, his study of which anticipated many of the developments in modern optics, physics, and astronomy. Though never formally canonized by Rome, Robert Grosseteste has long been regarded as a saint among English Christians, and the Anglican Communion venerates him as a saint today.

THE SCIENTIFIC METHOD

Drawing upon the philosopher Aristotle, Grosseteste formulated the proper method for scientific reasoning, what he called resolution and composition: repeatedly observing natural phenomena, generalizing from these particulars to a universal theory or law, then forming a hypothesis and seeking verification by repeated experimentation. The pioneers of the later scientific revolution would acknowledge their debt to Grosseteste's principles. (From Commentary on Aristotle's Posterior Analytics*)*

This, therefore, is how we arrive at simple universal statements from individual particulars through the help of the senses. In fact, beings like us whose minds are not purely spiritual can only acquire simple experimental universals through the medium of sense perception. For when our senses detect two observable events repeated a number of times, the one always associated with the other, it cannot at first readily detect the connection between the two. For example, let's say we see someone repeatedly eating a particular herb, and that person as a consequence repeatedly vomits up the contents of his stomach; the connection between the two events is not itself visible to the eye.

And yet the one who sees these things, drawing conclusions from the things he senses, begins to store them up in his memory, forging them together in a systematic way, then contemplating this system and wondering if it indeed explains the things he has seen. And seeking to confirm the relationship between these two things—his rational conclusions and his experimental observation—he seeks to administer that herb in different circumstances, in order to rule out the possibility of other causes, such as disease. But if he is able to remove all other possible causes, he can conclude that it is a universal principle that this herb leads to vomiting. And this is the path leading from the sensible observation of particular things to experimental universals.

HOW LIGHT AFFECTS SIGHT

From his study of rainbows (the treatise de Iride*) Grosseteste realized the ability of transparent mediums (such as drops of water) to refract light, causing magnification. He speculated how glass lenses might be lined up so as to enhance sight, laying the foundations for the invention of the telescope and microscope over four hundred years in the future.*

This part of optics, once it is perfectly understood, shows us the way that we can make the furthest things appear very close, and the tallest things appear very short, and the greatest things appear very small, so that we might be able to read small letters from an incredible distance, or to count grains of sand, grain, or grass, or any other miniscule thing. But even though these things astonish us, who wonder at them, we can see clearly how it is done. For a ray of light that is seen to penetrate through several different transparent mediums is fractured by them, and yet emerges at the angles of these transparent mediums joined together again.

HOW LIGHT AFFECTS MATTER

From his study of light and motion (his treatise de Motu Corporali et Luce)*, Grosseteste drew the surprising conclusion that the primary cause of physical motion is not matter but light. About seven hundred years later, many physicists would draw the same conclusion, using very similar reasoning, in connection with the big-bang theory.*

I claim, in fact, that the first *form* of bodies is the first *mover* of bodies. And this is *light*, which by itself multiplies and expands outward, setting in motion quantities of matter, being able to pass immediately through empty space, which is not so much motion as *change*. When light expands itself into different parts in this way, so as to incorporate matter, quantities of matter are caused to extend along with it; thus it causes the rarefaction of matter by increasing it. In this way, when light is joined together with quantities of matter, it can cause either compression or rarefaction.

Whenever light is emitted in one direction, it "drags" matter with it, causing physical motion. When light that is within matter emerges from it, and then light from outside matter enters within it, alternation is caused. And it should be clear, then, that the motion of bodies is caused by the increase of light, and this is a natural and bodily tendency.

ST. BONAVENTURE (1221–1274)

St. Bonaventure was a walking paradox, embodying a lifelong devotion to theological study while all the time lecturing his peers on the spiritual dangers of such study. Living at the height of the scholastic project of harmonizing faith and reason, Bonaventure would imitate his hero St. Francis by insisting that no one can embark upon such a project without an intense personal spiritual life of prayer, meditation, and active charity.

As a child he was saved from a near-fatal illness by the intercession of St. Francis, after which he eagerly entered the Franciscan order while still a teenager, perhaps in gratitude toward the man he referred to as his "blessed father." After showing intellectual promise, he was sent to the University of Paris to study under Alexander of Hales, who was striving to recruit pupils for a Franciscan theological school to rival the already-famous Dominicans.

He then taught in Paris until he was dismissed in 1256 along with all other friars. Jealous intellectuals had worked the public into outrage against the mendicants (beggars) who would not earn their own living decently like the more traditional monastics, but lived off the donations of others. Bonaventure's public defense of the mendicant way of life was so successful that the pope ordered the university to reinstate and promote the mendicants: St. Bonaventure and St. Thomas Aquinas were awarded their doctorates on the same day.

The next year, however, Bonaventure had to resign his academic position when he was elected head of the Franciscan order. The order was in chaos, split between so-called Spiritual Franciscans, who insisted on literal observance of absolute poverty with no exceptions, and the Relaxed Franciscans, who wanted to permit some commonly owned property in order to facilitate such tasks as academic study. Bonaventure negotiated a middle way between these groups, although rumor had it that he not only possessed a massive library of books, but also refused to let anyone borrow them!

Bonaventure struggled to keep up his writing during this period. He refused the archbishopric of York, but Pope Gregory X (whose election he had helped bring about—a tradition states that he threatened to lock the cardinals indoors until they agreed on a candidate!) finally convinced him to become a cardinal. When the papal envoys arrived with the cardinal's hat they found him washing dishes. He allegedly asked them to hang the hat on a tree until he could dry his hands. As cardinal, he helped secure a temporary union with the Greek Christians at the Ecumenical Council of Lyons in 1274 until he died during the proceedings, apparently poisoned, though the details remain mysterious.

He enjoyed veneration as a saint even during his lifetime. His teacher Alexander claimed that he had somehow escaped the curse of Adam's sin. Apparently, St. Thomas Aquinas once found Bonaventure in his cell writing a biography of St. Francis, but finding Bonaventure caught up in mystical rapture, he departed, saying, "Let us leave a saint to work for a saint." So great was his reputation among scholars that the arm and hand with which he wrote are the only relics of Bonaventure that have been preserved.

FRANCIS AS MODEL THEOLOGIAN

St. Bonaventure was, before all else, a Franciscan friar, who took St. Francis not only as his patron but also as a model of how to practice theology. Francis showed how theology was not exclusively an intellectual exercise: it was dependent on having a rightly ordered will, a holy relationship toward all of creation such as would replicate the state of man in the Garden of Eden. (From the Life of St. Francis*)*

True piety, which, according to the apostle, "is of value in every way" [1 Tm 4:8], had so penetrated the heart of Francis, and filled his whole being, that this man of God would seem to be entirely in its dominion. This piety, drawing himself upwards to God in devotion, transfiguring him into Christ in compassion, and inclining him to his neighbors through condescension, fashioned a universal connection toward all things, virtually recreating a state of innocence.

When he was drawn to all things through this piety, and in particular toward souls redeemed by the precious blood of Jesus Christ and yet contaminated by the stain of sin, with great compassion and tenderness he would weep bitterly, as a mother giving birth to Christ every day. And in particular he cared that God's ministers be given proper respect … and he wished that this be earned more by example than by word, more by cries of prayer than by prattling talk…. He said he preferred a simple and speechless brother whose good example inspired others to do good….

He rejoiced when he heard of holy friars traveling through the distant world proclaiming the Good News and bringing many to the path of truth. He blessed these friars as worthy of the most respect, who by word and work brought sinners to the love of Christ. Yet he turned angrily on those who brought disrespect to our religious state by their lives.

THE SPIRITUAL INTERPRETATION OF THE BIBLE

St. Bonaventure inherited the patristic tradition of seeing four levels (senses) of interpretation of the Bible: the literal, the allegorical, the moral, and the anagogical. But he connects the latter three spiritual senses firmly to the plain, literal, and historical meaning: unless one knows the literal well, one will fail at the spiritual! (From Breviloquium*)*

Now sacred Scripture has its own special procedure, and thus must be understood in its own way, and this we will seek to understand and set forth. Since a single word can veil multiple senses, the interpreter must strive to bring "the thing that is hidden … to light" (Jb 28:11) and must do this by means of other passages of Scripture. For example, one finds in the Psalms: "Take up shield and buckler, and rise for my help!" (Ps 35:2). We might suggest that the divine "buckler" is truth and a good will, and prove this by pointing to other passages of Scripture. For another passage says you cover the righteous "with favor as with a shield" (Ps 5:12), and another, "his faithfulness is a shield" (Ps 91:4).

One will not easily carry this out unless one has commended the Bible to memory by constant reading of the plain text; otherwise one will never be an excellent interpreter. Hence, just as those who disdain the basics of grammar, which governs all language, never learn the meaning of words or the construction of sentences, those who disdain the letter of sacred Scripture never penetrate to its spiritual understanding.

But the interpreter must be careful: not all passages are to be interpreted allegorically and mystically. For there are four senses of Scripture. The first is the literal, which deals with worldly things … such as the creation of the world.

The second is that which deals with the wanderings of the people of Israel, and by means of this signifies the future redemption of the human race.

The third is that by which the words signify and express the way we are saved through faith and morals.

The fourth is that by which the mystery of our salvation is expressed beforehand, in part through words, in part through obscure enigma. Thus all passages of Scripture should not be interpreted in the same, uniform way.

THE LOVE OF CHRIST AS THE KEY
TO THEOLOGICAL STUDY

Here, in The Mind's Road to God, *St. Bonaventure's indebtedness to Francis is very clear. One's ability to carry out theological study depends on one's ability to see all of nature as a reflection of God's beauty and goodness, and on one's purity and goodness of heart. This all comes home to Bonaventure as he recounts his insights into Francis' vision of the crucified Seraph while visiting the site at which it occurred.*

Therefore, following the example of the Blessed Father Francis, with panting spirit I sought this peace, I—a sinner—who has taken the place of the most Blessed Father himself as seventh Minister General after his passing, although entirely unworthy of it. It happened that, at the divine pleasure, about the thirty-third anniversary of the passing of Blessed Francis, I journeyed to Mount Alvernia, seeking a quiet place to find peace of spirit.

Arriving at that place I turned aside, and considering how the soul might arise to God I remembered that miracle which had happened to Blessed Francis in this same place, in the form of a vision of the winged Seraph in the likeness of the Crucified One. Reflecting on this steadily, it occurred to me that this vision showed not only the contemplative state achieved by our Father Francis, but also the path by which one might arise to such a state.

For in those six wings can be rightly understood six stages of illumination, by which the soul as if by certain steps or passages is disposed to pass over into peace through an ecstatic movement of Christian wisdom. The way is, however, none other but through the most ardent love of the Crucified One, just as Paul was caught up to the third heaven (see 2 Cor 12:2) only by being transfigured into Christ, as when he said, "I have been crucified with Christ; it is no longer I who live, but Christ who lives in me" (Gal 2:20). This was also the case with Francis, whose inner, spiritual state was manifested outwardly, since he carried in his own body the sacred passion of the Stigmata for two years before his death.

The six wings of the Seraph, therefore, depict the six stages of illumination, beginning with creatures and leading through them even to God himself, to whom no one rightly arises except through the Crucified. "He who does not enter the sheepfold by the door but climbs in by another way, that man is a thief and a robber" (Jn 10:1). If anyone goes through *this* door, "he will go in and out and find pasture" (Jn 10:9).

Because of this, John says in the Apocalypse: "Blessed are those who wash their robes [in the blood of the Lamb], that they may have the right to the tree of life and that they may enter the city by the gates" (Rv 22:14); as if to say that through contemplation one cannot step into the heavenly Jerusalem and arrive there except by the blood of the Lamb as through a gate.

That is, one may not be disposed to the contemplation of divine things, which lead to spiritual ecstasy, unless like Daniel one be a man of profound desire. Moreover, desire is inflamed in us in two ways, first, through loud cries of prayer, uttered through a groaning heart, and, second, by the radiance of contemplation, by which the soul moves directly to the divine light.

Therefore I invite the reader to cry in prayer to Christ crucified, through whose Blood we are purged from the filth of vice, lest at any time he believe that it is enough to read without anointing, to speculate without devotion, to investigate without wonder, to ponder without exultation, to labor without piety, to inquire without charity, to understand without humility, to study apart from divine grace, to speculate without divinely given wisdom.

Led beforehand, therefore, by divine grace, to the humble and pious, the repentant and the devout, those anointed with the oil of gladness, the lovers of divine wisdom and those inflamed with desire, free from the desire to be praised, wondering and thirsting after God, I propose the following considerations, suggesting that little to nothing will be seen in the external mirror, unless the internal mirror of our soul has been wiped and polished.

Therefore, O man of God, in the first place let the sting of your conscience bite you again before you raise your eyes toward the rays of wisdom glittering in His mirrors, lest by chance the sight itself of His radiance causes you to fall more deeply into the pit of shadows.

DEFENSE OF THE FRANCISCAN MOVEMENT

St. Bonaventure, as head of the Franciscan order, was called upon to defend the reputation of the order. More traditional monastics disliked the mendicants (beggars) because, unlike more traditional

monks (for example, the Benedictines), they did not support them-
selves by working with their own hands. Rather, like freeloaders
they depended on the generosity of others. In St. Bonaventure's Defense of the Mendicant*s, he argues that this was not only perfectly*
fitting, but also necessary for their task.

However, so that the road of errors may be closed, one must respond to the apparent scoffing of a critic, who strives to attack the
life of mendicants precisely in the most important part of their
work, namely, because of their lack of manual labor, the lack of
holding goods in common, and their begging for alms.

Now from that which the apostle commanded certain of
the Thessalonians, "to do their work in quietness and to earn
their own living" (2 Thes 3:12), and the fact that mendicants do
not work with their own hands, these reasons are pressed into
convicting them of idleness of life and violation of the apostolic
mandate. To this we, on the contrary, give answer that, as is clear
from the text, the apostle does not command all in general to
take on manual labor—as though all of them who do not do this
kind of labor were in a state of damnation, among whom would
be included the critic himself—but only those who were idle,
meddlesome, and restless; these he orders to live by the work of
their hands, lest they gain a living by their fawning flattery and
filthy gain, with the loss of salvation and a hindrance to the salvation of others.

The fact is, this sort of mendicant focuses on the saving of
souls, both their own and their neighbor's, using the sevenfold
activity prophetically expressed—that is, reading, meditating,
praying, contemplating, hearing, synthesizing, and proclaiming—which they are unable to attain without the aid of the Scriptures. And because they cannot gain a clear understanding of the
Scriptures except through careful study, this sevenfold activity
belongs properly to those who have adequate diligence.

And the difficulty of this study requires the attention of
the whole man, just as it is spelled out in Exodus, where the Lord
commanded that the poles which were used for supporting the

Ark would perpetually remain in place in its rings (see Ex 25:12–15)—on which St. Gregory explains, "Those who execute the office of preaching should never be withdrawn from the study of the sacred text … for it would be disgraceful for them to have to go learn the answer when questioned, when they should already be prepared to answer any question" [*Pastoral Rule* 2, 11].

Therefore, that some devote themselves entirely and diligently to this sevenfold activity, which is so sublime in itself, and yet so mentally taxing, is expedient and necessary for the people of the Church. Thus even if they do not labor with their hands, yet they are nonetheless worthy of support from the Church, according to the saying of Deuteronomy, "You shall not muzzle an ox when it treads out the grain" (Dt 25:4).

On this, the gloss says, "You shall not withdraw support from the preacher, so that he may give himself to prayer and preaching." And elsewhere the gloss says, "Those occupied with teaching are not able to provide for themselves." From this it is plainly evident that diligent study of wisdom, combined with the difficult labor of preaching, should be fully supported by the Church.

ST. THOMAS AQUINAS
(1225–1274)

Despite suffering an untimely death before he turned fifty, Aquinas managed to write more than sixty books (some, like the *Summa Theologica*, run over three thousand pages in length), often dictating to multiple scribes simultaneously. Yet he refused to finish his greatest book, renouncing all further writing in his later years because he thought it worthless—"straw," in his words—in comparison to the mystical experiences he had begun having in the chapel. Such was the enigma of St. Thomas.

Born to one of the noblest families in Italy, Thomas was trained by the best and brightest of his day at St. Benedict's own abbey school in Monte Cassino. His parents had groomed him to become abbot of the same wealthy monastery, but were shocked when this young scion announced his intention to join the Dominicans, the wandering beggars who often lived on the streets while preaching.

To save the family's honor, his brothers imprisoned him in a castle for a full year, even sending in a prostitute in the hope of giving him second thoughts about celibacy, but he chased her off with a hot poker and eventually managed a midnight escape through a window, at which point the pope utterly forbade his family to interfere with young Thomas' vocation.

The Dominicans fortunately realized Thomas' intellectual potential and sent him to Cologne to study under their great master, St. Albert the Great. After receiving his degree, Thomas taught for several decades in Cologne and Paris, until he was sent to help negotiate a theological agreement with the Greek bishops at the Second Council of Lyons in 1274. Riding a donkey to the council, he was struck by a falling tree branch and died from the injury.

Christendom certainly never knew a keener intellect. The *Summa Theologica*, which he dismissively introduces as "simple instruction for beginners," is undisputedly the most profound theological work ever written. St. Thomas was not only reportedly able to understand and remember everything he had ever read, but his most characteristic trait was his willingness to seek truth wherever it was found, no matter what the source. His *Summa* quotes pagan, Jewish, and Muslim philosophers nearly as often as it quotes Christians.

His goal was to collect all human knowledge and construct a grand synthesis with divine revelation, so as to integrate faith and reason to the utmost degree. His optimistic view of reason troubled some contemporaries, who thought he may have understated the effects of original sin, but Thomas' worldview assumed a very positive view of the created world itself: grace does not destroy or replace nature, he insisted—rather, it elevates and perfects it.

Though deeply controversial in his own day—only three years after Thomas' death, the bishop of Paris condemned several of his ideas—history would vindicate his views. Just three centuries later, when the Catholic bishops met at the Council of Trent to respond to the challenge of Protestantism, St. Thomas' *Summa* was placed on the high altar alongside the Bible during the opening Mass. Even later, Pope Leo XIII would name him "universal doctor" and make him the patron of all Catholic schools and universities.

ON FAITH AND REASON
(from the *Summa contra Gentiles*)

The truths about God that we believe fall into two categories. Some truths about God are entirely beyond the power of human reason—for example, that God is a Trinity. Other truths, however, are within the grasp of human reason—for example, that God exists and is one—and some philosophers have even proved these things using the light of human reason alone.

That there are truths about God which are entirely beyond the scope of human reason should be obvious…. The human mind does not have the power to reach the divine nature, since in the conditions of our present life our mind's power to understand begins with sense data, and objects that are not themselves sensed cannot be grasped by our mind unless it can gather some knowledge about them through the senses. But sense data cannot lead our mind to an understanding of the divine nature itself, since sensible things are so inferior to that which caused them. Nevertheless, our mind can still be led to *some* knowledge about God—for example, that he exists and some of the attributes He must have in order to be the First Cause of all things….

But if truths of this nature were left *solely* to human reason, three disadvantages would follow. First, only a few people would possess knowledge of God. For it takes extensive study to discover truth, and many are not up to this. Some are prevented by being constitutionally unfit, not being the type of people who acquire knowledge easily. These could never study enough to arrive at the highest levels of human knowledge, that is, the knowledge of God.

Others are prevented by the pressures of business and management of property, for there must always be some people who pay attention to these temporal affairs, and these could not possibly devote enough time in the scholarly pursuit of speculation to arrive at the highest levels of knowledge, that is, the knowledge of God. Others are prevented by laziness.

The knowledge of the truths that reason can discover about God requires a great deal of prior knowledge—indeed, almost the entire field of philosophical knowledge…. Therefore, it takes a great deal of work to arrive at these truths, and few are willing to undergo this for sheer love of knowledge.

A second disadvantage is that the few who *did* arrive at the knowledge of these truths would take a long time to do it, because these truths are so profound and have so many prerequisites to the study. And in youth and young adulthood, the soul is tossed around on the waves of passion, and not fit for the study of high truths: as the Philosopher [Aristotle] says, only in mature age does the soul become prudent and scientific. Thus if the only way to know about God were the power of reason, the human race would live in thick darkness of ignorance, since the knowledge of God (the best way people can become good and perfect) would belong only to a few, and to those few only after a great length of time.

A third disadvantage is that, due to the weakness of our judgment and the disturbances of our imagination, most of the investigations of our human reason contain some mixture of error. This would be a good reason for many to remain doubtful about even the most accurate demonstrations, misconstruing the force of a demonstration and seeing how so many supposedly wise people have so many different opinions. Besides, even in the midst of many proven truths there is sometimes an element of error, not demonstrated but asserted on the strength of some plausible and arcane reasoning that is wrongly taken for a demonstration.

Therefore, it was in fact necessary for the truth of divine things to be presented to the human race with a fixed certainty by way of faith. The arrangement of the divine mercy is very beneficial, therefore, since even the things which reason *can* investigate are still available for us to accept by faith, so that *all* people might *easily*, and *without doubt or error*, come to the knowledge of God....

Now, the things our reason discovers to be true must certainly be true. In fact, it is impossible to think false what my reason tells me is true. Yet it is also impossible to hold that the things we believe by faith are false, since they are clearly confirmed by God. Therefore, since only falsehood is opposed to truth, it is therefore impossible for the truths of faith to be contrary to the truths known by natural reason....

Therefore, the conclusion is obvious, that any arguments advanced against the teachings of our faith must not proceed logically from the first principles of nature, principles we already know to be true, and so do not amount to a true demonstration. They must be either probable or misleading, and there will always be a way to refute them....

In sum, there are two categories of divine truths for the wise person to study: one set that can be discovered by rational investigation, and another that is beyond all the power of reason.... To put forward the first set of truths we must proceed by demonstrative reasons that may convince our opponent. But because these reasons are not available for the second set of truths, we should not try to convince our opponent by argument, but rather should simply refute his arguments against the truth. We should be confident that this can be done, since natural reason cannot be contrary to the truth of faith....

There are, however, some *probable* arguments available to be put forward in defense of this second set of truths, to exercise the minds of believers and encourage them, but these should not be used to convince opponents. If we try to use them, we will simply strengthen them in their error, since they will conclude that we believe these truths on the basis of such weak arguments.

DOES GOD EXIST?

This extract from St. Thomas' masterpiece, the Summa Theologica, *illustrates the scholastic method: asking a question, advancing the best arguments on both sides, and attempting to reconcile them on the basis of both reason and revelation.*

Objection 1. It seems that God does not exist, because if there were two opposites and one of them were infinite, the other would be entirely destroyed. But by definition "God" is infinite goodness. If, therefore, God existed, we would not be able to discover any evil. But there is obviously evil in the world. Therefore God does not exist….

On the contrary, God himself says, "I AM WHO I AM" (Ex 3:14). I answer that, God's existence can be proven in five ways.

The first and clearest way is the argument from motion. It is certain and clear to our senses that in the world some things are in motion. Now whatever is in motion is put in motion by something else, for nothing can be in motion unless it is *potentially* that to which it is in motion, and a thing is in motion inasmuch as such potential is *actualized*, for motion is nothing else than the reduction of something from *potentiality* to *actuality*.

But nothing can be reduced from potentiality to actuality except by something already in a state of actuality. For example, only something *actually* hot (fire) makes something *potentially* hot (wood) actually hot, by moving and changing it. Now it is impossible for the same thing to be simultaneously both actual and potential in respect to the same thing, but only in respect to different things. For what is actually hot cannot simultaneously be potentially hot—rather, it is potentially cold. It is therefore impossible that a thing can simultaneously be both *mover* and *moved* in respect to the same thing, that is, that it should move itself.

Therefore, whatever is in motion must be put in motion by something else. If what puts it in motion is *itself* in motion, then this thing must also be put in motion by something else, and that by something else again. But this cannot go on into infinity, or else there would be no first mover, and if there is no first mover there would be no other movers, since other movers would move only if they were put in motion by the first mover. For example, a staff moves only because it is put in motion by the hand. Therefore it is necessary that there be a first mover, put in motion by nothing else, and this is what we understand to be God.

The second way is from the nature of the efficient cause. In the sensible world we find there is an order of efficient causes. There is no case known (indeed, it would be impossible) in which a thing is found to be its own efficient cause, for to be such it would have to be prior to itself, which is impossible. Now in efficient causes it is not possible to go on to infinity, because whenever causes follow one another in order, the first is the cause of the intermediate cause, and the intermediate is the cause of the last cause, no matter how many intermediate causes there are.

Now if the cause is removed, so is the effect. Therefore, if there were no first cause, there will be no last cause, nor any intermediate causes. And if it were possible to go on to infinity, there would never have been a first efficient cause, nor any last effect, nor any intermediate causes, all of which is plainly false. Therefore it is necessary that there be a first efficient cause, and this is what we understand to be God.

The third way is from possibility and necessity. We find in nature things that are possible to exist and possible not to exist, since they are found to begin and to end, and therefore can exist and not exist. But it is impossible for these always to exist, for whatever is possible not to exist at some time ceases to exist.

Therefore, if everything is possible not to exist, then at one time there would have been nothing in existence. Now, if this were true, nothing would exist now, because things are only brought into existence by things already in existence.

Therefore, if at one time nothing existed, it would have been impossible for anything else to come into existence, and thus even now nothing would exist—which is absurd. Therefore, it must be true that not everything that exists is able not to exist: some being must exist *necessarily* ... and this is what we understand to be God.

The fourth way is from the comparison to be found in things. Among things there are some things more and others less good, true, noble, and so on. But "more" and "less" are said of different things only to the extent that they are closer or further from some maximum. For example, one thing is hotter than another to the extent that it is closer to that which is hottest. So there must be something which is truest, best, noblest, and, ultimately, something which is the uttermost being....

Now the maximum in any category is the cause of all in that category, as fire (the maximum of heat) is the cause of all hotness in other things. Therefore, there must also be something that is the cause of the being, goodness, and every other perfection which is found in all things, and this is what we understand to be God.

The fifth way is from the governance of the world. We see that unintelligent things, such as natural bodies, act as though pursuing some goal. This is clear because they always (or nearly always) act in the same way, so as to obtain the best possible result. Therefore it is clear that they achieve this goal not by accident, but by design.

Now an unintelligent thing cannot move toward a goal unless it is directed toward it by something intelligent, as an arrow is shot toward its target by an archer. Therefore some intelligent being must exist which directs all natural things toward their goal, and this is what we understand to be God.

Reply to Objection 1. As Augustine says (*Enchiridion* xi): "Since God is the highest good, He would not allow any evil to exist in His works, *unless* His omnipotence and goodness were able to bring good even out of evil." This is part of the infinite goodness of God, that He should allow evil to exist, and out of it produce good.

HYMN FOR THE FEAST OF THE BODY AND BLOOD OF CHRIST

St. Thomas was commissioned by the pope to write a liturgy for this Eucharistic feast. One of his hymns, often known by the Latin title "Pange Lingua Gloriosi," is still well-known today.

> Sing, my tongue, the Savior's glory,
> Of His Flesh, the mystery sing;
> Of the Blood, all price exceeding,
> Shed by our Immortal King,
>
> Destined, for the world's redemption,
> From a noble Womb to spring.
> Of a pure and spotless Virgin
> Born for us on earth below,
> He, as Man, with man conversing,
> Stayed, the seeds of truth to sow;
> Then He closed in solemn order
> Wondrously His Life of woe.
>
> On the night of that Last Supper,
> Seated with His chosen band,
> He, the Paschal Victim eating,
> First fulfils the Law's command;
>
> Then as Food to all his brethren
> Gives Himself with His own Hand.
> Word-made-Flesh, the bread of nature
> By His Word to Flesh He turns;

Wine into His Blood He changes:
What though sense no change discerns.
Only be the heart in earnest,
Faith her lesson quickly learns.

Down in adoration falling,
Lo, the sacred Host we hail,
Lo, o'er ancient forms departing
Newer rites of grace prevail:

Faith for all defects supplying,
When the feeble senses fail.
To the Everlasting Father
And the Son who comes on high

With the Holy Ghost proceeding
Forth from each eternally,
Be salvation, honor, blessing,
Might and endless majesty.

Amen. Alleluia.

MEDIEVAL EASTERN CHRISTIANS

❧❧❧❧❧❧❧❧

A survey of medieval Christianity would be incomplete if it treated only Western Europe, ignoring the thriving churches that existed in the East during this period, especially because Christianity *began* in the East and only later spread to the West. "Eastern" Christianity generally refers to the churches that developed in Eastern Europe, the Balkans, and the Middle East, including Egypt. Christianity had also spread well into Africa, India, and the Far East during this time, but these churches had so little contact with the West that they will not be considered here.

The term *medieval* does not really apply to any of these regions outside Western Europe, since the events which mark the beginning and end of the Middle Ages—the collapse of the Latin Roman Empire, on the one hand, and the Renaissance and Reformation on the other—did not affect the East. But due to the frequent and fruitful interactions between East and West during the period in question, we should not omit at least a brief consideration of medieval Eastern Christianity.

In the early Church, the period of the Fathers, there was no clear distinction between East and West. Both shared a common literary and intellectual culture (inherited from Greece) and a shared political identity (the Roman Empire). More importantly, both shared a common commitment to the sources of the Christian faith: the Scriptures, the apostolic tradition, and the Church Fathers. While regional churches generally functioned autonomously in most matters, all Christians looked to the Church of Rome as a source of unity and purity of doctrine. Christians of all regions read one another's theological writings, venerated one another's saints, and shared communion with one another's bishops. This sense of being one family in Christ lasted well into the height of the medieval period.

The later separation of Eastern and Western Christianity, however, grew out of tensions that were evident even at a very early stage. While a common language, Greek, was shared in the first two centuries, by the third century Latin had replaced Greek in the West, which created a split in literary culture despite feverish translation attempts on both sides. The Western half of the empire collapsed under the weight of barbarian invasions in the fifth century, carved up into kingdoms ruled by immigrants who did not share Greco-Roman culture. The Eastern half of the Empire, with its base in Constantinople (Byzantium), however, continued to thrive, carrying on Greco-Roman culture for another millennium.

In relative isolation from the Church of Rome, the Byzantine emperor expanded his personal sway over the Church in the East in a way that alarmed Westerners. Meanwhile, in the absence of a strong Roman emperor in the West, the bishop of Rome expanded his jurisdiction over other churches, and even over political matters, in a way that went significantly beyond early precedents and naturally alarmed Easterners. Other theological disagreements flared up as well—over the role of the Holy Spirit in the Trinity, over the proper celebration of the Eucharist, over priestly celibacy, over the role of icons in religious worship, and more. And while most of these differences were rather subtle, they did have a cumulative effect, with each side growing more and more suspicious of the other's orthodoxy.

The fateful year of 1054 saw these tensions explode, and after a bitter exchange the bishops of Rome and Constantinople excommunicated each other, an event usually referred to as the Great Schism. But like any family feud, as time passed, some sense of friendly relations was restored, and Eastern and Western Christians continued to recognize one another as brothers and sisters in Christ. Theologians in the East and West continued to read one another's works, and feasts were celebrated in honor of one another's saints. Two ecumenical councils (Lyons II in 1274 and Florence in 1438) brought temporary reconciliations, but not lasting reunion.

Sadly, such a reunion has proven elusive in the modern period as well, although positive signs continue to appear, including the lifting of the mutual excommunications in 1965. Pope St. John Paul II famously asked the Church to "breathe with both lungs," so to speak, by overcoming the divisions between our two traditions. Perhaps a brief survey of Eastern medieval saints can help.

JUSTINIAN (483–565)

It may be difficult for Westerners to understand the appeal that Justinian—or St. Justinian the Great, as he is known in the East—has for Eastern Christians. The ideal of an anointed king like David or Solomon, whose personal piety shapes his rule, continued unchallenged in the East long after it had faded in the West. Perhaps this was furthered by the Greek, Platonic notion that earth should be a mirror image of heaven, so that God's (or Christ's) rule in heaven should find a parallel here below. The West, for its part, always harbored a lingering suspicion of tyranny and despotism, exacerbated by its experience of emperors and kings who used their "anointed" status to claim power even over the Church.

But this suspicion was more latent in the Greek East, and it may be that no ruler in history has better fitted the ideal of a Christian king than the great Justinian. The nephew of the previous emperor, Justinian rose to power while still in his thirties, filled with dreams of the ancient glory of the Roman Empire over which he now ruled. Yet in Justinian's day the empire was in tatters. The entire Western half (including Rome itself), had been lost, parceled into hundreds of barbarian kingdoms; the once-legendary Roman law was decrepit and unenforced, and the Christian Church that lay at its heart was threatened with schism.

Even today, Justinian's accomplishments baffle the intellect. In his reign of less than forty years, Justinian was able to reconquer much of the Western regions—Italy, North Africa, and much of Spain—ruling over a Roman Empire nearly as large as it had ever been in the past. He presided personally over a systematic rewriting of Roman law, producing a code of law (the *Corpus Juris Civilis*) so comprehensive in scope that it is still used by many nations today. His massive building projects were compared to those of Solomon and included the great Church of Hagia Sophia in Constantinople, one of the finest churches ever built in Christendom.

Perhaps most impressive of all, Justinian was able to steer the Church through the devastating Monophysite controversy, a heresy that combined Christ's divine and human natures into one, hybrid nature. He negotiated a compromise that kept the bulk of the Egyptian and Syrian bishops loyal to patristic tradition, and also in communion with the Roman Church in the West. In sum, Justinian seemed the perfect model of the Christian Roman emperor, reviving the glories of Rome in a day when they seemed a forgotten memory.

Even so, Christians in the Latin West remained, then as now, disturbed by some aspects of Justinian's legacy. After all, part of the Roman Imperial legacy was the alarming tradition of emperors claiming sovereignty over religious matters, and Justinian, like Constantine before him, considered himself both "priest and king," the head of Church as well as state. Alongside his civil-law code, Justinian promulgated a law code for the Church, envisioning himself as the supreme authority to which all bishops and councils must report. And the results were not always beneficial: Westerners complained that Justinian, under the influence of his Monophysite wife, Theodora, made far too many doctrinal concessions to the Monophysite bishops.

In fact, from a Latin point of view, Eastern emperors like Justinian seemed to claim powers Latin Christians ascribed to the pope; hence the derogatory term Caesaropapism, with Caesar playing the role of pope. In any case, even granting the validity of these concerns, no one can cast doubt upon the genuine accomplishments of this greatest of Roman emperors. Although not regarded as a saint in the West, Justinian has always had this honor in the East.

ON JUSTINIAN'S BUILDING PROJECTS

Our major source for Justinian's life is Procopius, one of the greatest historians of the period, who served as a legal advisor in Justinian's court and accompanied his armies on campaigns. In this selection from his On Buildings, *Procopius tells of Justinian's architectural accomplishments, especially the Church of Hagia Sophia (Holy Wisdom) in Constantinople. The Church survives today, converted into a Muslim mosque in the Turkish city of Istanbul.*

In our own age has been born the Emperor Justinian who, taking over the government when it was harassed by disorder, has not only made it greater in size, but also much more glorious. He did so by expelling the barbarians who had pressed hard upon it for a long time…. He has already added to the Roman Empire many regions that belonged to others in his own times, and has created countless cities that did not exist before. And finding that, up to his own time, religious belief was straying into errors and splintering in many directions, he cut off the paths leading into errors and ensured that it stood on the firm foundation of a united faith.

Also, having found that the laws were confusing, far more numerous than they should have been, and in disagreement with one another, he improved them by sorting out the confusion of words and smoothing out their disagreements. He also, of his own free will, dismissed the charges against those who tried to plot against him, he gave abundant wealth to the poor, and he plundered the wealth of their oppressors, bringing the entire nation to a prosperous condition. Even further, he strengthened the Roman Empire, which was highly vulnerable to barbarian attacks, with a great number of soldiers and built a long wall of strongholds along its frontiers.

However, I have already described most of the emperor's other achievements in other writings, so at present I will focus only on the benefits he brought as a builder. Many people say that the greatest king in history was the Persian Cyrus, who was chiefly responsible for founding the kingdom of Persia…. But in comparison with Justinian, the king of our times (and he did not only inherit the office of king, but it belonged by him by nature, since he was "gentle as a father," as Homer says), Cyrus' rule was mere child's play. The proof of this is that the Roman Empire, as I have said, has doubled in area and in power, while on the other hand, those who plotted against him and plotted his assassination are still alive, possessing their own property, serving as Roman generals, and even holding the same consular rank they once had, even though their guilt was proven with utter certainty.

But now we must proceed, as I have said, to the subject of the emperor's buildings, so that those who see them in the future will not be led astray by their great number and incredible size into thinking they are the works of many men—they will acknowledge them as the work of but one man….

Some of the commoners, the rabble of the city, once rose up against the Emperor Justinian in Byzantium in a rising that we call the Nika Revolt, which I have described in full detail in my book on the Wars. And to show that they revolted not only against the emperor, but also against God himself, the unholy wretches had the audacity to set fire to the Christian Church which the Byzantines call *Hagia Sophia* [Greek for "Holy Wisdom"]. "Wisdom" is their term for God, and they consider this His temple. And God permitted them to carry out this impious thing, foreseeing that this shrine would thereby be transformed into a much more beautiful one. So at that time the whole church became a charred ruin.

But the Emperor Justinian soon built a church so exquisitely shaped that if anyone had asked the Christians before the fire if they would like their church destroyed and one like this to take its place (showing them, perhaps, a model of the building we now see), they would have prayed for their church to be destroyed that very night, that they might witness its conversion into the new building. At any rate, the emperor, disregarding all questions of expense, eagerly pressed to begin the work of construction, and began to gather all the architects from the whole world … and he was able to select the most suitable men for this most important of his projects.

So the church has become a spectacle of marvelous beauty, overwhelming to those who see it, and altogether unbelievable to those who know it only by hearsay. For it soars to a height to rival the sky itself, and as if surging up from among the other buildings it stands on high and looks down upon the remainder of the city. All the while it dominates the whole city, while it towers to such a height that the whole city is viewed from there as from a watchtower. Both its breadth and its length have been so carefully proportioned that it can be said to be both exceedingly long and unusually broad, and it exults in an indescribable beauty.

For it proudly reveals its mass and the harmony of its proportions, having neither excess nor deficiency. It is both more ambitious than the buildings we are used to and considerably nobler than those that are merely large, and it abounds exceedingly in sunlight as the sun's rays reflect from its marble. Indeed, you might even say that its interior is illuminated not from outside, by the sun, but that the radiance shines out from within it, such an abundance of light bathes this shrine.

ON THE IMPORTANCE OF ROMAN LAW

This selection is from the preface to Justinian's collection of law codes (the Digest*), in which he gives his legal scholars their marching orders as they embark on the project of updating Roman legislation. Note especially his sense that God is the author and enforcer of law.*

Under the authority of God, whose heavenly majesty delivered it to me, I govern this empire, carry out its wars with success, adorn it with peace, perfect the framework of its government, and lift up the minds of its citizens to the contemplation of God. For we do not put our trust in weapons or soldiers, nor in generals or strategy, but we rest all our hopes in the guidance of the Supreme Trinity alone, from whom the whole universe has proceeded and by whom this entire world is governed.

Nothing is so worthy of respect as the authority of law, which makes all things—both divine and human—run smoothly, and expels iniquity. Yet I have found that the whole collection of our laws, which come to us from the days of Romulus and the foundation of the city of Rome, to be in such a state of confusion that they are infinitely long and are beyond the capacity of anyone to understand. Therefore, my first desire was to begin with the legislation of the earliest emperors, to update their laws and put them in a clear order, so they might be collected in one book, with all superfluous repetition and internal contradictions removed, and so all mankind might benefit from their clarity.

Now this has been done, and all laws are collected into one volume under my own name—since I put aside all insignificant and unimportant matters and made the full updating of the law a priority. All of Roman jurisprudence has been amended, rearranged, and presented in one volume, including all the scattered books of numerous authors. This is something no one even dared to hope for or to desire, and initially this task appeared to me to be impossibly difficult. We all lifted our hands to heaven, however, and prayed for divine aid. In this way we embraced this project in our minds, trusting in God, who is able in the magnitude of His goodness to grant and to complete even things which seem utterly desperate....

There is another thing of which we want you to make a priority. If you find anything in the old books which is not well written, anything superfluous or lacking in clarity, you should get rid of unnecessary verbosity, fix up what is lacking, and present the whole work in a fitting form and with an attractive appearance. You should at the same time further observe this: If you find anything expressed incorrectly in the ancient laws and regulations which the older writers cite in their books, you should fix it and put it in its correct form, so that whatever is selected and written by you will be seen as genuine, as the best version, and will be treated with the authority of the original, so that no one will refer to the ancient text and argue that your version is faulty.

Also, considering that by an ancient law, the so-called *Lex Regia*, all legal authority and power vested in the Roman people was transferred to the emperor himself, no authority lies in this or that particular source, but from my own legislative power. So how can antiquity interfere with my legislation?...

It is indeed a wonderful achievement that Roman jurisprudence from the time of the building of the city to my own rule, a period reaching nearly to a thousand and four hundred years, and shaken with civil war and confusion in Imperial legislation, has been collected nevertheless into one harmonious system. And this collection is without contradiction or repetition, and no two sets of laws deal with the same question. This is indeed impossible for mortal man, and must be attributed to heavenly Providence.

Therefore, having fixed our eyes on the aid of Immortality, we call upon the Supreme Deity, desiring that God himself be the author and guardian of the whole work…. We also rely on the heavenly Divinity to amend and correct anything that might be deficient within it.

JUSTINIAN'S REFORM OF CHURCH PRACTICE

As noted previously, Justinian saw himself as the guardian of the Church as well as of the state. For this reason he took legal measures to correct abuses in Christian liturgy and discipline. Note especially how he envisions his own role in this process. (From "Novel 137" in Civil Laws*)*

For the common good, I have taken measures to make more effective the civil laws, the enforcement of which God, due to His good will toward men, has entrusted to me. How much more reason, then, do I have for enforcing the sacred and divine laws that have been promulgated for the salvation of our souls? For those who observe these sacred laws become worthy of the assistance of our Lord God, while those who disobey them are liable to be punished by Him.

Therefore, the bishops whose job it is to enforce these laws are liable to severe penalties when they allow violations of these laws to remain unpunished. And, in fact, the sacred laws have not been strictly observed up until this time, and I have received several complaints about priests, monks, and even bishops, suggesting that they are not living in agreement with the divine laws. Indeed, there are some who do not even know how to say the Divine Liturgy or the ceremony of baptism, or do not perform them properly.

Therefore, granting the authority of the sacred laws, I promulgate this specific law, decreeing that any time a bishop must be consecrated in a city, the clergy and chief citizens of that city shall assemble together. They shall then, by proclamation, nominate three persons who will make an oath on the holy Gospels in agreement with the Scriptures. This oath, inserted in the proclamation, shall be worded as follows: that they did not select these three persons who were nominated due to any gifts or promises made to them, or through personal friendship or any kind of affection, but only because they knew these candidates they have chosen were steadfast in the Catholic faith and of honorable life, over thirty years of age and without wives, concubines, or children of any sort….

And the law requires that synods or councils of bishops should be held in every province. Since this is not happening it is the first thing that should be remedied…. I order that one synod shall assemble in each province in June or September…. I intend that ecclesiastical questions having reference to doctrine, to Church law, or the administration of Church property … and all matters in need of correction, should be debated and examined at each synod, and all abuses to be corrected in accordance with my laws and sacred regulations.

I order that all bishops and priests repeat the Divine Liturgy and prayers, when baptism is performed, not in an undertone but in a loud voice that can be heard by the faithful so that the minds of the listeners may be raised to greater devotion and a higher appreciation of the praises and blessings of God…. We notify all churchmen that if they violate any of these provisions, they must give an account of their conduct on that terrible day of our Lord and Savior Jesus Christ, and that if I am informed of any of these matters I will not disregard them or leave them unpunished.

I also order that if the governors of the provinces see that any of my regulations are not observed, they should first make sure the archbishops and other bishops call a synod and do what we have said. But if the bishops do not immediately obey, the governors should notify me of this fact so that I may promptly punish those who refuse to call these synods.

PSEUDO-DIONYSIUS THE AREOPAGITE (LATE FIFTH CENTURY)

It might be cynical to say that no one would be reading pseudo-Dionysius today if he hadn't lied about who he was, but that would be to misunderstand the way ideas were communicated in ancient and medieval cultures.

The *real* Dionysius was a Greek convert taught by St. Paul in Athens, who is mentioned in a single line of the New Testament (Acts 17:34) and then disappears from history. Disappears, that is, for nearly six hundred years, until several massive theological books showed up in Syria, whose author claimed to be the very same Dionysius! The Christian world quivered with excitement over such a discovery. After all, writings by a disciple of St. Paul were virtually the equivalent of the Bible itself, and everyone agreed that the theological and spiritual quality of the books was exquisite. Every Christian thinker raced to incorporate Dionysius' insights into his work; the great St. Thomas Aquinas quotes him seventeen hundred times, and his works reshaped the way Christians practiced theology.

Unfortunately, it was too good to be true, and in the fifteenth century the Italian scholar Lorenzo Valla exposed the books as a forgery, proving that the author clearly draws upon theological sources written centuries after the real Dionysius died. Modern scholarship still has not identified the real author—from that point onward known as pseudo-Dionysius, or "false Dionysius"—but has zeroed in on late fifth-century Syria as the point of origin.

But this does not mean that pseudo-Dionysius, the author of these treatises, is to be ignored as a Christian writer. Plagiarism, after all, is a modern concept. In the ancient and medieval worlds, pseudonymity, or writing under the name of a past author, was a common way of honoring that author, a sort of homage. Pseudo-Dionysius probably saw himself as carrying on the legacy of the real Dionysius, as trying to articulate what he *would* have written were he alive in the fifth century. And besides, as mentioned already, pseudo-Dionysius is a brilliant theologian in his own right, a fact no one disputes. Scholars such as Aquinas did not quote pseudo-Dionysius only because of his name; they quoted him because he was authentically and skillfully communicating the Christian theological and spiritual tradition.

The four books and ten letters left by pseudo-Dionysius possess their own unique character, however. They chart a cosmology where all things in creation emerge from the One Creator and are drawn back to Him in love, sort of a cosmic circle of grace. Pseudo-Dionysius places a strong emphasis on the otherness of God, who remains utterly distinct and separate from His creation, infinitely greater than all created things that no intellect can truly know Him.

In their desire to know God, humans tend to overuse their imaginations, picturing God in terms of created things and attributing to Him qualities such as passions, limitations, and a capacity for change. While this tendency is natural for the spiritually immature, it must be resisted by the spiritually advanced, as it can easily slip into idolatry, which drags God down into His creation.

While pseudo-Dionysius acknowledges the value of "positive theology"—that is, affirming positive statements that are true about God, such as "God is good," he strongly prefers "negative theology"—that is, negative statements that deny things of

God—for example, "God is not limited." In this way, like a sculptor chipping away at a block of stone, he reveals God's true nature by removing what does not belong to Him.

Some have complained that pseudo-Dionysius overemphasizes the unknowability of God, making Him dwell in absolute darkness. Yet for pseudo-Dionysius it is precisely this darkness that reveals the true nature of the Christian God, shining brilliantly in the true Light of Jesus Christ.

THE MYSTICAL THEOLOGY

This letter from Dionysius, addressed to St. Paul's co-worker St. Timothy, reveals pseudo-Dionysius' pattern of negative theology; it is included in the collection titled The Mystical Theology.

Mystical theology is like the ladder set up on earth whose top reached heaven, on which the angels of God were ascending and descending, and above which stood Almighty God. The angels descending are "negative" theology, which aims at showing how Almighty God is distinct from created things. For example, God is not matter, soul, mind, spirit, any particular being, or even being itself, but is above and beyond all of these. The angels descending are "positive" theology, which aims at affirming that God *is*, in fact, good, wise, powerful, being itself, and so forth. Theologians prefer negative theology, because it is more appropriate to discuss God by *distinguishing* Him from things, than by *comparing* Him with things.

O supernatural Trinity, highest God and highest good, guardian of the wisdom of Christians, direct us rightly to the most unknown, the most brilliant, the highest summit of mystical revelation. For here the simple, absolute, and changeless mysteries of theology lie hidden within the ever-brilliant darkness of silence, forever revealing hidden things. Here in the deepest darkness shines the ever-brilliant light, which, indescribable and invisible, fills our inner minds to overflowing with surpassing beauty. Let this, then, be my prayer.

But you, Timothy, since you have so persistently experienced these mystical visions, may leave behind all visible
perceptions and mental efforts, all sensible objects and understanding, all things that exist and do not exist. You may be
raised on high to union (as much as it is possible) with He who
is above every essence and understanding. You may be carried
on high by the irresistible and absolutely pure ecstasy, out of
yourself and out of everything else, to the supernatural light of
divine darkness, but only when you have cast away all things
and become free of them.

But be sure not to share these things with those who are
not ready for them—I mean, those who are entangled in existing things and are not ready to understand that there is something supernatural above all things which exist, who imagine that
they already understand the one who lives only in darkness. But
if even *these* should not be invited, how much more those even
more ignorant, who think of the Creator in terms of the lowest
created things? How much more those who think He is no more
than the false gods they make for themselves of various shapes?

In response to these, we must, of course, affirm that God
has all the attributes of things that exist, since He is the Cause of
them all; but we must more properly deny that He has all of these
attributes, since He is above all of them. And we must not imagine that these negations are in contradiction to the affirmations:
instead, we must simply say that God, being above all abstrac-
tions and definitions, is also above the negations.

This is why the great Bartholomew said that theology is
both great and small, and the Gospel is both lengthy and brief.
He must have understood this supernaturally—that the Cause of
all things is both long of speech and brief of speech, since no
speech or conception can encompass Him. This is because He is
supernaturally raised above all things, and manifested—in truth
and without veil—only to those who pass beyond all things, even
those which are pure and holy, high and exalted; only to those
who leave behind even sacred light and sounds and heavenly

words and enter into the darkness, where He who is beyond all things dwells.

For even Moses was required to be purified first, then separated from those who were not pure, and only after being cleansed did he hear the great trumpets and see the great light which radiated pure rays. Then he was separated from the crowd, and approached the mountain of divine ascent only with the chosen priests. And even then he did not meet with Almighty God himself, or even see Him (for He cannot be seen), but could only view the place where He was....

We pray to enter within this ever-brilliant darkness, and, by *not* seeing and knowing, we will come to see and to know that which is beyond all sight and knowledge. For this is true sight and knowledge, to supernaturally celebrate the Supernatural One, by negating and passing beyond all existing things. In the same way, those who make a statue chip away all of the obstructions which surround and obscure the clear view of the figure within, and, by chipping away in this fashion, they bring to light the genuine beauty concealed within the stone.

And we must, I think, celebrate these negations in the opposite way that we celebrate positive affirmations of God. For in the latter, we begin with the highest affirmations and then descend to the lower ones. But, in the former case, we ascend from the lowest places to the highest, chipping away in such a fashion that we may know the Unknowable One, who is hidden beneath all that which can be known. In this way we may see without veil that supernatural darkness, hidden beneath all the light of existing things.

In my other book, *Theological Outlines*, I celebrated the main affirmative expressions that we can make about God—how His divine and good nature is One, yet also Three, how He is Father, Son, and Spirit ... and in my book *Divine Names*, how He is Good, Being, Life, Wisdom, Power, and whatever else God can be named. Again, in my book *Symbolical Theology* I spoke of the names we can take from visible things and apply to God—forms, appearances, parts and organs, places and ornaments, anger and sorrow, wrath and joy, sickness, promises and curses, sleeping and waking, and all other representations which we can use to describe God in a symbolic way. And you must have noticed that the lower expressions required more words than the higher ones ... since, as we ascend to higher and more spiritual concepts, there is less to negate.

And, finally, when we enter into the darkness which is beyond understanding, we will find not only less speech, but a complete absence of it, and even an absence of understanding.... After the ascent is completed, our path contracts and our mouth becomes speechless, as we are entirely united to that which words cannot express.

Why, you ask, did we begin making our positive affirmations of God from the highest, and now we begin making negative statements from the lowest? Because if we are forced to imagine that He who is beyond all attributes actually has attributes, we should draw those attributes from those things that are highest and closest to Him. But when we deny that He has such attributes, we should begin with the easiest denials, that is, those things that are furthest removed from Him. Aren't life and goodness closer to Him than air and stone? Aren't wrath and corruption the most easily denied of Him?

I say, then, that the Cause of all things, which is above all things, is not nonexistent, nor lifeless, nor irrational, nor mindless, nor bodily, nor shaped, nor formed, nor qualified, nor quantifiable, nor material, nor locatable, nor visible, nor touchable, nor perceptible, nor disordered, nor confused, nor passionate, nor powerless, nor blinded, nor changeable, nor corruptible, nor divisible, nor deprived, nor moveable, and so forth.

On the other hand, we can ascend still further. We can say that He is not soul, nor mind, nor imagination, nor opinion, nor reason, nor conception, nor expressed, nor conceived, nor number, nor order, nor greatness, nor smallness, nor equality, nor inequality, nor similarity, nor dissimilarity, nor standing, nor moving, nor at rest, nor is power, nor has power, nor light, nor lives, nor is life, nor is essence, nor eternity, nor time, nor intelligible, nor knowing, nor truth, nor kingdom, nor wisdom, nor one, nor oneness, nor divinity, nor goodness, nor … any existing being.

Neither is He any nonexisting or existing thing, nor does any existing thing know Him as He is, nor does He know existing things (at least inasmuch as they exist), nor can He be expressed, nor named, nor known, nor is He darkness, nor light, nor error, nor truth, nor definable, nor abstractable. And when we affirm things of Him or deny things of Him, we do not affirm things of himself or deny them of himself, since the all-perfect and all-one Cause of all things is beyond every definition, preeminent over all things and freed from all things, being even beyond all negation.

ST. MAXIMUS THE CONFESSOR (580–662)

When Maximus retired from one of the most powerful positions in the Byzantine Empire to take up a life of prayer in a seaside monastery, he probably thought his troubles were behind him. But trouble would follow Maximus for the rest of his life: invasions, accusations, threats, and conspiracy chased him across three continents, culminating in one of the most gruesome fates imaginable for a man who wanted only to be left alone in contemplation of the God he loved.

Little is known of Maximus' early life, save that he served briefly as the chief secretary to the emperor in Constantinople before he took monastic vows in the monastery of Philippicus across the channel from the capital city. A sudden Persian invasion of the region, however, forced him to flee to Africa, where he found himself in the midst of a fiery theological debate. Although the Ecumenical Council of Chalcedon in 451 had affirmed that Christ had both a divine and a human nature, controversy continued over how many *wills* He had.

One school of thought, the Monothelite (Greek for "one will"), held that Christ would have only had a divine will but no human will, as a sinful, human will would have tainted His Incarnate divinity and made it possible for Him to sin. Maximus begged to differ: If Christ were truly human, He must have had a genuinely human will alongside the divine, or else He would not have been "a man like us in all things but sin" (cf. Heb 4:15).

Further, Maximus argued that if God was not fully united to humanity in the Incarnation, this endangered the possibility of humans becoming fully united to God in salvation. Maximus entered a public debate on this question with one of his close friends (and also his successor as abbot of the monastery), a Monothelite named Pyrrhus, and so bested him in debate that Pyrrhus renounced Monothelitism immediately.

Unfortunately, Pyrrhus would later retract this retraction and reembrace Monothelitism, and was also elected in 638 as the next bishop of Constantinople. Maximus, concerned that this error would spread, fled to Rome and helped convince Pope Martin I to condemn Monothelitism at a council in 649. It was too late, however. The Roman Emperor Constans II took the side of Pyrrhus and the Monothelites, and had both Maximus and the pope arrested for heresy. The pope died in captivity, and Maximus was taken in chains to Constantinople for trial.

Exiled and imprisoned repeatedly, he refused to renounce his belief in Christ's full humanity, and in 662 he was tortured, his hand cut off to prevent his further writing and his tongue cut out to prevent his further teaching. Maximus lingered on a few days before dying from his wounds. (The term *confessor* denotes one who "confessed" the true faith in the face of suffering and death, even if martyrdom did not immediately result.)

Within two decades, however, Maximus was vindicated. An ecumenical council held at Constantinople itself in 680 endorsed Maximus' position, that Christ had both a divine and a human will, and declared Maximus and Pope Martin I innocent of heresy. Maximus was almost immediately recognized as a saint and is one of the last saints recognized in both Western and Eastern Christianity.

Despite the tumultuous nature of his life and death, the bulk of his writings are contemplative, prayerful meditations on the spiritual life. Never a controversialist by nature, Maximus simply recognized that sound, orthodox theology was the necessary foundation for a life of prayer and holiness. As he put it, "Theology without practice is the theology of demons."

MYSTAGOGIA: CATECHESIS THROUGH LITURGY

In the early and medieval Church, most of the faithful learned their theology through the liturgy. Bishops and clergy would frequently give lectures and homilies (often to catechumens about to be baptized, or to the newly baptized) on the liturgy or the sacraments, using the various rituals and prayers as springboards for a deeper discussion of the mysteries of the faith, termed "mystagogia." In these selections from Maximus' Mystagogia, *he walks the reader through the main steps of the liturgy celebrated at Constantinople, pointing through the liturgy to God's great plan of salvation.*

What is symbolized by the first entry into the holy assembly, and the things done afterwards:

Having said these things … about the holy Church, we can now get ready to say even more briefly our reflections on the sacred assembly of the Church. First, when we see the bishop processing into the church to celebrate the liturgy with the sacred assembly, I was taught to see this as a symbol of the first coming of the Son of God, our Savior Jesus Christ, into this world in the flesh. In this way He delivered us and paid off the debt for the sin, violence, corruption, death, oppression, and diabolical tyranny to which the world had freely subjected itself.

He purchased the salvation of the whole world by His life-giving passion, releasing all from the captivity to which they were bound, taking upon himself their guilt, even though He had no guilt and was free from sin, returning us again to His kingdom. And when the bishop proceeds forward, entering the sanctuary itself, mounting and taking his seat, this is said to symbolically represent Christ's ascent to His throne in the heavens after making restitution for sins.

What, further, is symbolized by the entry of the people into the holy church:

The entry of the people into the church, together with their bishop, signifies the deliverance of unbelievers from ignorance and error, and the further progress of the faithful from depravity and ignorance to virtue and knowledge. On the one hand, the procession into the Church signifies the conversion of unbelievers to the one true God. And on the other, it signifies the further improvement of those of us who already believe, indeed, who have the pure name of the faithful, but who have until now lived a shameful and debauched life.

When these persons turn to the commandment of the Lord, we turn their sins to no account through works of repentance established to make amendment for them. This is true for each person, whether he is guilty of murder, adultery, thievery, pride, arrogance, violence, coveting, greed, mockery, not forgiving injuries, anger, insults, slander, complaining, envy, or drunkenness. To conclude (for this list could go on forever), a man guilty of any or all of these is found to be without fault, as soon as his free, deliberate consent has turned away from them and his will ceases to work evil, and preferring virtue to vice, he changes to a better life. This man is properly and truly understood to be with Christ our God and High Priest, who is symbolically understood to be the Church.

On the author and performer of the Mysteries, on the rites and ceremonies which are performed in the sacred assembly among the faithful, and those who are gathered in faith by the grace of the Holy Spirit:

In sum, the first entry of the bishop symbolizes the expulsion of unbelief, the growth of faith, the reduction of vices, the accretion of virtues, the abolition of ignorance, and the increase of knowledge. By hearing the divine readings, those things I just mentioned (faith, virtue, and knowledge) are more firmly held as fixed and irremovable habits. And by the divine songs that accompany them, the soul's power of free will is moved to consent to virtues, and the mind and spirit take pleasure and delight from these things.

By the sacred reading of the holy Gospel, worldly inclinations—those that belong to the world our senses perceive—are done away with. By the closing of the doors in succession is signified the passage and translation of the soul from this corruptible world to the spiritual world; also, the closing of the doors signifies the shutting of the doors of the senses, returning them from images of sin to pure things. Through our initiation into the holy Mysteries [that is, sacraments], we understand the most perfect, secret, and new dispensation of the knowledge and teaching of God.

The divine kiss and greeting, which all exchange with all, signifies the restoration of harmony with one another and with God, a consensus of souls in love. Our confession of faith in the creed is the fitting thanksgiving for the unheard of and wonderful design of our salvation. The Trisagion [the *Sanctus*] signifies our union with the holy angels, our elevation to equal rank with them, so that our harmonious singing of the glory of God will never end. Through that prayer in which we are privileged to call God Father, we recall our true adoption in the Spirit....

Through the holy things that are granted to us through the pure and life-giving Mysteries, we receive communion with Him who condescended to become mortal, accepting identity and likeness with us, so that man, as a consequence of this, may be joined to God. In this way, even while living this mortal life, through the grace that is in faith, we believe that we are made holy by receiving the gifts of the Spirit. Thus, in the future world, we will certainly have them ... according to the firm hope of our faith, and that which is assured by the indubitable certainty of his unchangeable promise.

When we will have kept his commands to the best of our ability, we believe that we will receive His gift, passing from that grace which is by faith to that grace which is by sight. You may be sure, God and our Savior Jesus Christ transform us into themselves, not shirking the corruption and mortality which mark our lives. Rather, through His design, earthly symbols are shown to us for the benefit of our senses at the present time, lavished upon us through these most ancient Mysteries.

THE CHURCH OF ROME AS GUARANTEE OF FAITH AND UNITY

When Maximus sensed that the unity of the Church was in danger during the Monothelite controversy, he looked to the Church of Rome as a touchstone of orthodoxy and as a guarantee of unity. Many of his efforts in the East consisted of attempting to convince Christians there to remain in unity with Rome. This is from his letter from Rome after the papal council.

The extremities of the earth, and all in every part of it who purely and rightly confess the Lord, look directly towards the most holy Roman Church and its confession and faith, as it were to a sun of unfailing light. They await from it the bright radiance of the sacred doctrines of our Fathers, according to what the six inspired and holy councils have purely and piously decreed, declaring most expressly the confession of faith.

For from the coming down of the incarnate Word amongst us, all the Churches in every part of the world have held that greatest Church alone as their base and foundation, seeing that according to the promise of Christ our Savior, the gates of hell do never prevail against it, that it has the keys of a right confession and faith in Him, that it opens the true and only religion to those who approach with piety, and shuts up and locks every heretical mouth that speaks injustice against the Most High.

ST. JOHN DAMASCENE (676–749)

All of a sudden, modern readers are finding John Damascene highly relevant. After all, he not only lived in a Muslim civilization, but also worked in the court of an Islamic ruler. Fluent in Arabic, he had read and commented on the Qur'an, and some of John's own works survive only in Arabic translations. As a Christian struggling to preserve intact the Christian tradition, while trying to engage intellectually and socially with an ascendant Islamic culture, St. John's legacy is as significant now as it ever was.

Syria, once the heart of Eastern Christianity, had succumbed to Muslim incursions by the seventh century and was incorporated into the Umayyad caliphate. The Muslim rulers (caliphs) normally retained Christian civil servants on their staff, and both John's father and grandfather had served the caliphs in Syria. John himself served as chief councilor at Damascus for the caliph Abdul Malik. His family, however, worked hard to keep their Christian faith alive, and John was educated by a Sicilian monk who had been taken as a prisoner of war and then bought out of captivity by John's father.

A Christian empire survived in the East, however, with its capital in Constantinople and its borders shrinking rapidly; yet the emperor in John's day was doing no favors for the Church. By long-standing Eastern custom, the Byzantine emperor had a firm grip on matters of doctrine and Church practice—the custom, as we saw under Justinian, that the West sarcastically called Caesaropapism. This worked reasonably well when the emperor was orthodox, but less well when he was a heretic. And, unfortunately, Emperor Leo the Isaurian was a heretic.

At question was the practice of using images such as pictures, statues, or icons in religious worship. Although the early Church had unhesitatingly incorporated such images into churches and liturgies, a vocal minority insisted that this amounted to idolatry, usually invoking the First Commandment against "graven images." Emperor Leo endorsed this view, over the protests of both the pope and the bishop of Constantinople, and issued numerous edicts in the 720s calling for *iconoclasm* (Greek for "destruction of icons") throughout the Byzantine Empire.

John of Damascus (or "Damascene") knew the Scriptures and tradition too well to fall for this. He issued three tracts defending the use of icons, including lengthy quotations from the Church Fathers endorsing his view. The clergy, the monks, and the vast majority of the faithful Christians in the East, stirred up by John's writings, rose up in rebellion against the emperor's iconoclastic policies. The emperor, not to be cowed, crushed the rebellions and, to protest the pope's defiance, seized jurisdiction over Italian territories. Unable to reach John directly—he wrote from the safety of the Muslim caliphate—Leo forged letters that painted John as a traitor plotting against his caliph.

John, however, had had enough of the controversy of public life. He retired to a monastery with his brother, sought ordination as a priest, and took up pastoral ministry. He left countless writings to posterity, including large collections summarizing the thoughts of the Church Fathers whom he loved so much. Latin writers such as Aquinas valued John's writings immensely, and he is recognized as a Doctor of the Church in both East and West. His greatest legacy, however, was as a defender of the use of icons. He would be pleased to know that, some decades after his death, his view would be vindicated at the seventh ecumenical council, Nicaea II, in 787, which condemned iconoclasm as a heresy.

ON THE HONOR GIVEN TO HOLY IMAGES

This treatise, titled On Holy Images, *embodies St. John's bold critique of the Greek emperor's iconoclastic policies, and a biblical defense of the practice of icon veneration.*

Since I am always convinced of my own unworthiness, I ought to have kept silent and confessed my shortcomings before God, but all things are good at the right time. Now I see the Church which

God founded on the apostles and prophets, its cornerstone being Christ His Son, tossed on an angry sea, beaten by rushing waves, shaken and troubled by the assaults of evil spirits. I see tears in the seamless robe of Christ, which wicked men have sought to rip in half, and His body cut into pieces—that is, the word of God and the ancient tradition of the Church.

Therefore I have judged it unreasonable to keep silence and to hold my tongue…. No, I have become even more inclined to speak out. The king's command is all-powerful over his subjects. And few men have been found until now who, while recognizing that the power of the earthly king comes from above [see Rom 13:1], have nonetheless resisted his demands when they were unlawful….

Now our opponents say: God's commands to Moses the lawgiver were: "You shall have no other gods before me. You shall not make for yourself a graven image, or any likeness of anything that is in heaven above, or that is in the earth beneath" (Ex 20:3–4)….

But, you see, the whole purpose of this is that we not adore a created thing more than the Creator, or give the worship of adoration to anyone but to Him alone. By "worship," therefore, God always intends the worship of adoration. For, again, He says, "You shall not bow down to them or serve them; for I the Lord your God am a jealous God" (Ex 20:5). And again: "You shall tear down their altars, and dash in pieces their pillars, and burn their Asherim [idols] with fire; you shall hew down the graven images of their gods, and destroy their name out of that place. You shall not do so to the Lord your God" (Dt 12:3–4). And a little further on, "You shall make for yourself no molten gods" (Ex 34:17).

You see that He forbids image-making because of the danger of idolatry, since it is impossible to make an image of the immeasurable, uncircumscribed, invisible God. You have not seen any likeness of Him, the Scripture says, and this was St. Paul's testimony as he stood in the midst of the Areopagus: "Being then God's offspring, we ought not to think that the Deity is like gold, or silver, or stone, a representation by the art or imagination of man" (Acts 17:29).

These commands were given to the Jews because of their tendency to idolatry. Now we, on the contrary, are no longer immature children…. We have passed the stage of infancy, and reached the perfection of adulthood. We receive our habit of mind from God, and know what may be imaged and what may not. Scripture says, "You cannot see my face" (Ex 33:20). How wise is the Lawgiver! For how can we depict the invisible? How can we picture the inconceivable? How can we give expression to the limitless, the immeasurable, the invisible? How can we give a form to immensity? How can we paint immortality? How can we outline a mystery?

But, on the other hand, once you reflect that God, who is a pure spirit, has become man for your sake, you will clearly be able to depict Him in a human form. When the Invisible One becomes visible to flesh, you may then draw a likeness of His body. When He who is a pure spirit, without form or limit, immeasurable in the boundlessness of His own nature, existing as God, takes upon himself the form of a servant in substance and in stature, and a body of flesh, then you may draw His likeness, and show it to anyone willing to look at it.

Depict His ineffable condescension, His virginal birth, His baptism in the Jordan, His transfiguration on Mount Tabor, His all-powerful sufferings, His death and miracles, the proofs of His Divinity, the deeds which He worked in the flesh through divine power, His saving Cross, His Tomb, and Resurrection, and Ascension into heaven. Give to it all the permanence of engraving and color. Have no fear or anxiety….

Now, as long as we are talking about images and worship, let us analyze the exact meaning of each. An image is a likeness of the original with a certain difference, for it is not an exact reproduction of the original…. Again, visible things are images of invisible and intangible things, and which show some faint reflection of them. Holy Scripture describes God and the angels in a physical form, and the saint [Pseudo-Dionysius] explains why. Sensible things can only give a suitable picture of what is beyond the senses, and can only give a form to what is intangible, by doing so in a fully physical way, which does not require a great mental effort to understand.

Holy Scripture, therefore, meets our needs perfectly, and whenever it tries to communicate something intangible to us, it clothes it in flesh. In this way, Scripture makes an image that is suited to our natures, and brought down to the level of our desires. A certain sense perception thus takes place in the brain that was not there before, and is transmitted to the intellect, and added to the mental store.

Gregory, who is so eloquent about God, says that the mind that decides to go beyond corporeal things is incapable of doing it. For the invisible things of God since the creation of the world are made visible through images (cf. Rom 1:20). We see images in creation which remind us faintly of God, as when, for instance, we speak of the holy and adorable Trinity, imaged by the sun, or light, or burning rays, or by a running fountain, or a full river, or by the mind, speech, or the spirit within us, or by a rose bush, or a sprouting flower, or a sweet fragrance....

Worship is the way we show veneration and honor. Now, understand that there are different degrees of worship. First of all, there is the worship of adoration, which we show to God, who alone is worthy of worship by nature. Then, for the sake of God who is worthy of worship by nature, we also honor His saints and servants....

In ancient times, God the incorporeal and uncircumscribed was never depicted. Now, however, when we see God clothed in flesh, and having conversation with men, I will make an image of the God whom I see. I do not worship matter; I worship the God who made matter, who became matter for my sake, who condescended to inhabit matter, who worked out my salvation through matter. I will not stop honoring the matter that works my salvation. I honor it, but not as I honor God....

Do not despise matter, for it is not despicable. Nothing that God has made is despicable. This is the Manichean [or, Gnostic] heresy. The only despicable thing is what does not come from God, but is our own invention, the spontaneous choice of will to disregard the natural law—that is to say, sin....

We proclaim Him also by our senses on every side, and we sanctify the noblest sense, which is that of sight. The image is a memorial to the sight, just what words are to a listening ear. What a book is to the literate, that is what an image is to the illiterate. The image speaks to the sight as words to the ear; it brings us understanding.

SERMON ON THE FEAST OF THE ASSUMPTION

St. John Damascene is remarkable for the depth of his devotion to Mary. He is one of the strongest early witnesses for the doctrine of the Assumption—that is, the belief that Mary was taken up into heaven, body and soul, at the end of her life. This text is taken from one of his sermons on the feast of the Assumption.

There is no one alive who is able to praise adequately the holy death of God's Mother, even if he had a thousand tongues and a thousand mouths. Not if all the most eloquent tongues could be united would their praises be sufficient. She is greater than all praise....

Today the holy Virgin of Virgins is presented in the heavenly temple. Virginity in her was so strong as to be a consuming fire. Virginity is generally lost by childbirth, but she is always a virgin, before the event, in the birth itself, and afterwards. Today the sacred and living ark of the living God, who conceived her Creator himself, takes up her abode in the temple of God, not made by hands.

David, her forefather, rejoices. Angels and Archangels are in jubilation, Powers exult, Principalities and Dominations, Virtues and Thrones are in gladness: Cherubim and Seraphim magnify God. Not the least of their praise is it to refer to the Mother of glory. Today the holy dove, the pure and guileless soul, sanctified by the Holy Spirit, put off the ark of her body, the life-giving receptacle of Our Lord. Today she found rest for the soles of her feet, taking her flight to the spiritual world, and dwelling securely in the sinless country above. Today the Eden of the new Adam receives the true paradise, in which sin is remitted and the tree of life grows....

The Lord and Creator of heaven, the Architect of all things beneath the earth and above, of creation, visible and invisible, who is not circumvented by place (if that which surrounds things is rightly termed place), created himself, without human cooperation, as an Infant within her. He made her a rich treasure house of His all-pervading and infinite Divinity, subsisting entirely in her without passion, remaining entire in His universality and himself unlimited....

The bosom of the earth was no fitting receptacle for the Lord's dwelling place, the living source of cleansing water, the corn of heavenly bread, the sacred vine of divine wine, the evergreen and fruitful olive branch of God's mercy. And just as the all holy body of God's Son, which was taken from her, rose from the dead on the third day, it followed that she should be snatched from the tomb, that the mother should be united to her Son. And as He had come down to her, so she should be raised up to Him, into the more perfect dwelling place, heaven itself.

It was fitting that she, who had sheltered God the Word in her own womb, should inhabit the tabernacles of her Son. And as Our Lord said it was fitting for Him to be concerned with His Father's business, so it was fitting that as His mother she should dwell in the courts of her Son, in the house of the Lord, and in the courts of the house of our God. If all those who rejoice dwell in Him, where must the very cause of joy itself abide?

It was fitting that the body of her who preserved her virginity unstained in her motherhood should be kept from corruption even after death. She who nursed her Creator as an infant at her breast had a right to be in the divine tabernacles. The place of the bride whom the Father had espoused was in the heavenly courts. It was fitting that she who saw her Son die on the cross, and received in her heart the sword of pain which she had not felt in childbirth, should gaze upon Him seated next to the Father. The Mother of God had a right to the possession of her Son, and as handmaid and Mother of God to the veneration of all creation.

GREGORY PALAMAS (1296–1359)

The figure of Gregory Palamas embodies in his very person some of the deepest tensions between Eastern and Western Christianity. Long regarded as a heretic in the West, Palamas is one of the most beloved saints in the East, which honors him with not one but two feast days!

By Gregory's day, Eastern and Western Christianity had already drifted apart. Aggravated by disagreements about the role of the Holy Spirit and the authority of the bishop of Rome over worldwide Christianity, the bishops of East and West refused to recognize one another. Though relations had thawed a bit by the fourteenth century, the "hesychast" controversy caused them to flare up again.

This controversy remains one of the most difficult for Westerners to understand. The practice of *hesychasm* (literally "quietness") refers to a set of meditative practices carried out by Eastern monks—inner quietness, controlled breathing, chin pressed into the chest, and the constant repetition of the "prayer of the heart": "Lord Jesus Christ, Son of God, have mercy on me, a sinner." Monks who practiced this routine claimed that it allowed them to see the light of God himself, the same as Jesus' disciples saw at the Transfiguration. They did not claim to see the divine essence itself, of course, but only the uncreated "operations" or "energy" of God, which they explained using the analogy of the sun and its rays.

This practice—and its theoretical foundations—certainly built upon a long Eastern spiritual tradition, especially the writings of the great pseudo-Dionysius, but they also represented something of a fresh development of this tradition. The controversy erupted when Barlaam, an Italian visitor to an Eastern monastery, witnessed these practices. Trained in Latin scholastic theology, Barlaam was scandalized by what he saw and heard. The meditative practices he dismissed as silly—he called the hesychasts *omphalopsychoi*, "men with their souls in their navels." But he took offense at the distinction between God's essence and His "energies," which conflicted with the doctrine of the absolute simplicity and unity of God which was so prized in the Latin West. If God's essence and His "energies" were both divine, yet distinct from each other, wasn't this polytheism?

At this point, Gregory Palamas entered the fray. The son of a Byzantine civil servant who had been raised in the Imperial court, Gregory had retired from public life to pursue a monastic vocation on Mount Athos, the most celebrated monastery in the East and one where hesychasm was central to the monks' spirituality. Gregory, who claimed to have seen the divine light personally through the practice of hesychasm, wrote over sixty works defending the practice against Barlaam and its other detractors. The debate continued to swirl, requiring no fewer than six councils at Constantinople to settle.

Though Gregory suffered significantly for his defense of hesychasm, even being excommunicated by one of the earlier councils, he was vindicated in the end. In 1351, the last council closed, endorsing both the practice of hesychasm and the doctrine of the divine "energies" behind it. Gregory's works were so influential in this debate that the latter doctrine is often known as Palamism.

Unfortunately, this debate aggravated East-West relations even further. Barlaam, finding himself condemned by the council, converted to the Roman, Latin Church and was ordained a bishop in the West. Western opposition to Palamism only hardened the Eastern commitment to it, and the six councils at Constantinople came to be regarded, collectively, as the Ninth Ecumenical Council in the East.

Most Western theologians no longer view Palamas' doctrine of the divine energies as heretical, though they still remain controversial in Western theology. Regardless, many in the West (especially the late Pope St. John Paul II) came to appreciate Palamas' theological system and spirituality as a legitimate development of the Greek theological tradition.

A SERMON ON THE HOLY SPIRIT

In this homily on the feast of Pentecost, Gregory speaks of the role of the Holy Spirit in the divine plan of salvation. Note the strong emphasis on the doctrine of the Trinity and the Incarnation, as well as the way these are connected to the doctrine of theosis, or "deification": because Christ and the Spirit share equally in the Father's divinity, they can impart that divinity to the human race. Note also a brief reference to the distinction between the essence and "energy" of the Holy Spirit.

A short while ago, with the strong eyes of faith, we beheld Christ ascending no less clearly than those accounted worthy to be eyewitnesses, nor are we less favored than they. "Blessed are those who have not seen and yet believe," says the Lord (Jn 20:29), referring to those who have found assurance through hearing, and see by faith. Recently, we saw Christ lifted up from the ground bodily (Acts 1:9). Now, through the Holy Spirit sent by Him to His disciples, we see how far Christ ascended and to what dignity He carried up the nature He assumed from us. Clearly, He went up as high as the place from which the Spirit sent by Him descended....

It follows that at His Ascension Christ went up to the Father on high, as far as His Fatherly bosom, from which comes the Spirit. Having been shown, even in His human form, to share the Father's glory, Christ now sent forth the Spirit who comes from the Father and is sent by Him from heaven. But when we hear that the Spirit was sent by the Father and the Son, this does not mean that the Spirit has no part in their greatness, for He is not just sent, but also himself sends and consents to be sent....

The Holy Spirit is not just sent, but himself sends the Son, who is sent by the Father. He is therefore shown to be the same as the Father and the Son in nature, power, operation, and honor. By the good pleasure of the Father and the cooperation of the Holy Spirit, the only begotten Son of God, on account of the boundless ocean of divine love for mankind, bowed down the heavens and came down (see Ps 18:9). He appeared on earth after our fashion, lived among us, and did and taught great, wonderful, and sublime things truly worthy of God, which led those who obeyed Him towards deification and salvation.

After willingly suffering for our salvation, being buried, and rising on the third day, He ascended into heaven and sat down on the right hand of the Father, whence He cooperated in the descent of the divine Spirit upon His disciples by sending down together with the Father the power from on high....

When the fiftieth day after the Resurrection had come, the day we now commemorate, all the disciples were gathered with one accord in the upper room, each having also gathered together his thoughts (for they were devoting themselves intently to prayer and hymns to God). "And suddenly," says Luke the Evangelist, "a sound came from heaven like the rush of a mighty wind, and it filled all the house where they were sitting" (Acts 2:2)....

Those miracles accomplished by the Lord in the flesh, which bore witness that He was God's only-begotten Son in His own Person, united with us in the last days, came to an end. On the other hand, those wonders began which proclaimed the Holy Spirit as a divine Person in His own right, so that we might come to know and contemplate the great and venerable mystery of the Holy Trinity. The Holy Spirit had been active before: it was He who spoke through the prophets and proclaimed things to come. Later, He worked through the disciples to drive out demons and heal diseases. But now He was manifested to all in His own Person through the tongues of fire, and by sitting enthroned as Lord upon each of Christ's disciples, He made them instruments of His power....

The fact that the divine Spirit sat upon them is proof not just of His lordly dignity, but of His unity. He sat, it says, "on each one of them. And they were all filled with the Holy Spirit" (Acts 2:3–4). For although divided in His various powers and energies, in each of His works the Holy Spirit is wholly present and active, undividedly divided, partaken of while remaining complete, like the sun's ray. They spoke with other tongues, other languages, to people from every nation, as the Spirit gave them utterance. They became instruments of the divine Spirit, inspired and motivated according to His will and power. Anything taken hold of by somebody outside itself, sharing in the energy but not the essence of the one acting through it, is his instrument....

The promise was now fulfilled and the Holy Spirit, given and sent by both the Father and the Son, descended. He shone round about the holy disciples and with divine power kindled them all like lamps, or, rather, He revealed them as heavenly lights set above the whole world, who had the word of eternal life, and through them He illuminated all the earth. If from one burning lamp someone lights another, then another from that one, and so on in succession, he has light continuously. In the same way, through the apostles ordaining their successors, and these successors ordaining others, and so on, the grace of the Holy Spirit is handed down through all generations and enlightens all who obey their spiritual shepherds and teachers.

Each hierarch in his turn comes to give the city this grace and gift of God and the enlightenment of the divine Spirit through the Gospel. Those who reject any of them, as can happen, interrupt God's grace, break the divine succession, separate themselves from God, and deliver themselves up to sinful rebellions and all kinds of disasters....

Christ had ascended bodily into heaven, so if He had not sent His Holy Spirit to accompany and strengthen His disciples and their successors in following generations who taught the Gospel of grace, He would not have been preached to all nations, nor would the proclamation have been passed down to us. That is why the Lord, in His all-surpassing love for mankind, showed at Pentecost that His disciples were partakers, fathers, and ministers of everlasting light and life, who bring us to new birth for eternal life and make those who are worthy children of the Light and fathers of enlightenment. Thus He himself is with us unto the end of the world, as was promised through the Spirit (see Mt 28:20).

For He is One with the Father and the Spirit, not according to hypostasis, but in His divinity, and God is One in Three, in one tri-hypostatic and almighty divinity. The Holy Spirit always existed and was with the Son in the Father. How could the Father and divine Mind be without beginning if the Son and Word were not also without beginning? How could there be a pre-eternal Word without there also being a pre-eternal Spirit? Thus the Holy Spirit ever was and is and will be, co-Creator with the Father and the Son, together with them renewing that which has suffered corruption, and sustaining the things that endure … [and] will stay with those who are worthy in the age to come, making them immortal and filling their bodies as well with eternal glory, as the Lord indicated by telling His disciples, "I will ask the Father, and he will give you another Counselor, to be with you for ever" (Jn 14:16).

"It is sown," says the apostle (meaning buried and committed to the earth), "a physical body"—that is, to say, an ordinary created body with a created soul, stable and capable of movement. "It is raised" (that is, comes back to life), "a spiritual body" (1 Cor 15:44), which means a supernatural body, framed and ordered by the Holy Spirit, and clothed in immortality, glory, and incorruption by the Spirit's power (cf. 1 Cor 15:53).… Who are these heavenly people? Those who are steadfast and immovable in their faith, who always abound in the Lord's work and bear the image of the heavenly Adam through their obedience to Him....

But let us, brethren, I beseech you, abstain from deeds and words hateful to God, that we may boldly call God our Father. Let us truly return to Him, that He too may turn back to us, cleanse us from all sin and make us worthy of His divine grace. Then shall we keep festival both now and forever, and celebrate in a godly and spiritual way the accomplishments of God's promise, the coming of the All-holy Spirit among men and His resting upon them; the fulfillment and perfection of the blessed hope in Christ himself Our Lord.

For to Him belong glory, honor, and worship, with His Father without beginning and the all-holy, good, and life-giving Spirit, now and forever and unto the ages of ages. Amen.

Bibliography

*Note: Translated texts by the author are indicated below. The majority of the translations used are in the public domain; they have been adapted for readability. The author has benefited immensely from the numerous projects underway to digitize and scan public-domain books, such as the Internet Archive (*https://archive.org/*), Christian Classics Ethereal Library (*http://www.ccel.org/*), and Project Gutenberg (*http://www.gutenberg.org*). Without such projects, a book like this would be nearly impossible.*

Sources have been categorized by section.

Map
Muir, Ramsay. *Philip's New Historical Atlas for Students*. London: G. Philip, 1911.

Medieval Missionaries

Columba
Adamnan. *Life of Saint Columba, Founder of Hy*. Edited by William Reeves. Edinburgh: Edmonston and Douglas, 1874.

Bede. *The Ecclesiastical History of the English Nation*. Translated by Lionel Cecil Jane. London: J. M. Dent & Co., 1903.

Stone, S.J. *Lays of Iona and Other Poems*. London: Longmans, Green & Co., 1897.

Augustine of Canterbury
Bede. *The Ecclesiastical History of the English Nation*. Translated by Lionel Cecil Jane. London: J. M. Dent & Co., 1903.

Gregory the Great. "Register of Letters." Translated by James Barmby. *Nicene and Post-Nicene Fathers*, Second Series, Vol. 13. Edited by Philip Schaff and Henry Wace. Buffalo, NY: Christian Literature Publishing Co., 1898.

Willibrord
Talbot, C. H. *The Anglo-Saxon Missionaries in Germany, Being the Lives of SS. Willibrord, Boniface, Leoba and Lebuin together with the* Hodoepericon *of St. Willibald and a selection from the correspondence of St. Boniface*. London and New York: Sheed and Ward, 1954.

Boniface
Talbot, C. H. *The Anglo-Saxon Missionaries in Germany, Being the Lives of SS. Willibrord, Boniface, Leoba and Lebuin together with the* Hodoepericon

of St. Willibald and a selection from the correspondence of St. Boniface. London and New York: Sheed and Ward, 1954

Cyril and Methodius

Jahn, Otto, ed. *Vita Constantini. Entfuhrung der Europa auf Antiken Kunstwerken. Vorgelegt in der Sitzung der Philosophisch-Historischen Classe.* 1869. Translated by J. Blosser.

Shipman, A. "Slavonic Language and Liturgy." *The Catholic Encyclopedia*. New York: Robert Appleton Company, 1912.

Medieval Leaders

Gregory the Great

Bede. *The Ecclesiastical History of the English Nation*. Translated by Lionel Cecil Jane. London: J. M. Dent & Co., 1903.

Gregory the Great. "Book of Pastoral Rule." Translated by James Barmby. *Nicene and Post-Nicene Fathers*, Second Series, Vol. 12. Edited by Philip Schaff and Henry Wace. Buffalo, NY: Christian Literature Publishing Co., 1895.

_____. "Commentary on Job." Translated by J. O'Donnell (http://faculty.georgetown.edu/jod/texts/lastmoralia.english.html). Used with permission.

_____. "Register of Letters." Translated by James Barmby. *Nicene and Post-Nicene Fathers*, Second Series, Vol. 13. Edited by Philip Schaff and Henry Wace. Buffalo, NY: Christian Literature Publishing Co., 1898.

Alcuin of York

Alcuin of York. "On the Saints of the Church at York." *Library of the World's Best Literature, Ancient and Modern*. Edited by Charles Dudley Warner. Vol. 1. New York: R. S. Peale and J. A. Hill, 1896.

_____. *Propositiones Alcuini doctoris Caroli Magni imperatoris ad acuendos juvenes*. PL 101. Translated by J. Blosser.

Page, Ralph Barlow, ed. *The Letters of Alcuin*. New York: R. B. Page, 1909.

Charlemagne

Einhard, *Life of Charlemagne*. Translated by S. E. Turner. New York: Harper and Brothers, 1880.

Grant, A. J., ed. and trans. *Early Lives of Charlemagne by Eginhard and the Monk of St. Gall*. London: Chatto & Windus, 1926.

Munro, D. C., trans. *Translations and Reprints from the Original Sources of European history*. Vol. 6. Philadelphia: University of Pennsylvania Press, 1900.

Elizabeth of Hungary

Jacobus de Voragine. *The Golden Legend or Lives of the Saints*. Translated by William Caxton. Edited by F. S. Ellis. London: J. M. Dent, 1900.

King Louis IX

De Joinville, John. *The Memoirs of the Lord John de Joinville: A New English Version.* Translated by Ethel Wedgwood. New York: E.P. Dutton and Co., 1906.

Louis IX. "Saint Louis' Advice to His Son." *Medieval Civilization.* Translated and edited by Dana Munro and George Clarke Sellery. New York: The Century Company, 1910.

Munro, Dana C., trans. "Letters of the Crusaders." *Translations and Reprints from the Original Sources of European History.* Vol. 1:4. Philadelphia: University of Pennsylvania Press, 1896.

Medieval Martyrs

Boethius

Boethius. *Consolation of Philosophy.* Translated by H. R. James. London: Elliot Stock, 1897.

Wenceslaus

Pekar, Josef. *Die Wenzels und Ludmila Legenden und Die Echtheit Christians.* Prague: 1906. Translated by J. Blosser.

Thomas Becket

Roger of Hoveden. *The Annals of Roger de Hoveden.* Translated by Henry T. Riley. 2 vols. London: Bohn, 1853.

Joan of Arc

Champion, Pierre, ed. *The Trial of Jeanne d'Arc.* Translated by W. P. Barrett. New York: Gotham House, 1932.

De Vireville, Vallet, ed. *Chronique de la Pucelle, ou Chronique de Cousinot.* Translated by Belle Tuten. Paris: Adolphe Delahaye, 1859.

Medieval Monastics

Benedict of Nursia

Benedict. *The Holy Rule of St. Benedict.* Translated by Boniface Verheyen. Atchison, KS: St. Benedict's Abbey Press, 1949.

Gregory the Great. *The Second Book of the Dialogues of Saint Gregory.* Translated by P. W. Paris: 1608.

Odo of Cluny

Bruel, A., ed. "Recueil des Chartes de L'Abbaye de Cluny." *Select Historical Documents of the Middle Ages,* edited by Ernest F. Henderson. London: George Bell and Sons, 1910.

Eadmer of Canterbury. *Life of St. Odo.* PL 133. Translated by J. Blosser.

Dominic de Guzman

Jordan of Saxony. *Libellus de principiis ordinis praedicatorum*, ed. by H. Chr. Scheeben, *Monumenta ordinis praedicatorum historica* 16. Rome: 1935. Translated by J. Blosser.

Francis of Assisi

Francis of Assisi. *The Writings of St. Francis of Assisi.* Translated by Paschal Robinson. Philadelphia: Dolphin Press, 1906.

Thomas of Celano. *St. Francis of Assisi.* London: J. M. Dent & Co., 1904.

Clare of Assisi

De Chérancé, Léopold. *St. Clare of Assisi.* New York: Benziger Bros., 1910.

Gilliat-Smith, Ernest. *Saint Clare of Assisi: Her Life and Legislation.* London: J. M. Dent & Sons, 1914.

Seton, Walter. *Some New Sources for the Life of Blessed Agnes of Bohemia, Including a Fourteenth Century Latin Version.* Aberdeen: The University Press, 1915.

Thomas of Celano. *St. Francis of Assisi.* London: J. M. Dent & Co., 1904.

Gerard Groote

Thomas à Kempis. *The Imitation of Christ.* Milwaukee: Bruce Publishing Company, 1940.

_____. *Founders of the New Devotion. Being the Lives of Gerard Groote, Florentius Radewin and their Followers.* London: B. Herder, 1905.

Medieval Mystics

Bernard of Clairvaux

Bernard of Clairvaux. *On the Love of God.* Translated by Marianne Caroline and Coventry Patmore. London: Kegan Paul, 1881.

_____. *Life and Works of Saint Bernard, Abbot of Clairvaux.* Vol. 4. Translated by Samuel J. Eales and Jean Mabillon. London: J. Hodges, 1896.

_____. *Liber ad milites templi de laude novae militiae.* PL 182. Translated by J. Blosser.

William of St. Thierry. "Life of St. Bernard." *A Source Book of Mediaeval History: Documents Illustrative of European Life and Institutions from the German Invasions to the Renaissance.* Edited by Frederic Austin Ogg. New York, 1907.

Hildegard of Bingen

Steele, Francesca Maria. *The Life and Visions of St. Hildegard.* London: Cranton & Ousely, 1914.

Meister Eckhart

Meister Eckhart. *Meister Eckhart's Sermons.* Translated by Claud Field. London: H. R. Allenson, 1909.

Jan van Ruysbruck

Van Ruysbruck, Jan. *The Adornment of the Spiritual Marriage*. Translated by Dom C. A. Wynschenk. Edited by Evelyn Underhill. London: J. M. Dent, 1916.

Julian of Norwich

Julian of Norwich. *Revelations of Divine Love*. Translated by Grace Warrack. London: Methuen, 1901

Catherine of Siena

Catherine of Benincasa. *Letters of Catherine Benincasa*. Translated by Vida D. Scudder. J. M. Dent & Sons, 1905.

Catherine of Siena. *The Dialogue of Saint Catherine of Siena*. Translated by Algar Thorold. London: Kegan Paul, Trench, Trubner & Co., 1907.

Bl. Raymond of Capua. *Life of Saint Catharine of Siena*. Translated by the Ladies of the Sacred Heart. Philadelphia: Peter F. Cunningham, 1859

Medieval Thinkers

Augustine of Hippo

Augustine of Hippo. *Confessions. Nicene and Post-Nicene Fathers*, First Series, Vol. 1. Edited by Philip Schaff. Buffalo, NY: Christian Literature Publishing Co., 1887.

_____. *On the Trinity. Nicene and Post-Nicene Fathers,* First Series, Vol. 3. Edited by Philip Schaff. Buffalo, NY: Christian Literature Publishing Co., 1887.

_____. *On Nature and Grace. Nicene and Post-Nicene Fathers*, First Series, Vol. 5.

Edited by Philip Schaff. Buffalo, NY: Christian Literature Publishing Co., 1887.

_____. *City of God. Nicene and Post-Nicene Fathers*, First Series, Vol. 2. Edited by Philip Schaff. Buffalo, NY: Christian Literature Publishing Co., 1887.

_____. *On Christian Doctrine. Nicene and Post-Nicene Fathers*, First Series, Vol. 2. Edited by Philip Schaff. Buffalo, NY: Christian Literature Publishing Co., 1887.

Anselm of Canterbury

Anselm. *Proslogium; Monologium: An Appendix in Behalf of the Fool by Gaunilo; and Cur Deus Homo*. Translated by Sidney Norton Deane. Chicago, Open Court Publishing Company, 1903.

_____. *The Devotions of Saint Anselm, Archbishop of Canterbury*. Edited by Clement C. J. Webb. London, 1903.

Robert Grosseteste

Baur, Ludwig, ed. *Die Philosophischen Werke des Robert Grosseteste, Bischofs von Lincoln*, Beiträge zur Geschichte der Philosophie des Mittelalters, 9, Münster: Aschendorff Verlag, 1912. Translated by J. Blosser.

Dales, Richard C., ed. *Roberti Grosseteste episcopi Lincolniensis commentarius in viii libros Physicorum Aristotelis*, Boulder: University of Colorado Press, 1963. Translated by J. Blosser.

Bonaventure

Bonaventure. *Opera omnia*. Rome: Collegium S. Bonaventurae, 1882. Translated by J. Blosser.

Thomas Aquinas

Chambers, John David. *Laude Syon: Ancient Latin Hymns of the English and Other Churches*. London: J. Masters, 1855.

Thomas Aquinas. *Summa contra Gentiles*. Translated by Joseph Rickaby. London: Burns and Oates, 1905.

_____. *Summa Theologica*. Second and Revised edition. Translated by Fathers of the English Dominican Province. Burns and Oates, 1920.

Medieval Eastern Christians

Justinian

Justinian. *The Digest of Justinian*. Translated by John Henry Monro. Cambridge: Cambridge University Press, 1904.

_____. "Novel 137." *The Civil Laws*. Translated by S. P. Scott. Cincinnati, OH: Central Trust Co., 1932.

Procopius. *On Buildings*. Translated by H. B. Dewing. Boston: Harvard University Press, 1940.

Pseudo-Dionysius the Areopagite

Pseudo-Dionysius the Areopagite. *Mystic Theology*. Translated by John Parker. Oxford: J. Parker, 1897.

Maximus the Confessor

Chapman, John. "St. Maximus of Constantinople." *The Catholic Encyclopedia*. Vol. 10. New York: Robert Applegate Co., 1911.

Maximus the Confessor. *Opera. Tomus secundus*. Translated by Francisci Combefis. Paris: Andream Cramoisy, 1675. Translated by J. Blosser.

John Damascene

John Damascene. *On Holy Images; followed by Three Sermons on the Assumption*. Translated by Mary H. Allies. London: Thomas Baker, 1898.

Gregory Palamas

All translations by John Sanidopoulos (http://www.johnsanidopoulos.com). Used with permission.